Ready® | K Mathematics PRACTICE AND PROBLEM SOLVING

W9-BDS-811

Vice President-Product Development: Adam Berkin
Editorial Director: Cynthia Tripp
Editorial: Pamela Halloran, Djana Paper, Susan Rogalski
Project Manager: Grace Izzi
Cover Designer: Matt Pollock
Book Designer: Scott Hoffman
Illustrator: Sam Valentino

ISBN 978-1-4957-1678-2
©2016—Curriculum Associates, LLC
North Billerica, MA 01862

15 14 13 12

Table of Contents

Family Letter available with every lesson.

Table of Contents

Unit 3: Counting and Cardinality, Numbers to 10

Unit 4: Operations and Algebraic Thinking

Family Letter available with every lesson.

Table of Contents

Family Letter available with every lesson.

Table of Contents

Family Letter available with every lesson.

Dear Family,

This week your child is learning about counting.

In class, your child will discuss reasons that people count and why counting is an important part of everyday life. For example, a teacher might count the books on a shelf to make sure there are enough for each child. Or a child might count the number of days until his or her birthday.

By counting objects in groups of 1 to 4, your child will also develop the understanding that when counting a group of objects, each number is associated with one object, and the last number counted tells the total amount in the group. For example, when counting a group of 4 crayons, you might touch each crayon while saying a number: *1, 2, 3, 4. There are 4 crayons.* Or you might move each crayon to the side as it is counted.

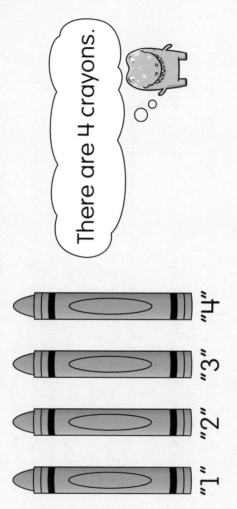

There are 4 crayons.

"1"   "2"   "3"   "4"

Through learning what it means to count and developing strategies for keeping track of objects being counted, your child will start to build a strong foundation for success in math.

Invite your child to share what he or she knows about counting by doing the following activity together.

NEXT

Materials: 3 cups, 9 pennies (or other small objects such as buttons or dried beans)

Do the following activity to help your child practice counting strategies.

- Fill each of the cups with 2, 3, or 4 pennies (a different number in each cup).

- Have your child pour the pennies out of one cup and onto the table. Ask how many pennies are on the table.

- If your child has trouble counting the pennies, guide him or her to use a strategy such as touching each penny as it is counted, moving each penny to the side as it is counted, or putting each penny in the cup as it is counted.

- Have your child put the pennies back in the cup and repeat with the other two cups. Then change the order of the three cups and do the activity again.

If your child needs an extra challenge, here's a way to take the activity further. Have your child close his or her eyes and listen while you drop 1 to 4 pennies into a cup. Ask your child how many pennies are in the cup. Repeat several times.

Understand Counting

Name _____

Why do we count?

Draw something you would count.

Have your child draw a picture of something he or she has counted or might like to count, such as stickers or blocks.

Why might people count at home?

Draw something you count at home.

Discuss with your child things to count at home and why people might count things at home. Then have your child draw something he or she has counted at home, such as stuffed animals or cups.

Understand Counting

Name _____

Example

Have your child match each object to a tile to find the number of objects. Guide your child to draw a line from each object to a number, starting with 1 and continuing in order. Ask your child to circle the number that tells how many objects are in each group.

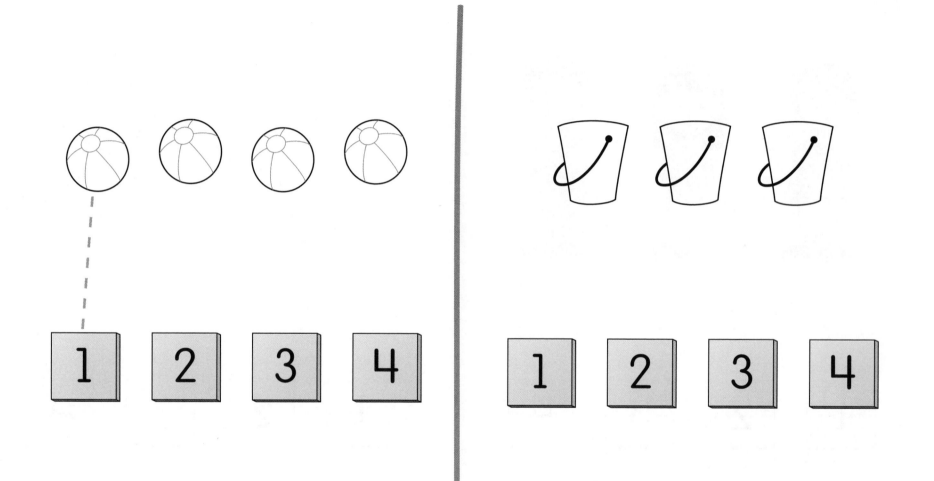

Have your child match each object to a tile to find the number of objects. Guide your child to draw a line from each object to a number, starting with 1 and continuing in order. Ask your child to circle the number that tells how many objects are in each group.

Understand Counting

Name _____

Example

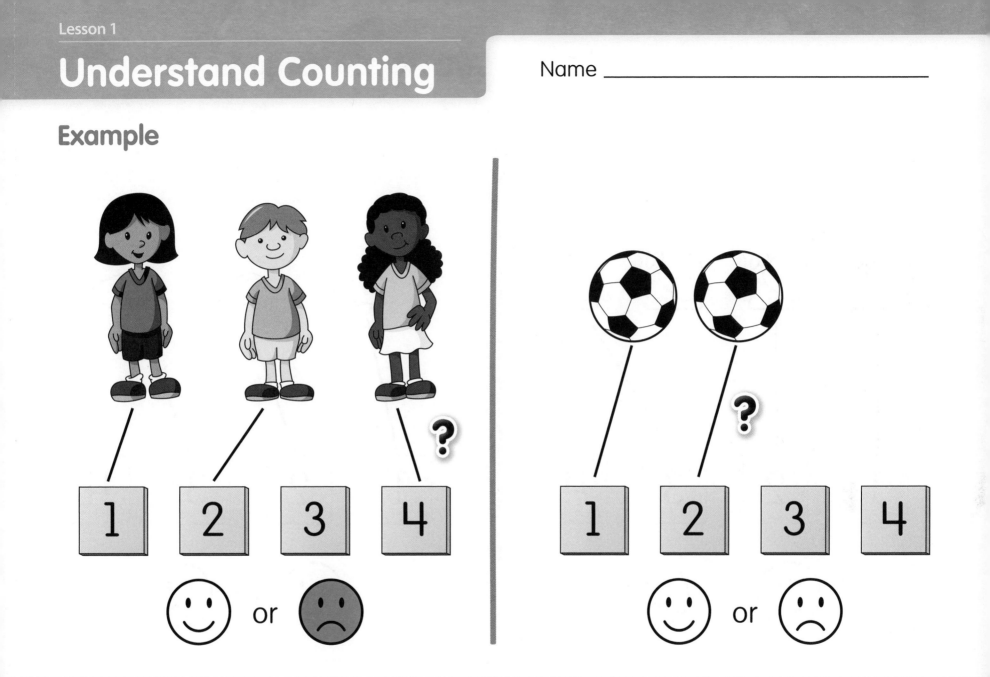

Discuss with your child whether or not the objects are counted correctly. Have your child color the happy face if the objects are counted correctly or the sad face if they are not. Guide your child to describe how the counting is correct or how it is wrong.

Lesson 1 *Understand* Counting

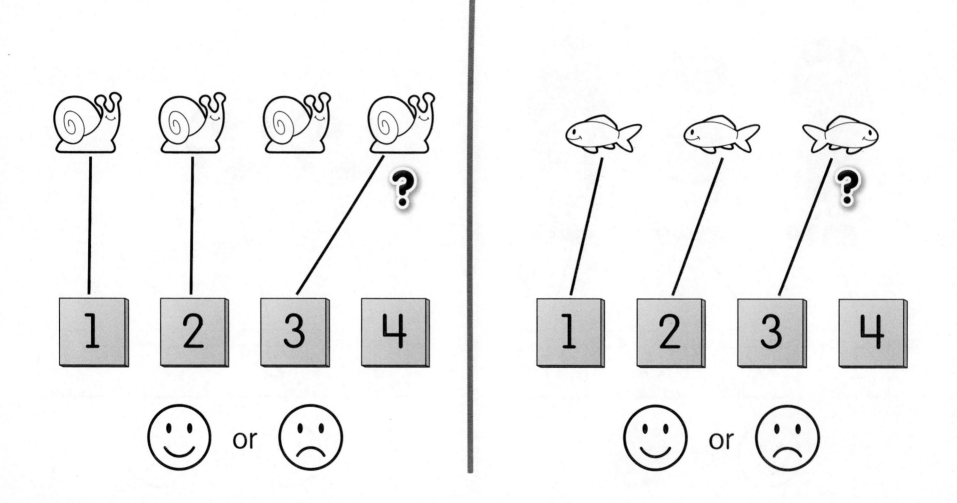

Discuss with your child whether or not the objects are counted correctly. Have your child color the happy face if the objects are counted correctly or the sad face if they are not. Guide your child to describe how the counting is correct or how it is wrong.

Dear Family,

This week your child is building counting skills with the numbers 1, 2, and 3.

Counting skills include learning to recognize and count groups of 1, 2, and 3 objects. An example of this is finding groups of 1, 2, and 3 objects in pictures and in the classroom. Your child will continue to develop the understanding that when objects are counted, each number is associated with one object, and the last number counted tells the total amount in the group. He or she will also continue exploring strategies for keeping track of objects while counting, such as by pointing to or touching each object as it is counted.

This lesson begins to explore the idea that numbers can be represented in various ways. For example, the dots below can be colored in more than one way to show 3.

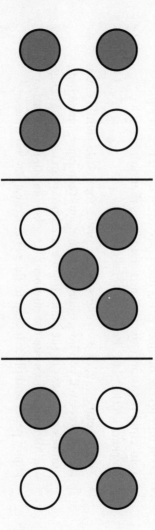

Your child will also practice writing the numbers 1, 2, and 3. Working with the numbers 1, 2, and 3 will help your child build a strong foundation for success in math.

Invite your child to share what he or she knows about counting 1, 2, and 3 by doing the following activity together.

Materials: index cards or slips of paper, pencil, plate, bowl of 5 bite-sized crackers (or other small objects such as dried beans, pennies, or buttons)

Use index cards or slips of paper to make number cards for the numbers 1, 2, and 3.

- Ask your child to place 1, 2, or 3 crackers on the plate. For example, say: *Show me 2 crackers.* He or she should take that number of crackers from the bowl and place them on the plate. Count the crackers on the plate together to check. Repeat several times with different numbers from 1 to 3.

- Then mix up the number cards and place them facedown in a pile. Your child turns over the top card and places that number of crackers on the plate. Repeat several times.

- Finally, place 1, 2, or 3 crackers on the plate. Your child should count the crackers, tell you how many there are, and then place a matching number card next to the plate. If your child needs an extra challenge, ask him or her to write the number of crackers on an index card or slip of paper and place it next to the plate. Repeat several times.

Count 1, 2, and 3

Name _____

Have your child color groups of 1, 2, and 3 objects. Use a different color for each number. Then have your child color the rest of the picture.

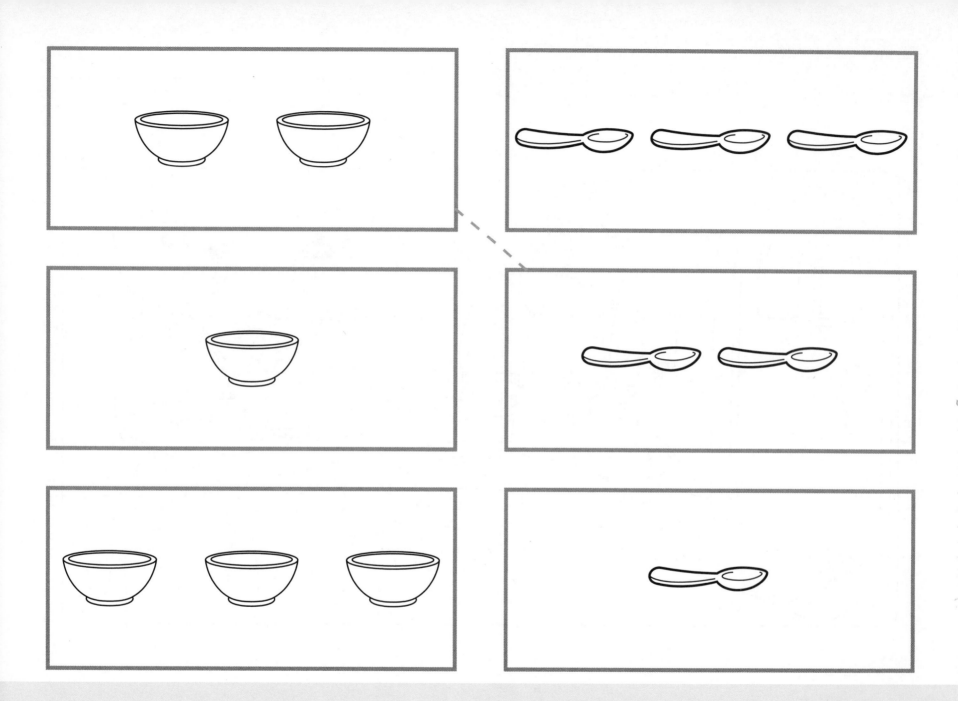

Have your child count the number of objects in each group. Then have your child draw lines to match groups that show the same number of objects.

Count 1, 2, and 3

Name _____

Example

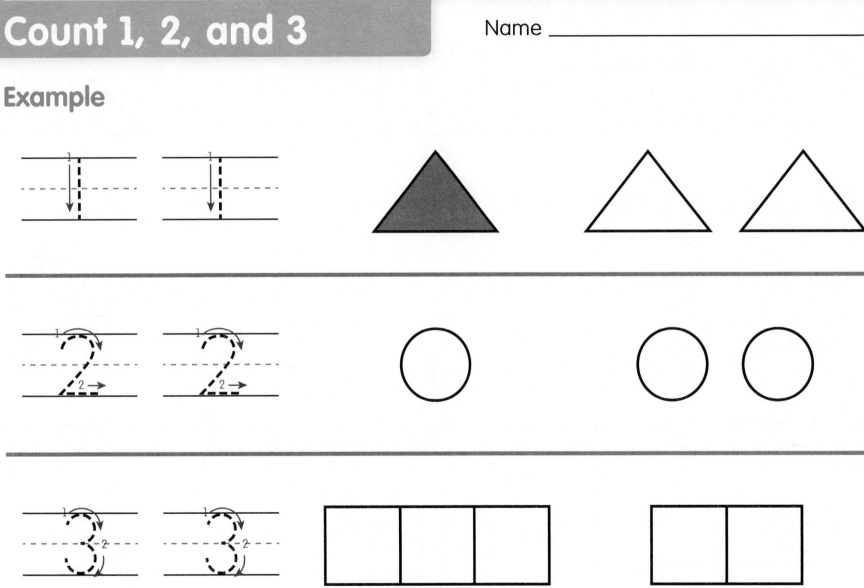

Have your child trace the numbers and identify 1, 2, or 3 shapes. Ask your child to trace the two numbers. Then guide him or her to color the group that has that number of shapes.

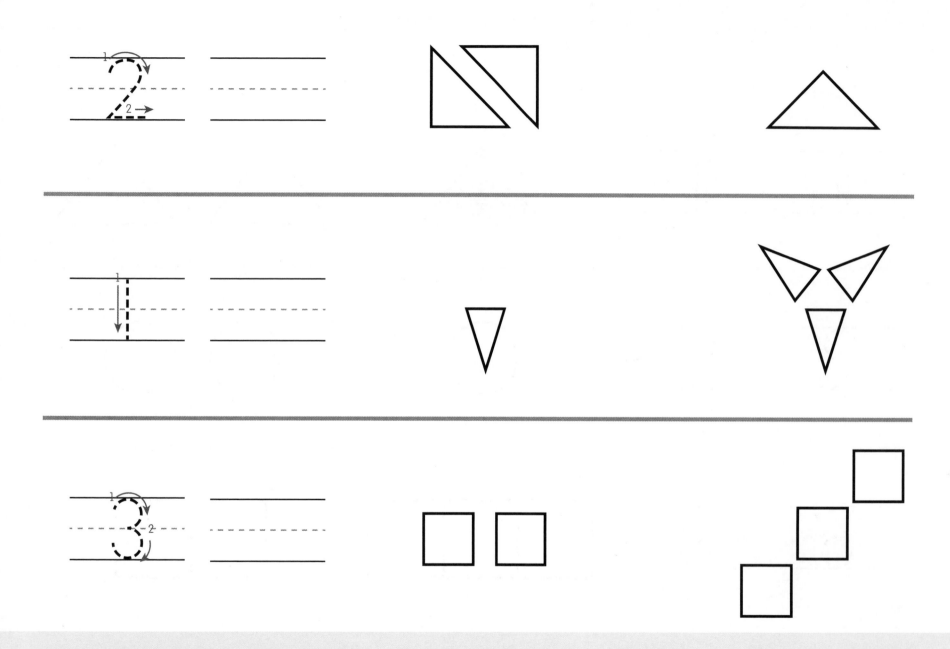

Have your child practice writing numbers and identifying 1, 2, or, 3 shapes. Ask your child to trace and then write the given number. Then guide him or her to color the group that has that number of shapes.

Count 1, 2, and 3

Example

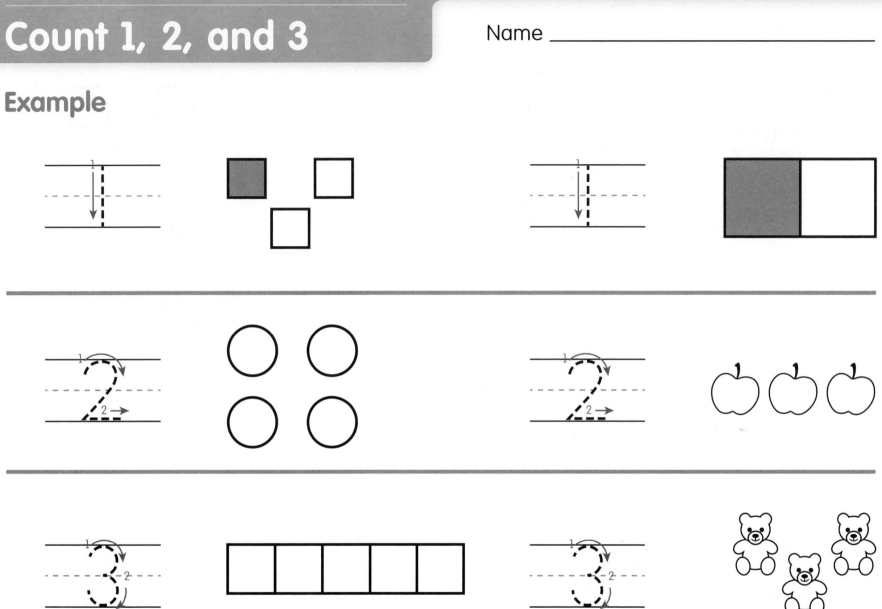

Have your child practice writing numbers and counting out shapes or objects. Ask your child to trace the number. Then guide him or her to color that number of shapes or objects.

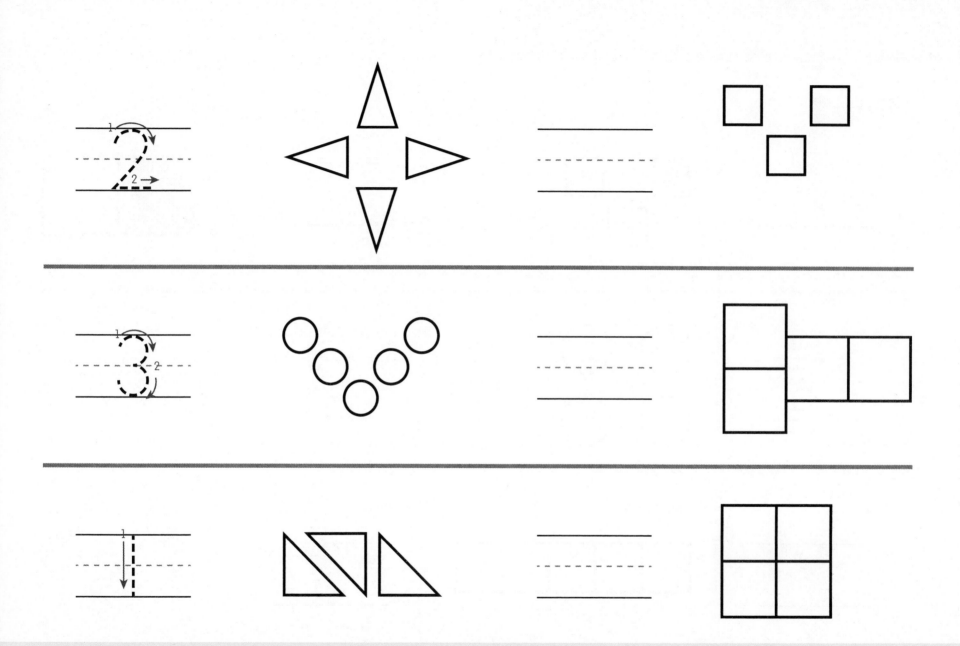

Have your child practice writing numbers and counting out shapes. Ask your child to trace and then write the number. Then guide him or her to color that number of shapes. Color 2 shapes in each group in the top row, 3 in the middle row, and 1 in the bottom row.

Dear Family,

This week your child is building counting skills with the number 4.

This skill involves learning to recognize and count groups of 4 objects in various arrangements. For example, 4 dots can be arranged in a single row or in 2 rows of 2 dots.

Your child will also explore the different ways that 4 objects can be counted and begin to think about 4 in relation to other numbers. For example, the 4 flowers below can be counted from left to right, from right to left, or as a group of 2 and another group of 2. By exploring the various ways that 4 can be counted, and how 4 relates to other numbers, your child will begin preparing to add and subtract, which will be a focus later in the year.

4 flowers

This lesson also includes practice with writing the number 4.

Invite your child to share what he or she knows about counting up to 4 objects by doing the following activity together.

NEXT

Materials: plates, cups, napkins, spoons, forks (at least 5 of each)

Tell your child you are going to pretend that 4 people will be eating dinner together. Have your child lead you in setting the table, encouraging him or her to focus on the number 4 and to count 4 objects.

Ask questions such as: *How many plates do we need? How do you know there are 4 cups? Can you count 4 spoons and put them next to the forks?* When you have finished setting the table have your child count the objects to make sure there are 4 of each.

Then tell your child that this time 2 people will be eating together. Have your child lead you in resetting the table for 2 people. Ask questions to help your child focus on the number 2. When the table is set, have your child count the objects to make sure there are 2 of each. You may wish to repeat the activity by setting the table for 3 people or 1 person.

Throughout the day point out other objects that are in groups of 1, 2, 3, or 4. For example, ask how many knobs are on the door or how many shoes your child is wearing. Have your child count 3 drawers in a dresser. Point out 4 wheels on a toy car, and so on.

Count 4

Have your child color groups of 4 similar objects red. Then have your child color the rest of the picture using different colors.

Have your child practice finding groups of 4 objects. Ask your child to count the number of fish and number of fishbowls. Have him or her circle the group of 4. Then have your child count the number of birds and number of worms, and circle the group of 4.

Count 4

Example

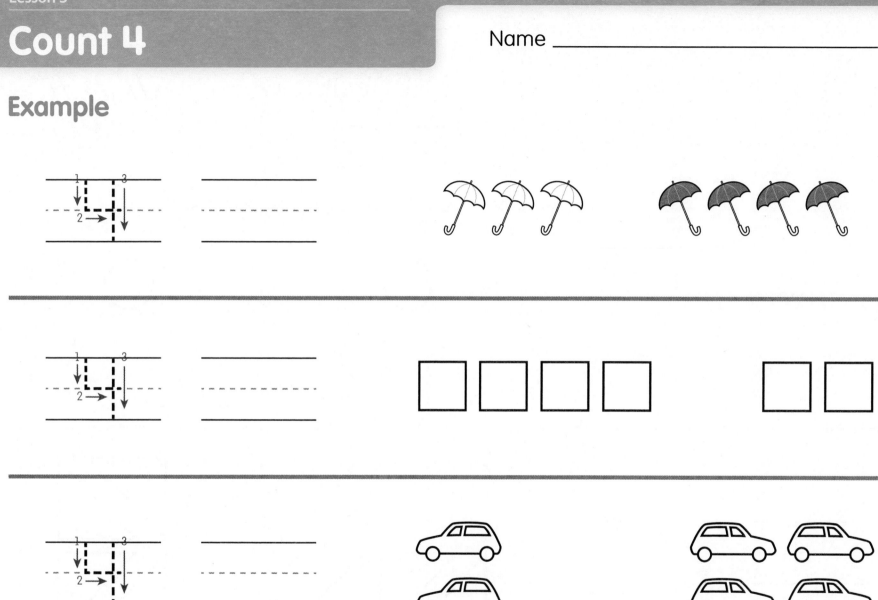

Have your child practice writing the number 4 and finding groups of 4 objects. Ask your child to trace and then write the number 4. Guide him or her to color the group of 4 objects in each problem, as shown in the Example.

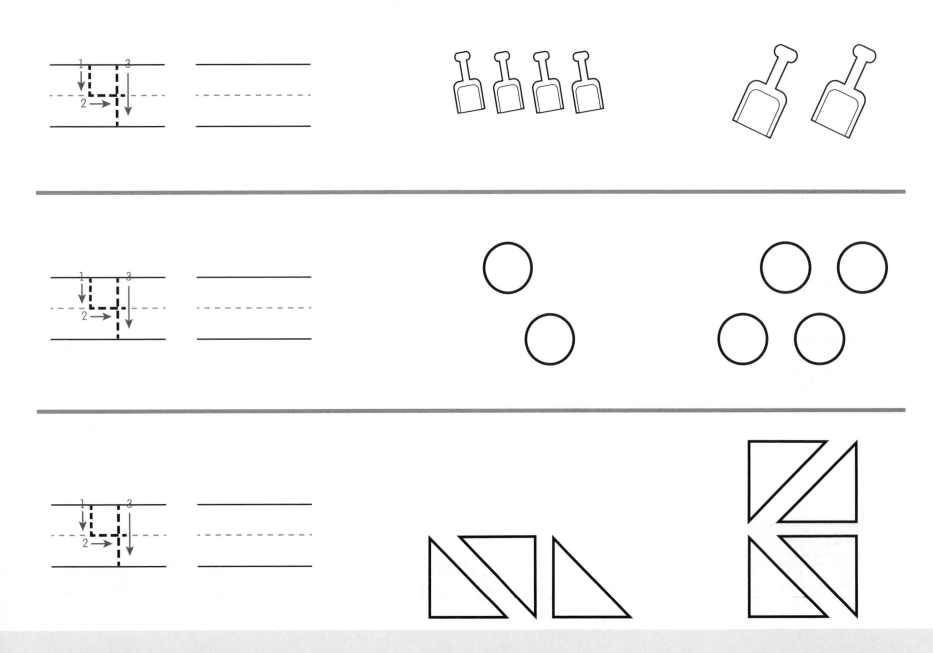

Have your child practice writing the number 4 and finding groups of 4 objects. Ask your child to trace and then write the number 4. Guide him or her to color the group of 4 objects in each problem.

Count 4

Example

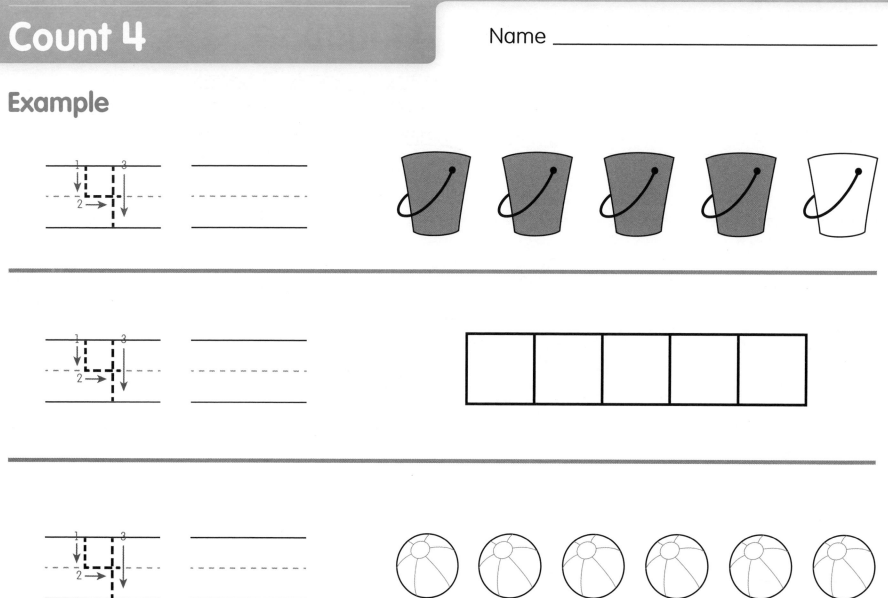

Have your child practice writing the number 4 and counting out 4 shapes or objects. Ask your child to trace and then write the number 4. Guide him or her to color 4 shapes or objects in each problem, as shown in the Example.

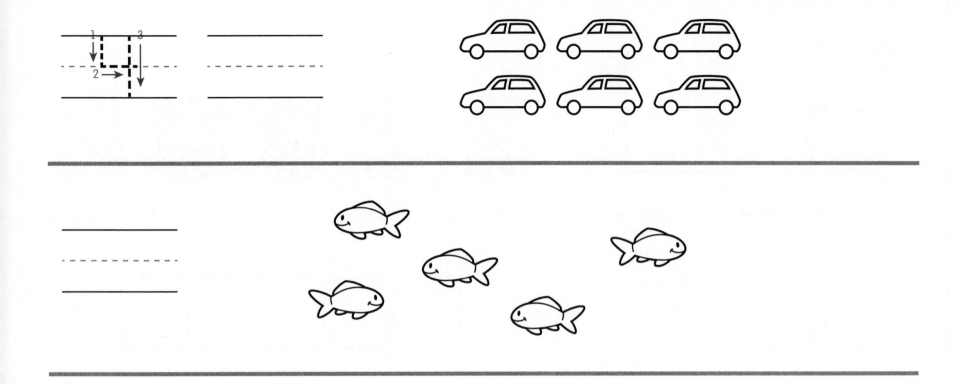

Have your child write 4, count out 4, and draw 4. In the first row, have your child trace and write the number 4, and then color 4 objects. In the middle row, have your child write the number 4 and color 4 objects. In the last row, ask your child to write the number 4 and draw a picture to show 4 objects.

Dear Family,

This week your child is building counting skills with the number 5.

This skill involves learning to recognize and count groups of 5 objects in pictures and in the classroom. Building on previous lessons, your child will explore how 5 is related to other numbers. For example, 5 is more than 4, and 5 can be shown as groups of 4 objects and 1 object, or groups of 3 objects and 2 objects. Understanding the quantity 5 and how it relates to other numbers will help your child prepare for later work with greater numbers.

Another helpful counting strategy is using fingers to count groups of 5, raising one finger at a time while counting until all 5 fingers on one hand are raised.

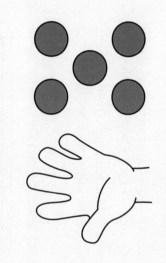

This lesson also includes practice with writing the number 5.

Invite your child to share what he or she knows about counting 5 by doing the following activity together.

Materials: shallow plastic container with lid or shallow metal baking pan, $\frac{1}{2}$ to 1 cup of salt or sugar, colored paper (optional)

In this activity, your child will use his or her finger to practice writing the numbers 1 to 5 in a layer of salt or sugar.

• Pour $\frac{1}{2}$ to 1 cup of salt or sugar into a shallow plastic container or shallow metal pan.

• Spread out the salt or sugar info a fairly thin layer.

• Have your child use his or her finger to practice writing the numbers 1 to 5 in the salt or sugar. (Note: If your child is working on a white table, you may wish to place a sheet of colored paper under the container so that the numbers are easier to see.)

• Show your child how to wipe a hand across the salt or sugar each time he or she is ready to write a new number.

• When your child is done with the activity, you can cover the container and save the salt or sugar for future use with the same activity.

Count 5

Name _____

Have your child color groups of 5 similar objects blue. Then ask your child to color the rest of the picture using different colors. Finally, have your child circle the number 5 in the picture.

Example

Have your child count and draw lines to match objects. Ask your child to draw a line to connect each shovel to a pail. Encourage your child to count as he or she draws each line. Next have your child connect each child to a shell, counting as he or she draws each line.

Count 5

Example

Have your child practice writing the number 5 and finding groups of 5 objects. Ask your child to trace and then write the number 5. Guide him or her to color the group of 5 objects in each problem, as shown in the Example.

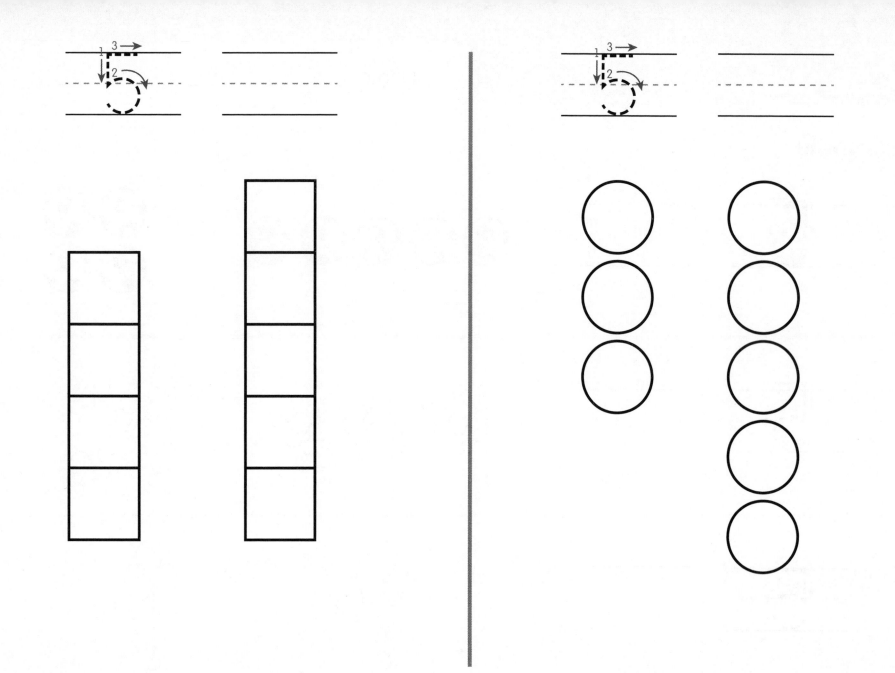

Have your child practice writing the number 5 and finding groups of 5 shapes. Ask your child to trace and then write the number 5. Guide him or her to color the group of 5 shapes in each problem.

Count 5

Name _____

Example

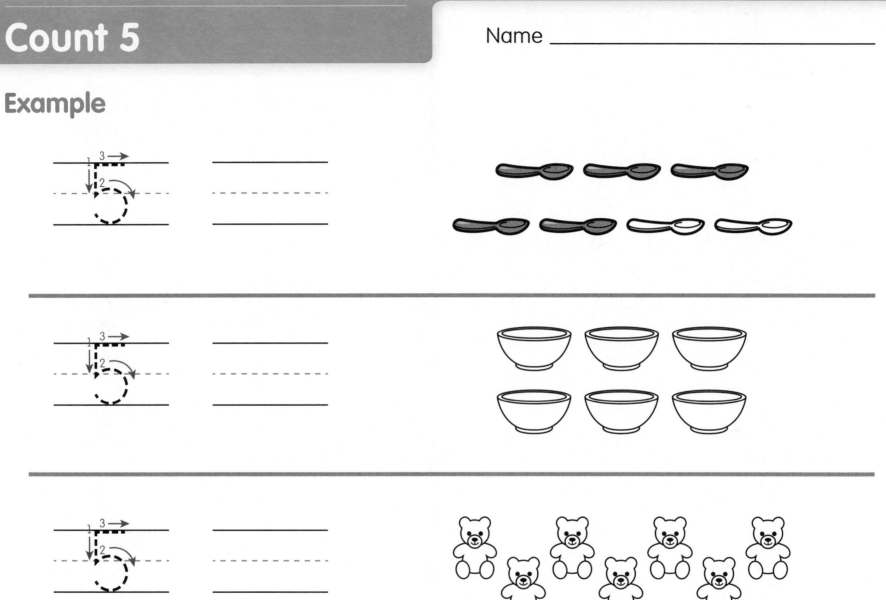

Have your child practice writing the number 5 and counting out 5 objects. Ask your child to trace and then write the number 5. Guide him or her to color 5 objects in each problem, as shown in the Example.

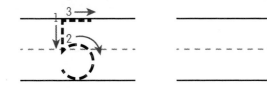

Have your child trace and write 5, count out 5, and draw 5. On the left, have your child trace and write the number 5 and then color 5 apples. On the right, ask your child to write the number 5 and then draw a picture to show 5 objects.

Dear Family,

This week your child is learning to compare within 5.

The lesson includes comparing groups of up to 5 objects. For example, your child may compare a group of 3 hats and a group of 4 blocks to find that there are more blocks. Comparing groups of objects to find which has more and which has less helps to prepare your child to compare the actual numbers in the future. This also prepares them for later work finding out how much more or less is in one group than another. These are important mathematical and real-world skills.

Your child will explore various strategies for comparing, such as lining up the groups of objects being compared in separate rows to see which group has more objects and which group has fewer objects. Another strategy includes crossing out one object from each group of objects until one group has no more to cross out. Or your child may be able to recognize which group has more by just looking at the groups.

5 is more than 4.

Invite your child to share what he or she knows about comparing within 5 by doing the following activity together.

NEXT

Materials: 2 sets of dot cards made by drawing 1 to 5 dots on each of 10 index cards or slips of paper (there should be two cards for each number)

Tell your child that you are going to practice comparing numbers by playing two games: "Go for More" and "Go for Less."

- To play "Go for More," you and your child each get a facedown set of dot cards, shuffled. For each round, you each turn over the card on the top of your pile.

- Your child compares the number of dots on each card and says which card shows more. For example, if your dot card shows 4 dots and your child's shows 2 dots, your child should say, "4 is more than 2." If the cards show the same number of dots, turn over the next card.

- The person who turned over the dot card showing more gets 1 point. Play until someone gets 10 points.

- Then play "Go for Less." In this game, your child says which dot card shows less. For example, "2 is less than 4." This time, the person whose dot card shows less gets 1 point.

4 is more than 2.

Compare Within 5

Name _____

Have your child find a group of more than 4 similar objects and color those objects green. Then have your child find a group of fewer than 4 similar objects and color those objects orange. Ask your child to color the rest of the picture using different colors.

Example

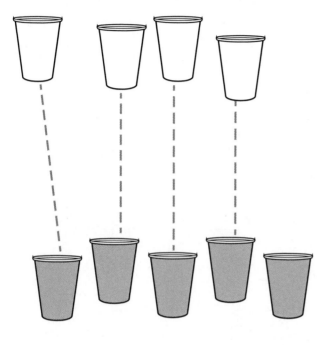

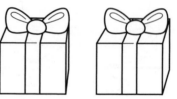

Compare Within 5

Name _____

Example

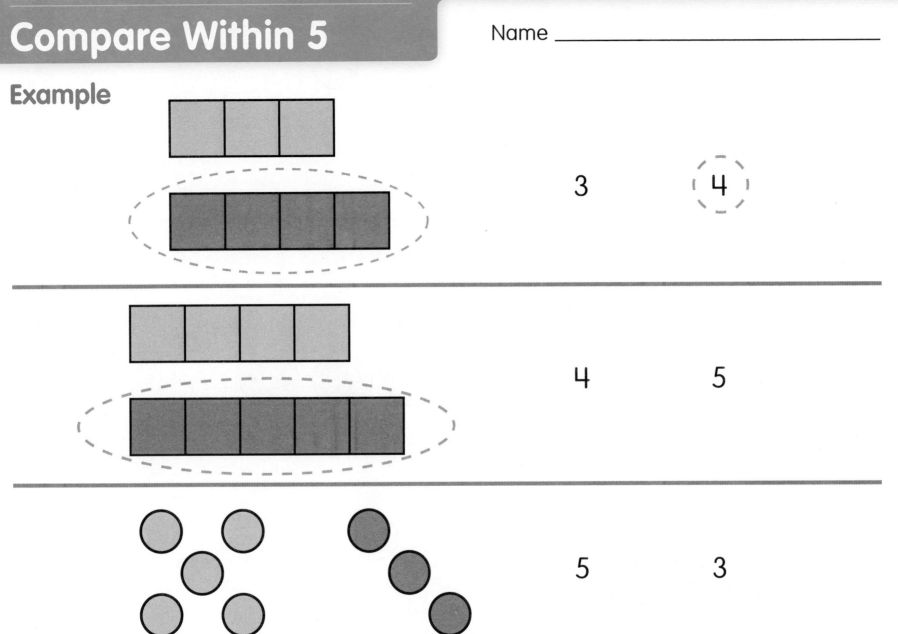

3   (4)

4   5

5   3

Have your child compare the two groups of shapes and circle the group with more. Then ask your child to circle the number that is more.

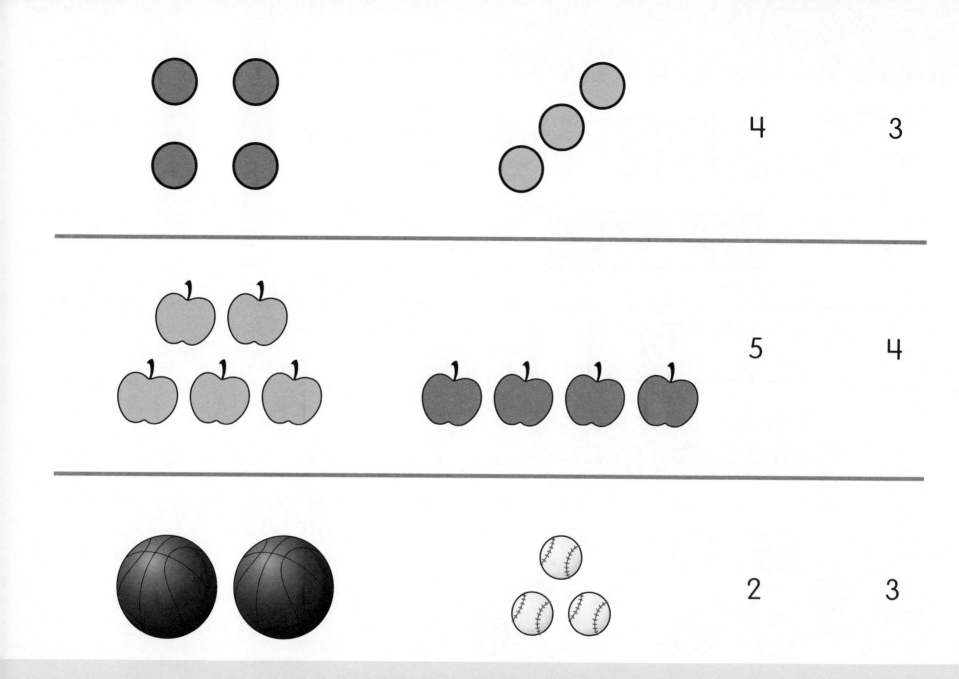

4   3

5   4

2   3

Have your child compare the two groups of shapes or objects and circle the group with more. Then ask your child to circle the number that is more.

Compare Within 5

Name _____

Example

Which is less?

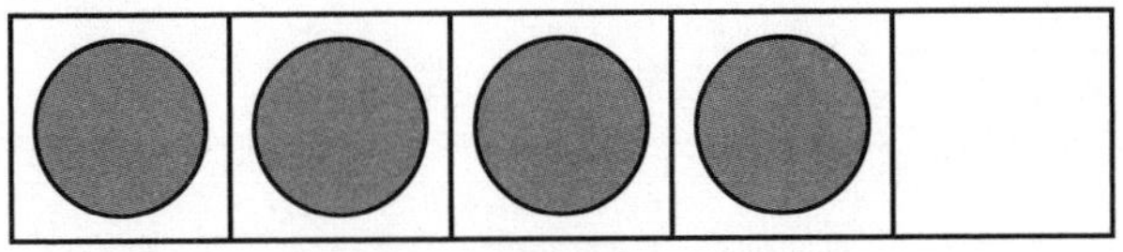

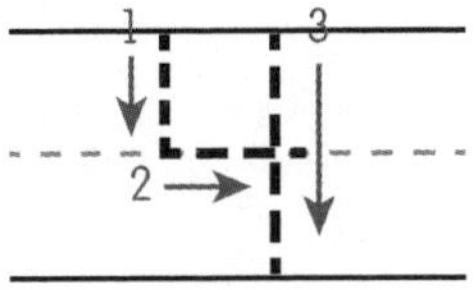

or   (1)

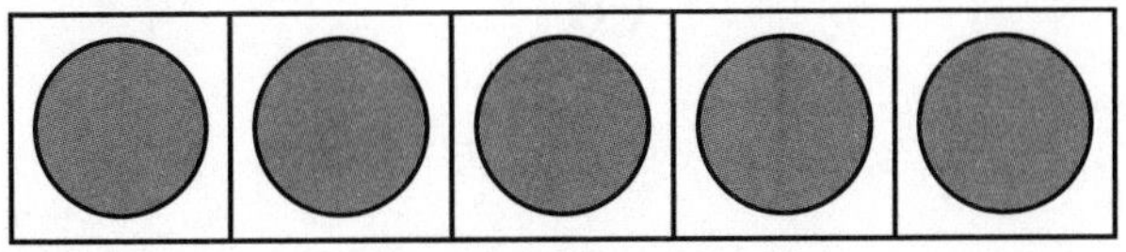

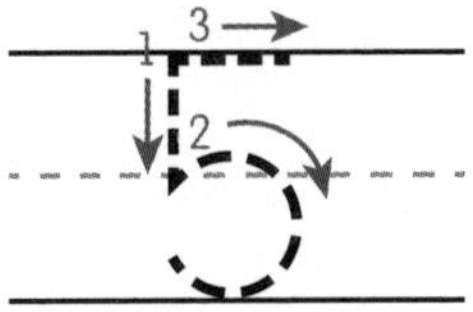

or   2

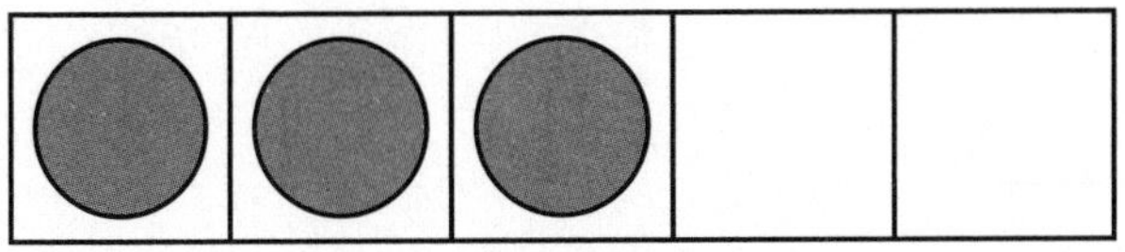

or   5

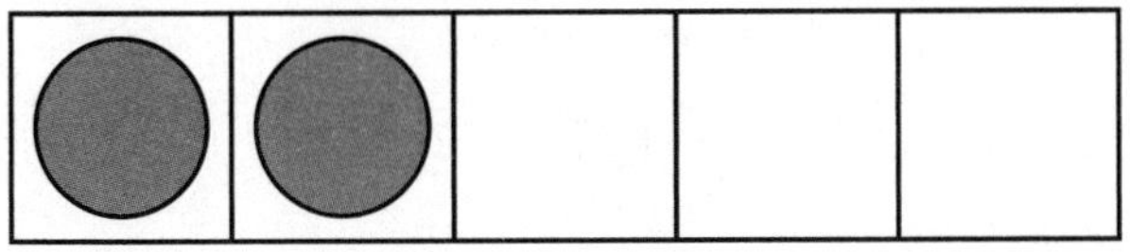

or   3

Have your child count and write how many counters are shown. Ask your child to compare the number he or she wrote with the number on the right. Have your child circle the number that is less, as shown in the Example.

Which is less?

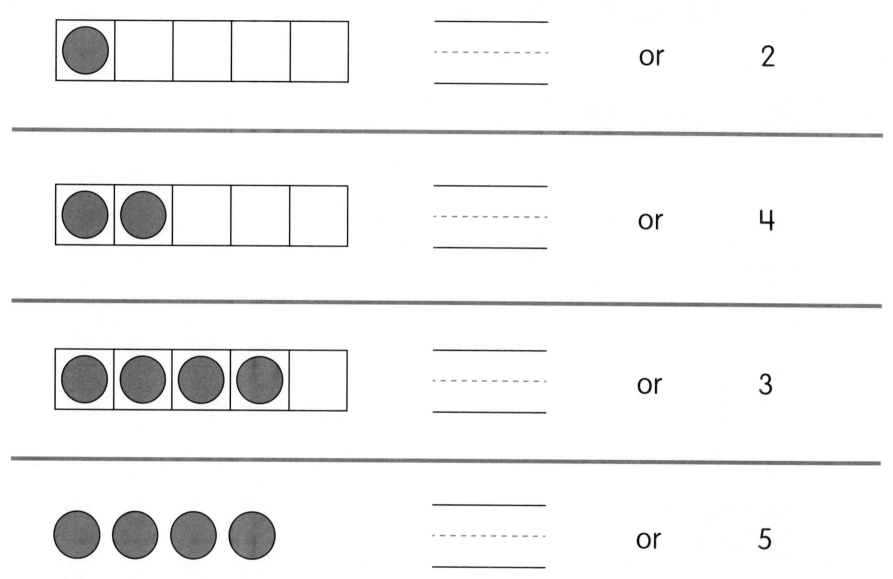

_____ or 2

_____ or 4

_____ or 3

_____ or 5

Have your child count and write how many counters are shown. Ask your child to compare the number he or she wrote with the number on the right. Have your child circle the number that is less.

Dear Family,

This week your child is learning to find the numbers that make 3, 4, and 5.

Numbers can be thought of as being made up of combinations of other numbers. For example, 4 is made up of 1 and 3, 2 and 2, or 3 and 1. Thinking of numbers this way will help your child prepare for adding and subtracting numbers. For example, knowing that 1 and 3 make 4 lays the foundation for solving 1 + 3 = 4. The ways to make 3, 4, and 5 are listed below.

Ways to Make 3	**Ways to Make 4**	**Ways to Make 5**
1 and 2	1 and 3	1 and 4
2 and 1	2 and 2	2 and 3
	3 and 1	3 and 2
		4 and 1

In class, your child will explore ways to make 3, 4, and 5 using pictures and objects. For example, putting together connecting cubes of different colors helps to visualize the ways to make 4, as shown below.

1 and 3   4

Invite your child to share what he or she knows about making 3, 4, and 5 by doing the following activity together.

Materials: 5 small objects (such as pasta shapes, dried beans, cereal pieces, buttons, or paper clips), paper plate or sheet of paper

Do the following activity to help your child find ways to make the numbers 3, 4, and 5.

- Draw a line down the center of a paper plate or sheet of paper.

- Give your child 3 small objects. Have your child count the objects and then place them on the plate or paper.

- Show your child how to place the objects on both sides of the line to show a way to make 3. Encourage him or her to tell how the objects make 3. For example, if 1 object is on the left and 2 objects are on the right, your child might say: "1 and 2 make 3." Then have your child rearrange the objects to show another way to make 3. If there are 2 objects on the left and 1 on the right, he or she might say: "2 and 1 make 3."

- Repeat the activity, starting with 4 objects and then 5 objects. Try to find and describe all the ways to make each number.

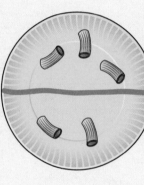

Make 3, 4, and 5

Name _____

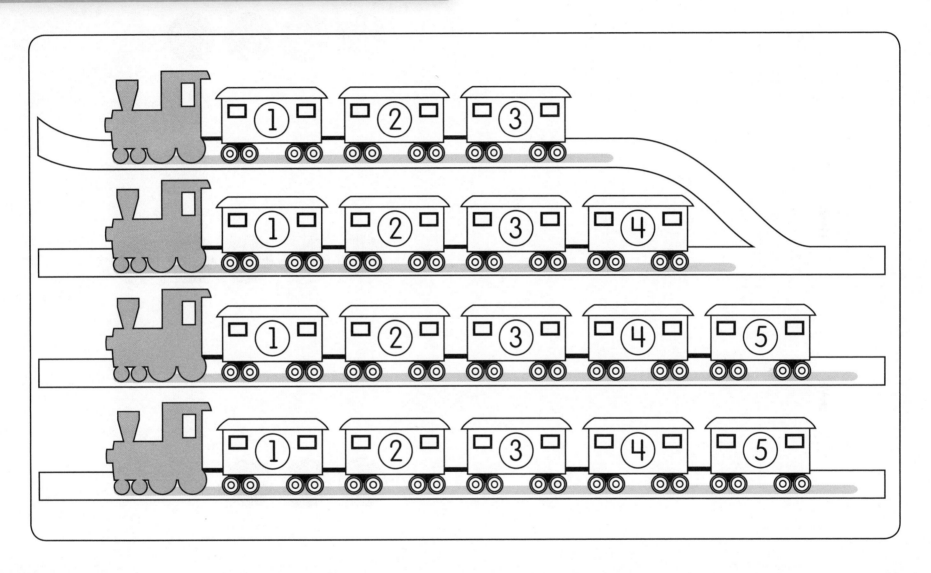

Have your child use green to color 1 car on the top train, 2 cars on the second train, and 3 cars on the third train. Have him or her color the rest of the cars in those trains purple. Ask your child to color the bottom train green and purple to show another way to make a train with 5 cars. Encourage your child to describe the trains with statements such as, "This train has 1 green car and 2 purple cars. 1 and 2 make 3."

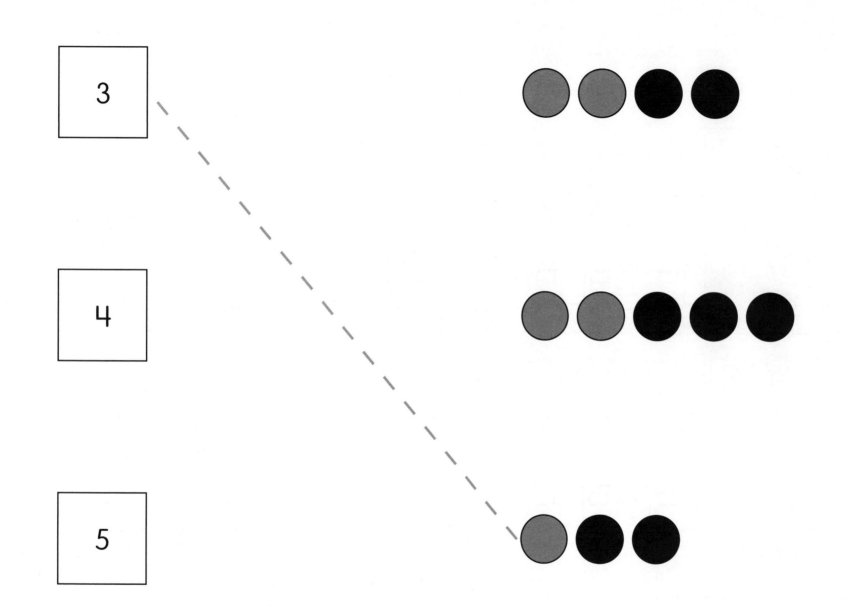

Have your child draw lines to match each number to a group of counters that shows a way to make that number. Ask your child to trace the dashed line as an example. Have your child describe how each number is made. For example, your child might say, "1 and 2 make 3."

44   Lesson 6 Make 3, 4, and 5

©Curriculum Associates, LLC   Copying is not permitted.

Make 3, 4, and 5

Name _____

Example

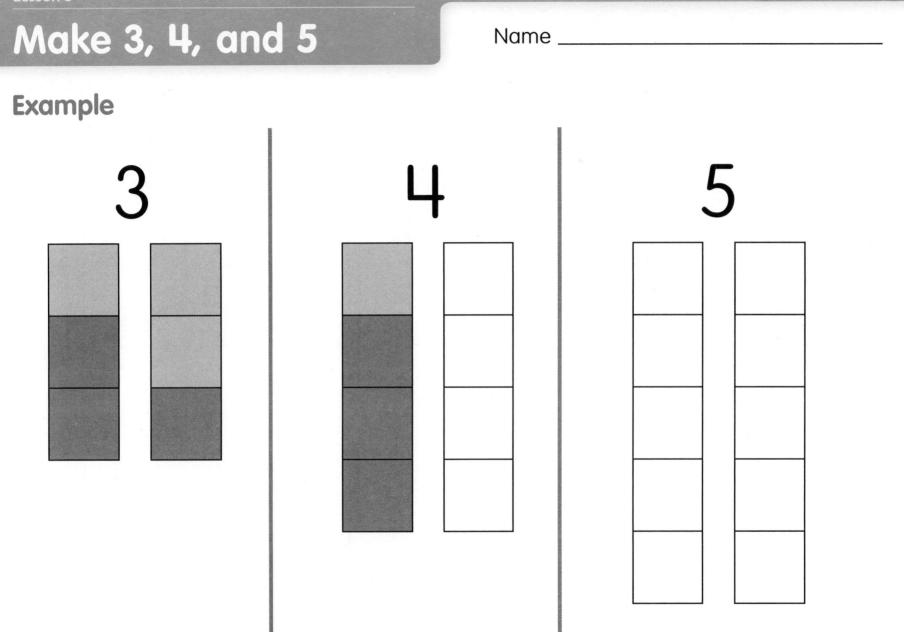

Have your child use two colors to show different ways to make the number at the top of each problem. In the Example problem, point out to your child that the first group of boxes shows that 1 and 2 make 3, and the second group of boxes shows that 2 and 1 make 3. Then have your child use two colors to show different ways to make 4 and 5.

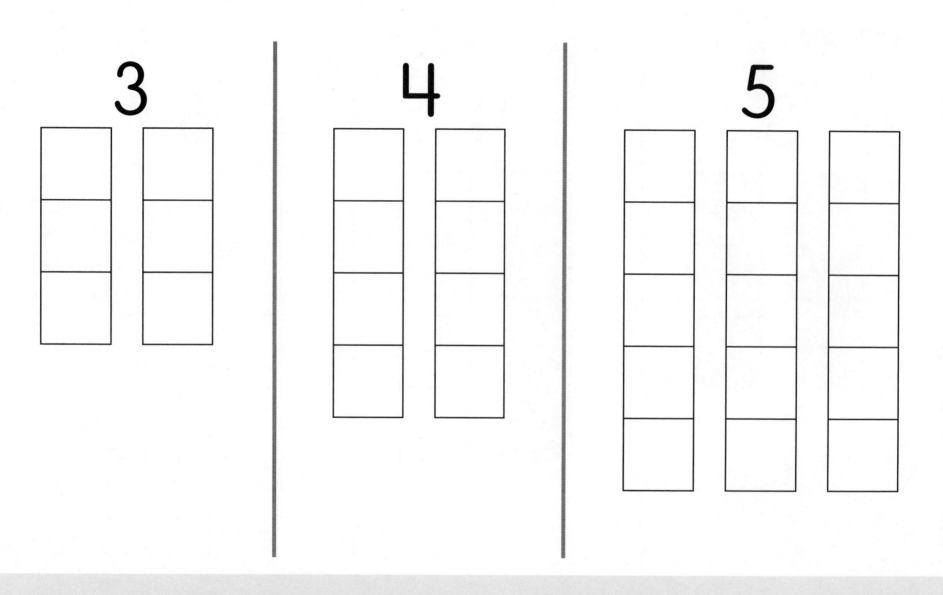

Have your child use two colors to show different ways to make 3, 4, and 5. In the first two problems, have your child show two different ways to make 3 and 4. In the last problem, have your child show three different ways to make 5.

Make 3, 4, and 5

Name _____

Example

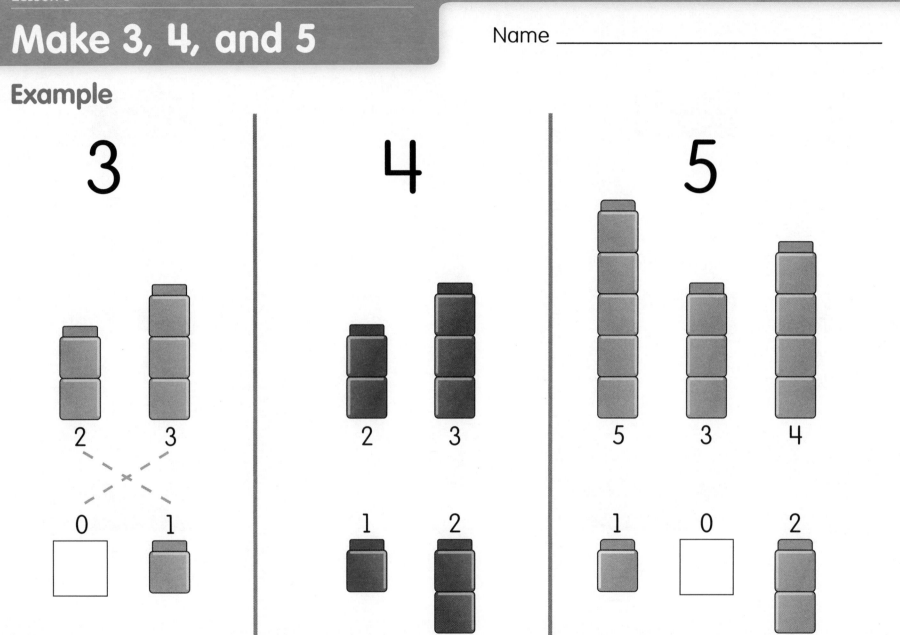

Have your child draw lines to match the cubes on the top to the cubes on the bottom to make cube trains of 3, 4, and 5. Point out to your child that in the Example problem, the empty box shows zero cubes. Have your child name the number pairs that make each target number. For example, to name the number pairs in the Example problem, your child might say, "2 and 1 make 3; 0 and 3 make 3."

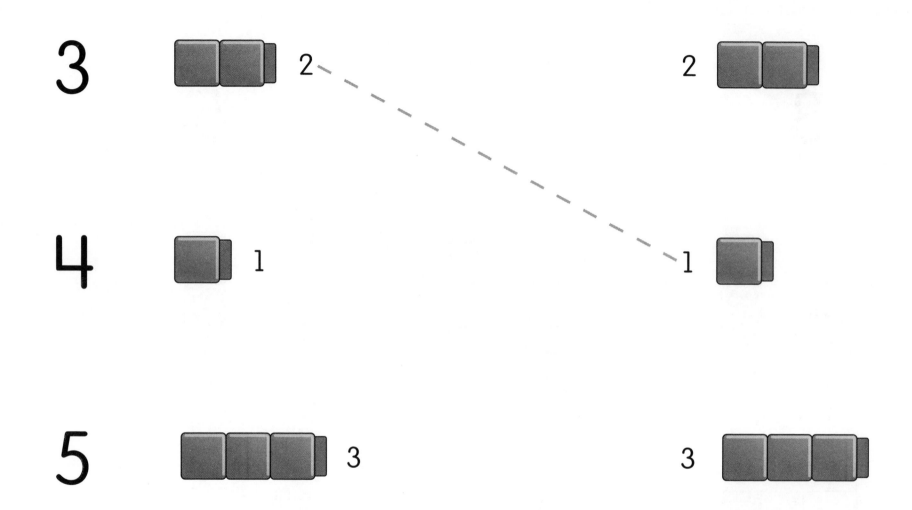

Have your child draw lines to match the cubes on the left to cubes on the right to make trains of 3, 4, and 5. Have your child name the number pairs used to make each target number.

Numbers 1 to 5

Name _____

Color 4 △ blue.

Color 5 △ green.

Color 5 △ red.

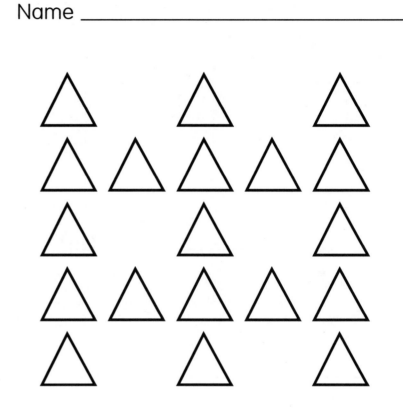

How many △ are white? _____

Explain to children that this is a problem that can be solved in different ways. Have children color 4 triangles blue, 5 triangles green, and 5 triangles red. Then count how many triangles are white and write the number.

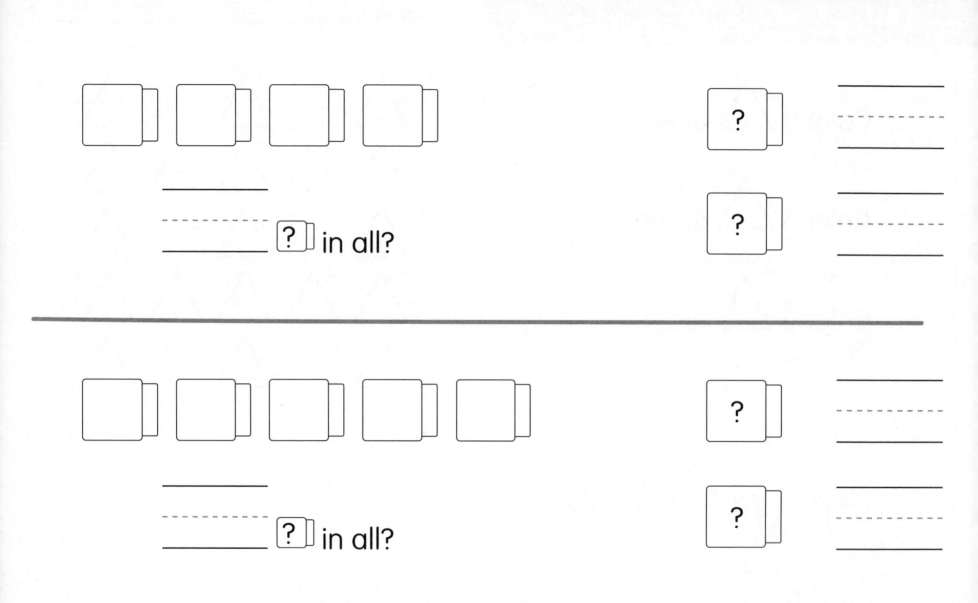

_____

- - - - - - - ?⃞ in all?

_____

- - - - - - - ?⃞ in all?

Explain to children that this is a problem that can be solved in different ways. Have children color some cubes red and some blue.
Then write the number of cubes that are red. Write the number that are blue. Write how many cubes in all.

Roll and Count

Name _____

1 _____

- - - - - - - -

_____

2 _____

- - - - - - - -

_____

3 _____

- - - - - - - -

_____

4 _____

- - - - - - - -

_____

5 _____

- - - - - - - -

_____

Materials For each child: number cube 1–5, 15 counters or small objects (dried beans, counting bears, etc.), Roll and Count Game Board
How to Play Roll the number cube. Find the box with that number. Write the number, then put that number of objects on the box. Skip a turn if a box is already full. The first player to fill all the boxes wins.

Dear Family,

This week your child is building counting skills with the numbers 6 and 7.

This skill involves counting groups of 6 and 7 objects, and exploring how these numbers are related to other numbers. For example, 6 is 1 more than 5, and 7 is 1 more than 6.

Exploring how 6 and 7 relate to other numbers, in particular the number 5, will be important for later work involving greater numbers. This is because grouping objects as 5 and some more can be helpful in keeping track of larger amounts.

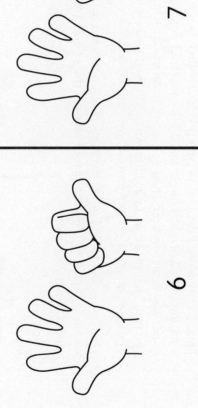

6   7

Your child will also practice writing the numbers 6 and 7.

Invite your child to share what he or she knows about counting 6 and 7 objects by doing the following activity together.

Materials: paper, pencil, 14 small objects (such as buttons, dried beans, or cereal pieces), dot cube (or homemade number cards 1–6)

Trace your child's hand and your own hand on separate sheets of paper. Use these hand pictures to play "Get to 6."

• You and your child should each have 6 buttons (or other small objects). Have your child roll a dot cube (or turn over a number card) and put that number of buttons on his or her hand picture by placing 1 button on each finger. Then you roll the dot cube and place that number of buttons on your own hand picture.

• Take turns rolling the dot cube and placing more buttons on your hand pictures until the first person gets to 6, which is shown by 1 button placed on each finger and 1 button placed next to the hand. Make sure to stop when you get to 6, no matter what number you roll. You might get to 6 right away, or it might take a few turns. The first person to get to 6 wins. Play several times.

• Then play "Get to 7." Follow the same rules, but now try to get to 7, which is shown by 1 button placed on each finger and 2 buttons placed next to the hand.

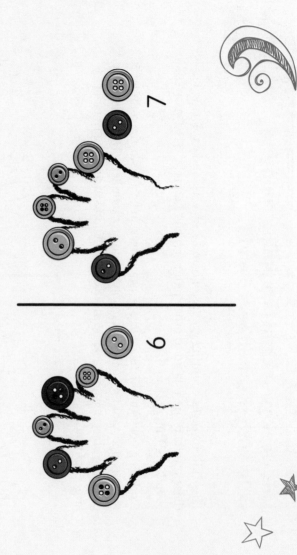

Count 6 and 7

Name _____

Have your child color a group of 6 similar objects blue. Then have your child choose any 7 windows on the buildings to color yellow. Finally, ask your child to color the rest of the picture using different colors.

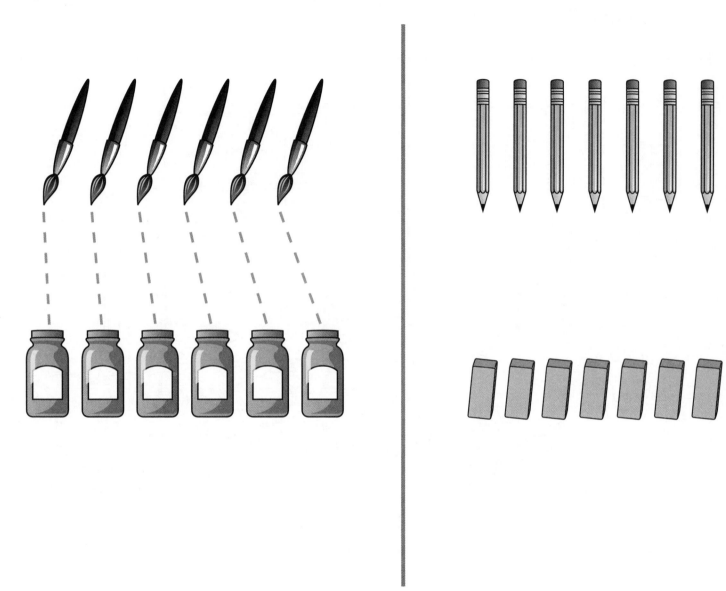

Have your child count and draw lines to match objects. Ask your child to draw a line to connect each paintbrush to a jar. Encourage your child to count as he or she draws each line. Then have your child connect each pencil to an eraser, counting as he or she draws each line.

Count 6 and 7

Example

Have your child practice writing 6 or 7 and finding groups of 6 or 7 objects. Ask your child to trace and then write the number at the beginning of each problem. Guide him or her to color the group with that number of objects, as shown in the Example.

Have your child practice writing 6 or 7 and finding groups of 6 or 7 objects. Ask your child to trace and then write the number at the top of each problem. Guide him or her to color the group with that number of objects.

Count 6 and 7

Example

Have your child practice writing 6 or 7 and counting out 6 or 7 objects. Ask your child to trace and then write the number at the beginning of each problem. Then guide him or her to color that number of objects, as shown in the Example.

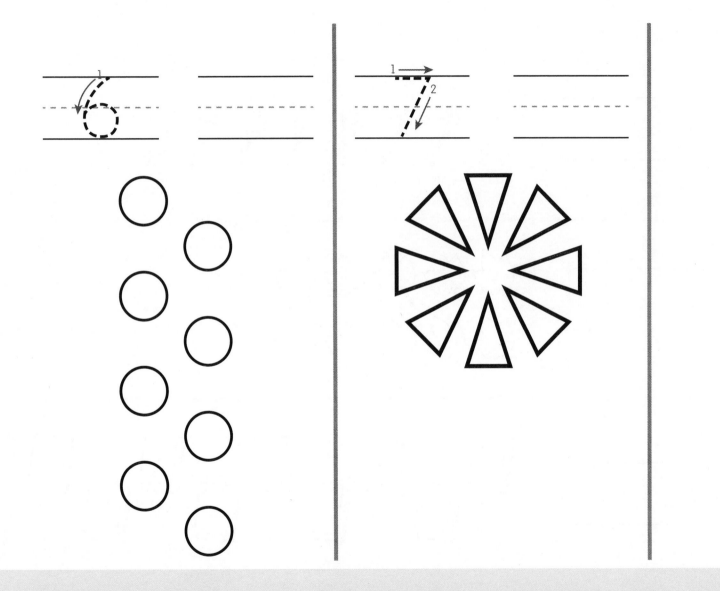

Have your child practice writing 6 or 7, count out and color that number objects, and draw 7 objects. In the first two problems, have your child trace and write the number and then color that many objects. In the last problem, ask your child to write the number 7 and then draw a picture to show 7 objects.

Dear Family,

This week your child is learning to find the numbers that make 6 and 7.

As discussed in an earlier letter, numbers can be thought of as being made up of combinations of other numbers. The number 6 can be made up of 2 and 4, 3 and 3, or 5 and 1, with the addends in either order. Learning to make numbers from combinations of other numbers will help your child prepare for adding and subtracting. For example, knowing that 2 and 4 make 6 lays the foundation for solving 2 + 4 = 6.

In class, your child will show different ways to make 6 and 7 with counters on a 10-frame. A 10-frame is a grid with 5 spaces in the top row and 5 spaces in the bottom row. Working with a 10-frame will help your child visualize numbers as amounts. It also helps to develop an understanding of how various numbers relate to 5 and 10, which will be important for later work with greater numbers.

Make 6 on a 10-frame.

5 and 1

Make 7 on a 10-frame.

3 and 4

Invite your child to share what he or she knows about making 6 and 7 by doing the following activity together.

NEXT

Materials: pencil, paper, cup, 7 pennies (or other coins)

Help your child find ways to make 6 and 7 by doing the following activity.

- Write "Make 6" at the top of a sheet of paper and draw a two-column chart with the headings "Heads" and "Tails."

- Show your child a penny and explain that the side with the face is called "heads," and the other side is called "tails."

- Place 6 pennies in a cup. Have your child pour the pennies onto the table and sort them by heads and tails. He or she writes how many there are of each in the chart.

- Have your child put the pennies back in the cup and repeat pouring, sorting, and filling in the chart each time a new combination of 6 appears.

- Repeat until all the ways to make 6 have been found. Then draw a new chart titled "Make 7" and have your child do the activity with 7 pennies.

Ways to Make 6
1 and 5
2 and 4
3 and 3
4 and 2
5 and 1

Ways to Make 7
1 and 6
2 and 5
3 and 4
4 and 3
5 and 2
6 and 1

Make 6

Heads	Tails
4	2
1	5

Make 6 and 7

Name _____

For each set of objects (bears, ducks, planes), encourage your child to color some of them one color and the rest a second color. Then have your child color the balls and draw more to show a total of 7. Have your child color the rest of the page.

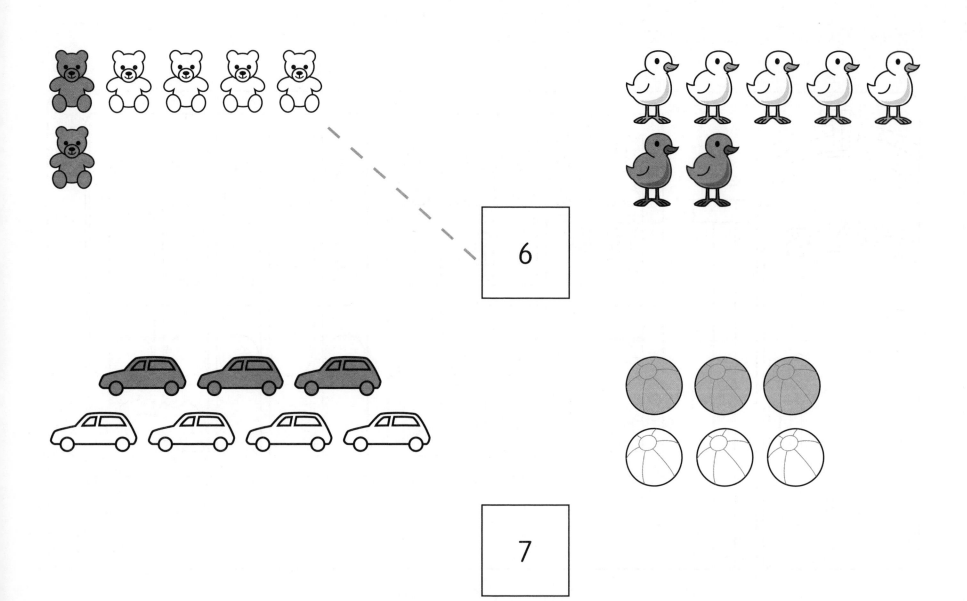

Have your child draw lines to match each number to two groups of objects that show different ways to make that number. Then have your child describe how each number is made. For example, your child might say, "2 gray bears and 4 white bears make 6."

Make 6 and 7

Example

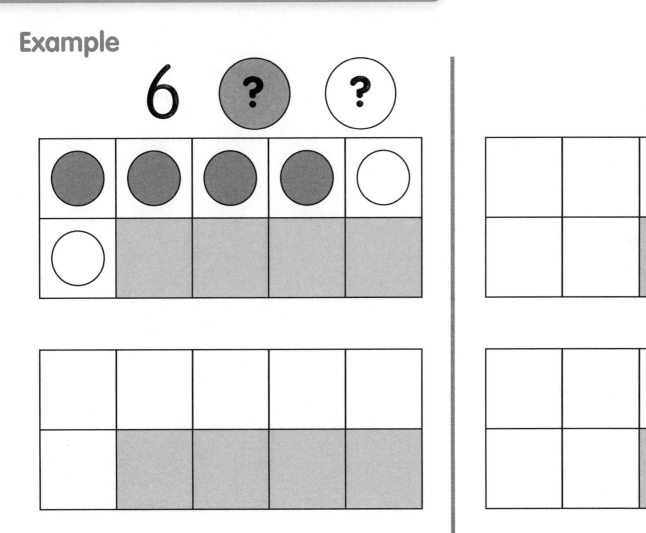

Guide your child to use coins or counters that are different on each side to make totals of 6 or 7. Point out that in the Example problem, the number pair shown for 6 is 4 and 2. Then have your child show and use two colors to record a different way to make 6. On the right, have your child show and record two ways to make 7.

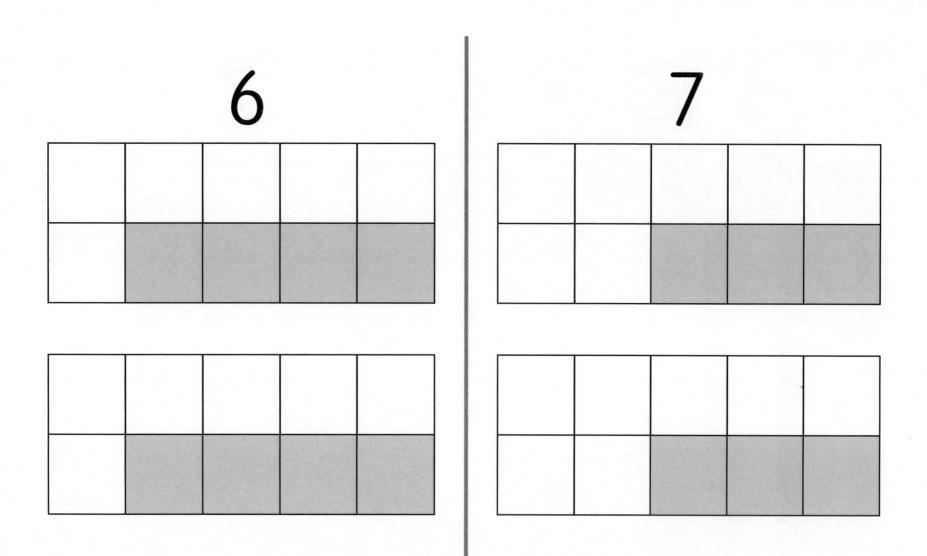

6

7

Guide your child to use coins or counters that are different on each side to show ways to make 6 or 7. For the first three problems, have your child use two colors to record his or her work. For the last problem, challenge your child to use one color to make 7 and tell the number pair shown (7 and 0).

Make 6 and 7

Name _____

Example

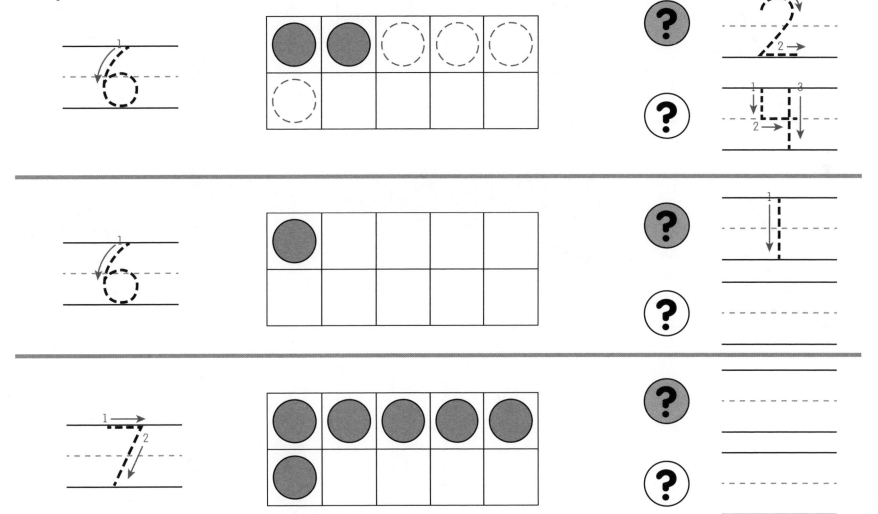

Guide your child to trace the numbers on the left and draw more counters in the 10-frames to show a total of 6 or 7. On the right, have your child write the number of gray counters shown and the number of counters that he or she drew to make the total.

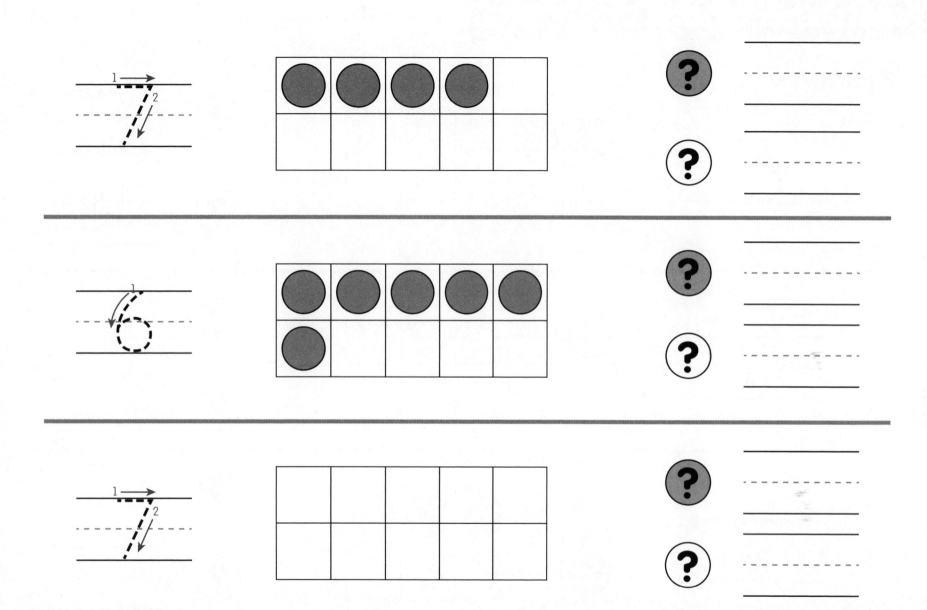

Guide your child to trace the numbers on the left and draw more counters in the 10-frames (if needed) to show a total of 6 or 7. For the first two rows, have your child write the number of gray counters shown and the number of counters that he or she drew to make the total. For the last row, have your child use two colors to draw counters that show another way to make 7 and write the number pair.

Dear Family,

This week your child is building counting skills with the numbers 8 and 9.

The lesson includes practice with counting 8 and 9 objects. Strategies for keeping track of what has been counted remain important, especially when counting these larger groups. For example, touching or pointing to each object or object in a picture or marking each object as it is counted are ways to ensure that no items have been missed.

Building on earlier lessons, your child will also explore how 8 and 9 relate to other numbers. For example, pictures show how 8 and 9 visually relate to 5 and 10. This will help prepare for later work with greater numbers.

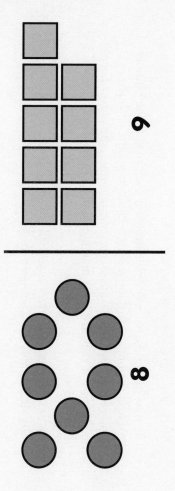

8   9

Your child will practice writing the numbers 8 and 9 and continue to practice counting groups of 1 to 7 objects so that each new number can be related to those already learned.

Invite your child to share what he or she knows about counting up to 9 by doing the following activity together.

NEXT

Materials: 18 index cards (or pieces of paper), pencils or crayons, small stickers (optional)

To review counting and writing the numbers 1 through 9, help your child make the cards described below and then use them to play a matching game.

- Have your child make number cards by writing the numbers 1 to 9 on index cards (or pieces of paper). Use crayon or pencil so the numbers do not show through the backs of the cards.

- Show your child how to make object cards by placing 1 to 9 stickers or drawing 1 to 9 small pictures on the rest of the cards.

- When finished, place the number cards facedown in a row and the object cards facedown in another row.

- The first player turns over one card from each row. If the number card and the object card are a match (such as a card with the number 8 and a card with 8 stickers or pictures), the player keeps both cards. If they are not a match, the player turns the cards facedown again.

- The next player turns over two cards to try to find a match. Play until all the matches have been found.

Count 8 and 9

Name _____

Have your child color a group of 8 similar objects. Then have your child use a different color to color a group of 9 similar objects. Have your child color the rest of the picture.

Have your child count and draw lines to match objects. Have your child draw a line to connect each umbrella to a child. Encourage your child to count as he or she draws each line and tell the total number of lines drawn. Then have your child connect each child to a rain hat, counting as he or she draws each line.

Count 8 and 9

Name _____

Example

Have your child practice writing 8 or 9 and finding groups of 8 or 9 objects. Ask your child to trace and write the number at the beginning of each problem. Then have your child color the group with the correct number of shapes or objects.

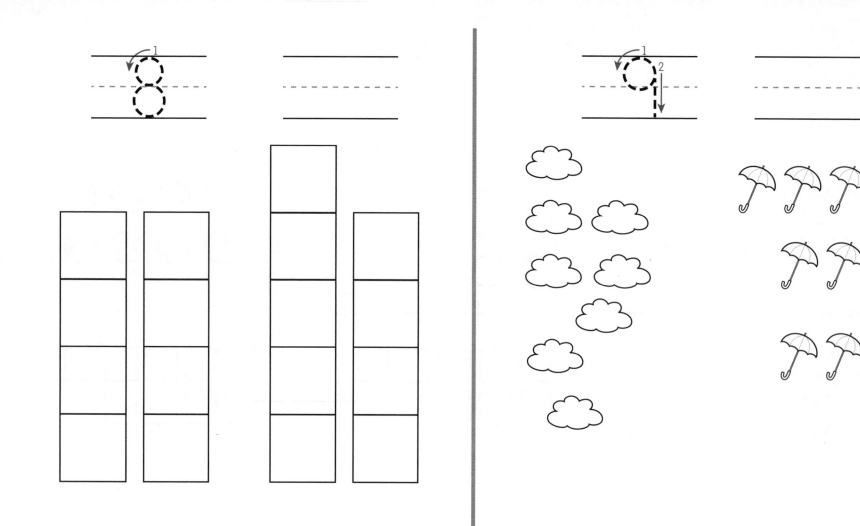

Have your child practice writing 8 or 9 and finding groups of 8 or 9 objects. Ask your child to trace and write the number at the beginning of each problem. Then have your child color the group with the correct number of shapes or objects.

Count 8 and 9

Name _____

Example

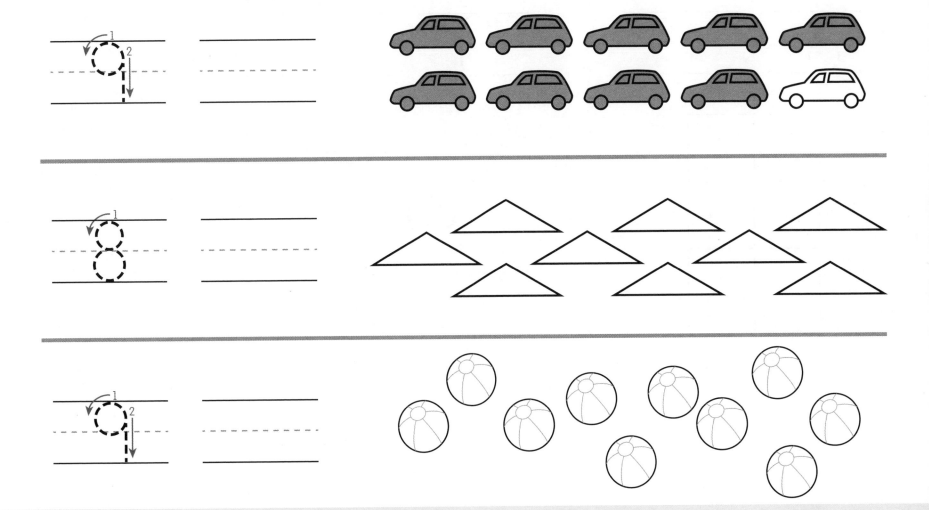

Have your child practice writing 8 or 9 and counting out 8 or 9 objects. Ask your child to trace and then write the number at the beginning of each problem. Then have your child color that number of objects.

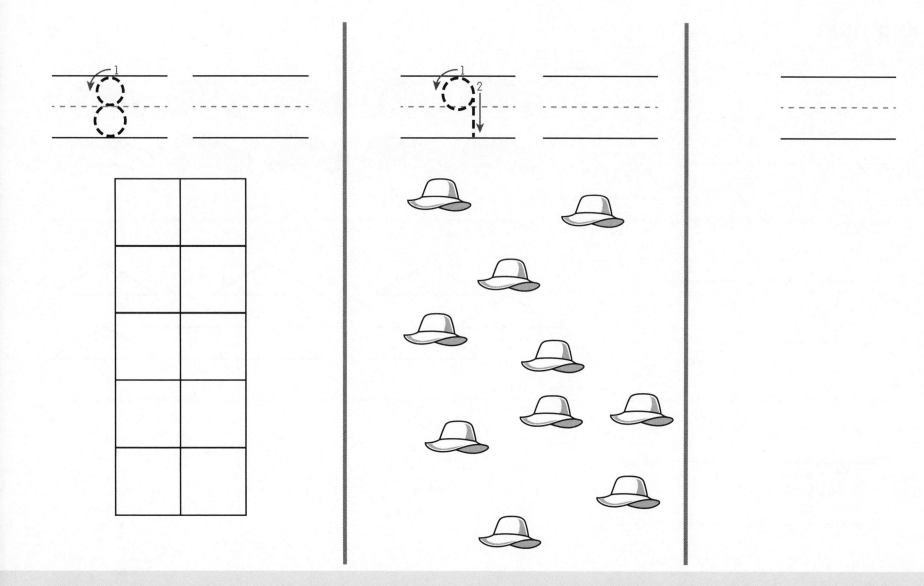

Have your child practice writing 8 or 9, count out and color that number of objects, and draw 9 objects. In the first two problems, have your child trace and write the number and then color that many shapes or objects. In the last problem, have your child write the number 9 and then draw a picture to show 9 objects.

Dear Family,

This week your child is learning to find the numbers that make 8 and 9.

As discussed in earlier letters, numbers can be made up of combinations of other numbers. In this lesson, drawings and 10-frames are used to explore the various ways to make 8 and 9.

Using 10-frames will help your child visualize the numbers that make 8 and 9, as well as help develop an understanding of how 8 and 9 relate to 5 and 10. For example, 8 is 5 and 3 more, and 9 is 1 less than 10. Being able to quickly relate numbers to 5 and 10 will help your child succeed in later work with greater numbers and with addition and subtraction.

Ways to Make 8	
1 and 7	7 and 1
2 and 6	6 and 2
3 and 5	5 and 3
4 and 4	

Ways to Make 9	
1 and 8	8 and 1
2 and 7	7 and 2
3 and 6	6 and 3
4 and 5	5 and 4

Make 8 on a 10-frame

2 and 6

Make 9 on a 10-frame

5 and 4

Invite your child to share what he or she knows about making 8 and 9 by doing the following activity together.

NEXT

Making 8 and 9 Activity

Materials: 18 small objects in two colors (9 of each color such as buttons, beads, dried beans, small blocks, pennies, nickels), paper bag or other container, 10-frame (provided below)

Help your child practice finding ways to make 8 and 9.

- Place 16 small objects in a paper bag. Make sure there are 8 objects of each color.

- Have your child remove 8 objects from the bag. After he or she has counted to check that there are 8 objects, your child sorts the objects by color into two groups.

- Then have your child place the objects on the 10-frame, starting from the top left and keeping same-colored objects together.

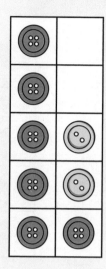

- Your child uses the objects in the 10-frame to tell you a way to make 8. For example, using the 10-frame above, your child might say, "6 and 2 make 8."

- After doing the activity several times, add 1 more object of each color to the bag and have your child find ways to make 9.

Make 8 and 9

Name _____

Have your child use two different colors to color a group of 8 similar objects. Then have your child use two different colors to color a group of 9 similar objects. Have your child color the rest of the page.

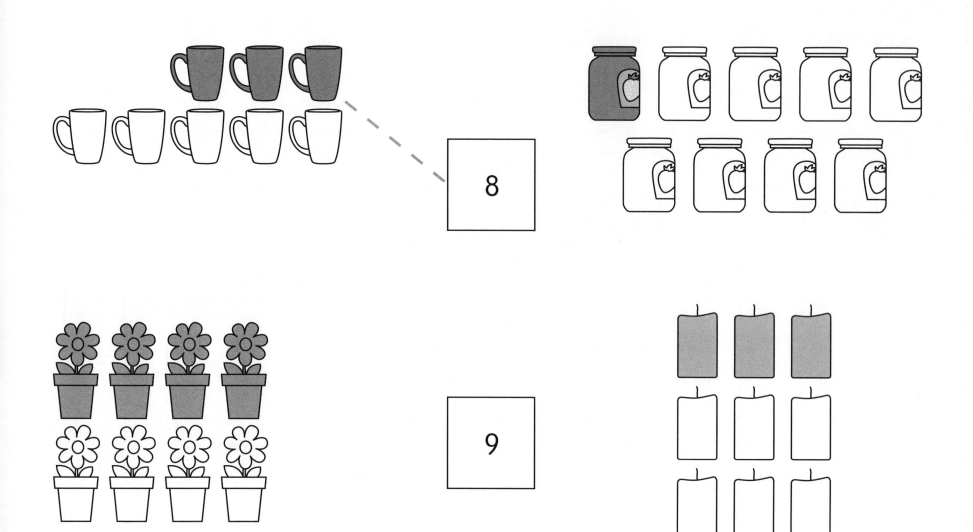

Have your child draw lines to match each number to two groups of objects that show different ways to make that number. Then have your child describe how each number is made. For example, your child might say, "3 gray cups and 5 white cups make 8."

Make 8 and 9

Name _____

Example

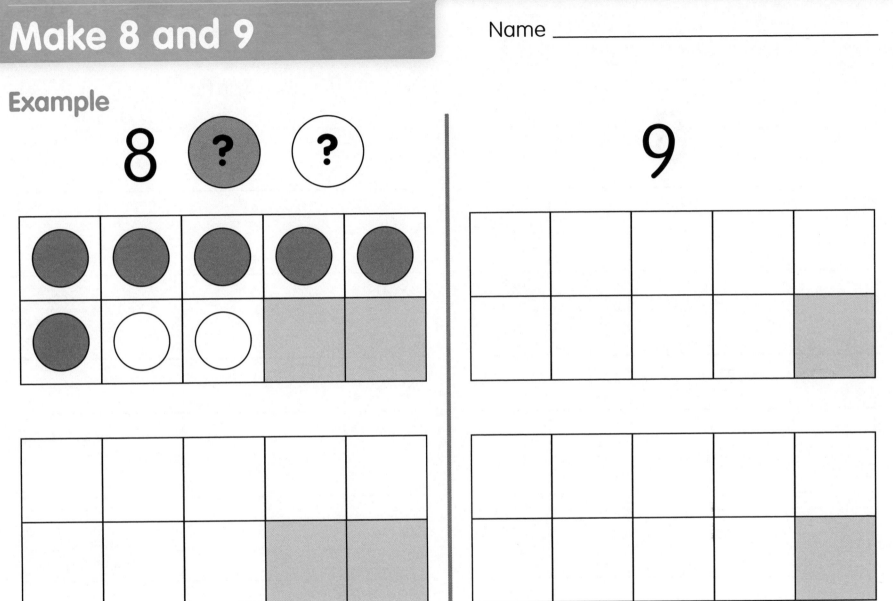

8   ?   ?

9

Guide your child to make 8 and then 9 using coins or counters that are different on each side. Point out that in the Example problem, the number pair shown for 8 is 6 and 2. Then have your child show and use two colors to record a different way to make 8. On the right, have your child show and record two ways to make 9.

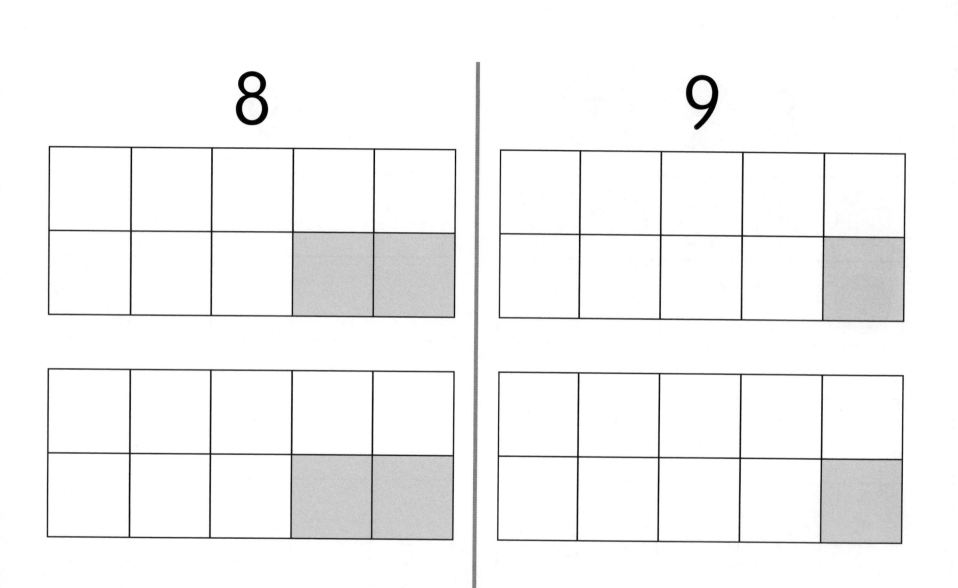

Guide your child to make 8 and then 9 using coins or counters that are different on each side. For the first three problems, have your child use two colors to record his or her work. For the last problem, challenge your child to use one color to make 9 and tell the number pair shown (9 and 0).

Make 8 and 9

Name _____

Example

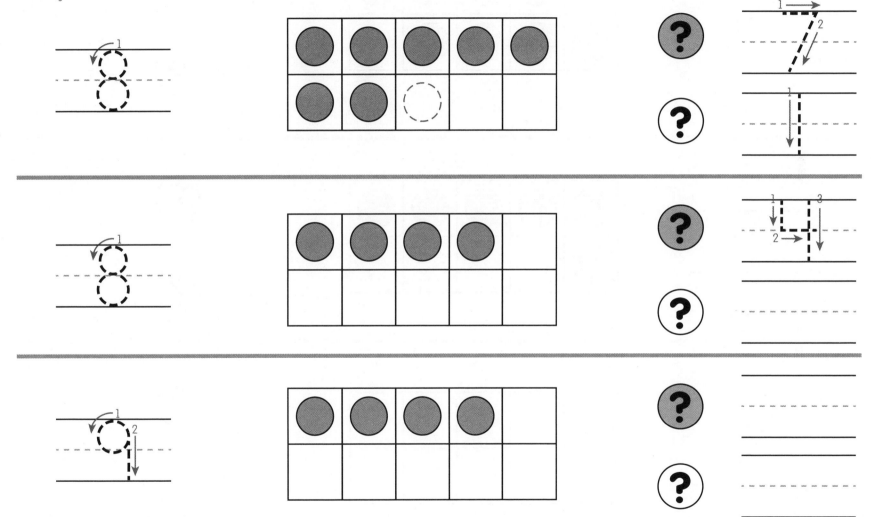

Guide your child to trace the numbers on the left and draw more counters in the 10-frames to show a total of 8 or 9. On the right, have your child write the number of gray counters shown and the number of counters that he or she drew to make the total.

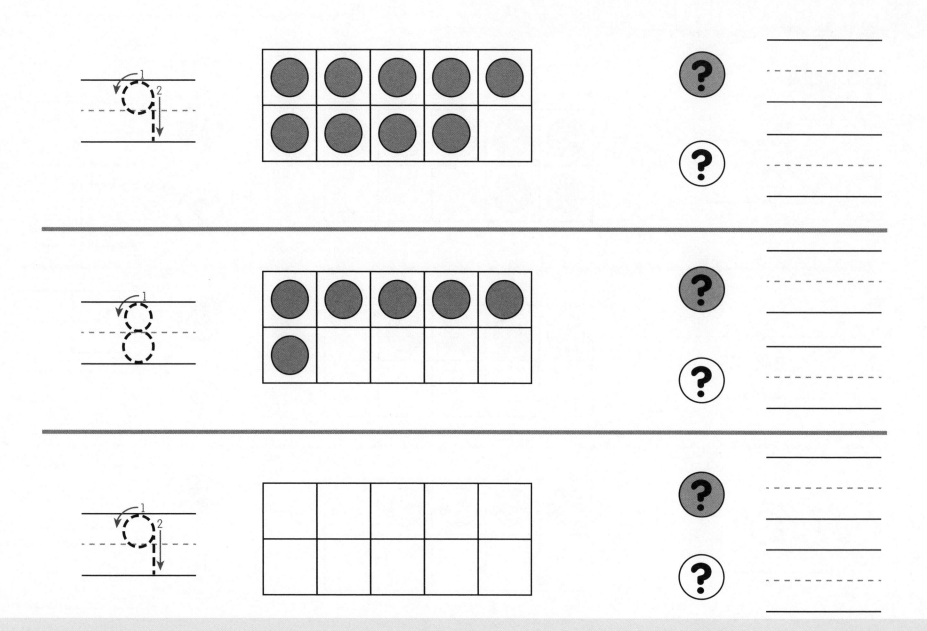

Guide your child to trace the numbers on the left and draw more counters in the 10-frames (if needed) to show a total of 8 or 9. For the first two rows, have your child write the number of gray counters shown and the number of counters that he or she drew to make the total. For the last row, have your child use two colors to draw counters that show another way to make 9 and write the number pair.

©Curriculum Associates, LLC   Copying is not permitted.

Numbers 6 to 9

Name _____

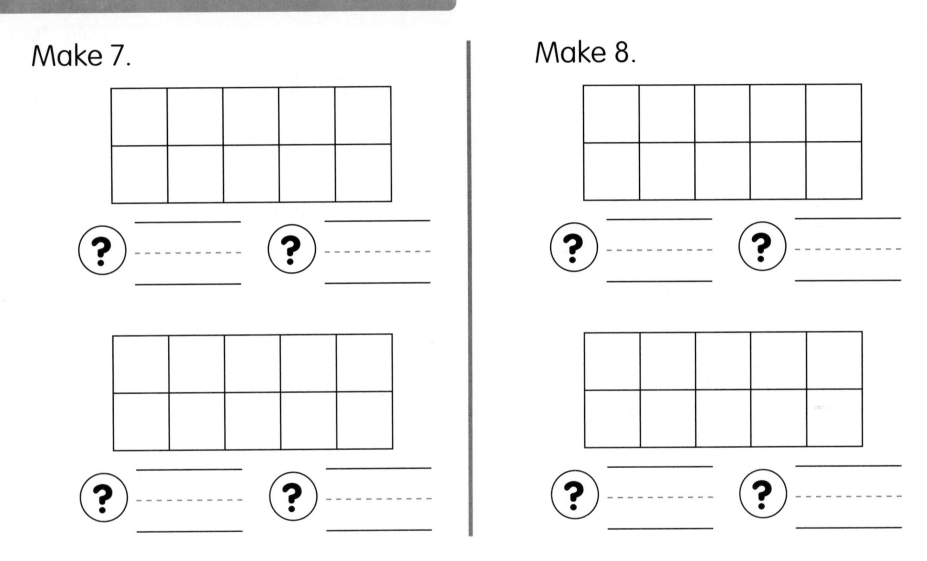

Make 7.

Make 8.

Have children draw red and blue counters to make 7 and 8 two different ways. Explain to children that these problems can be solved in different ways. Have children count and write the number of counters of each color they drew.

How many dogs? _____

Draw 1 🦴 for each dog.

Have children count and write the number of dogs, then draw one bone for each dog pictured. Allow children to find their own strategies for determining how many bones to draw.

Match 6, 7, 8, and 9

Name _____

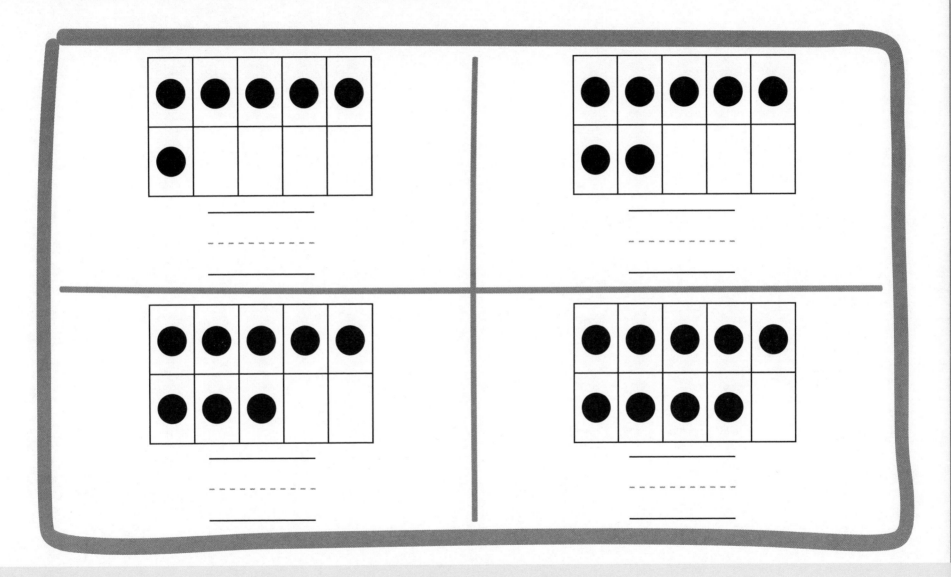

Materials For each pair: 1 set of Dot Cards; for each child: Match 6, 7, 8, and 9 Game Board
How to Play Take a dot card. Tell how many dots are on the card. Find the 10-frame with that many dots. Write the number to label that 10-frame. Skip a turn if the 10-frame is already used. The first player to label all the 10-frames wins.

Dear Family,

This week your child is building counting skills with the number 10.

This skill includes practice with counting groups of 10 objects in various ways. Using counters, pictures, 10-frames, and other tools help to visualize and count 10. Examining and counting groups of 10 in 2 rows of 5, 2 columns of 5, and other common arrangements strengthen the visualization of 10. Understanding 10 will provide your child with a strong foundation for working within our place-value number system, including solving problems involving greater numbers and using various addition and subtraction strategies.

Building on earlier lessons, your child will also explore how 10 relates to other numbers. For example, 10 is one more than 9, and 10 is 2 groups of 5. To reinforce the relationships between numbers and to review numbers learned previously, your child will continue to practice counting groups of 1 to 9 objects. Learning to write the number 10, which involves writing two digits, is also an important part of this lesson.

Invite your child to share what he or she knows about counting 10 by doing the following activity together.

Counting 10 Activity

Materials: paper, pencil, 10 small objects (such as buttons, dried beans, or cereal), dot cube (or homemade number cards 1–6)

Trace your child's two hands on a sheet of paper. Help your child use the hand picture to do the following activity.

- Roll a dot cube (or turn over a number card) and count out that number of buttons. Place 1 button on each finger.

- Keep rolling and placing buttons until you get to 10—when all fingers are covered. Make sure to stop when you get to 10, no matter what number you rolled. Repeat the activity several times.

- You may want to have your child count the covered fingers to emphasize the relationship between two hands and the number 10.

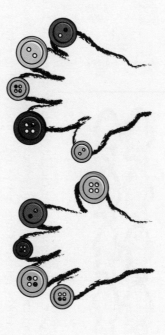

In addition to doing the above activity, practice counting 1 to 10 objects with your child whenever you can. For example, encourage your child to count spoons, apples, crackers, buttons, books, stairs, etc. Also, point out numbers you see in the world around you, such as on signs, clocks, food labels, license plates, and sports uniforms.

Count 10

Name _____

Have your child use different colors to color groups of 10. Then have your child color the rest of the picture.

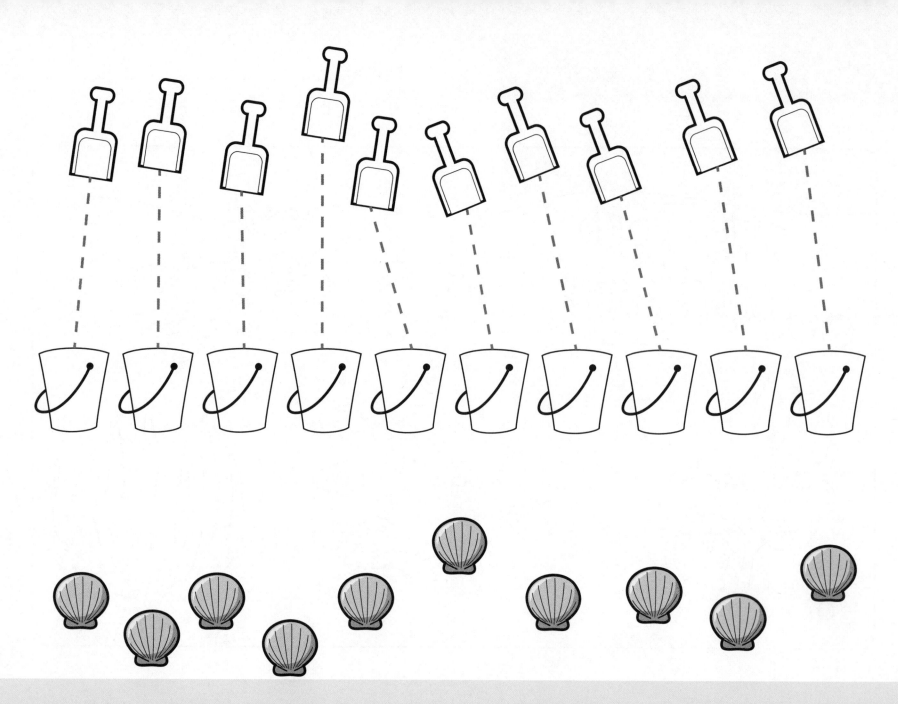

Have your child count and draw lines to match objects. Have your child count as he or she traces lines to connect each shovel to a pail. Ask your child to tell the total number of pails. Then have your child connect each pail to a shell, counting aloud as he or she draws lines.

Count 10

Example

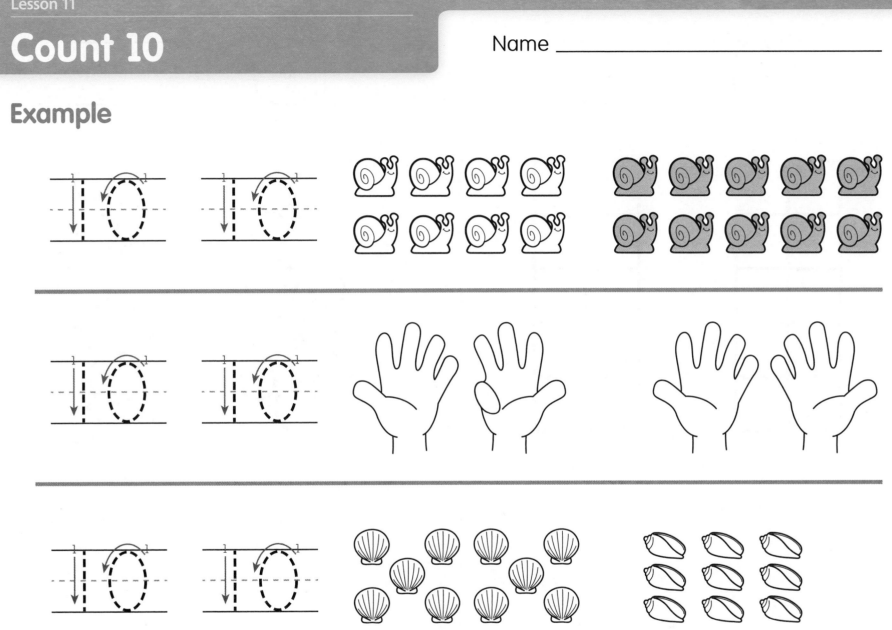

Have your child trace the number 10 and color the group that has 10 objects. Have your child count the number of objects in each of the two groups. Discuss different ways to count the objects. Then have him or her color the group that has 10.

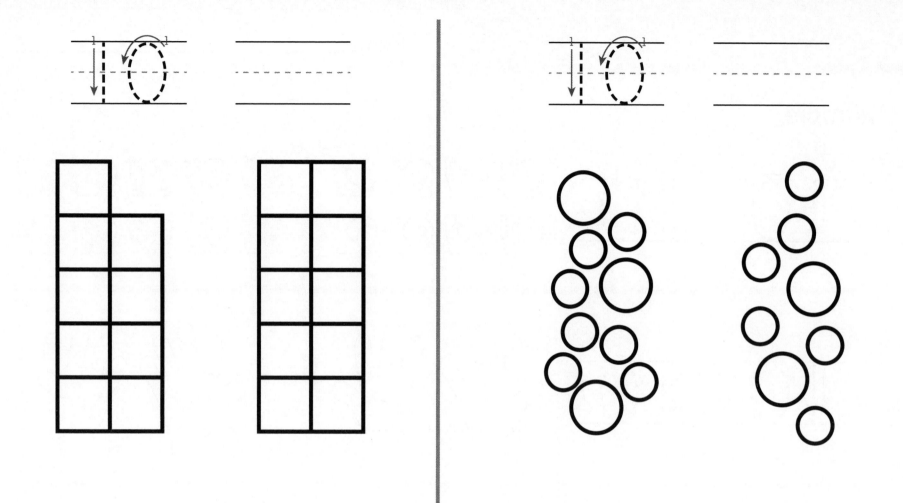

Have your child trace and write the number 10 and color the group that has 10 objects. Have your child count the number of squares or circles in each group. Discuss different ways to count the objects. Then have him or her color the group that has 10.

Count 10

Example

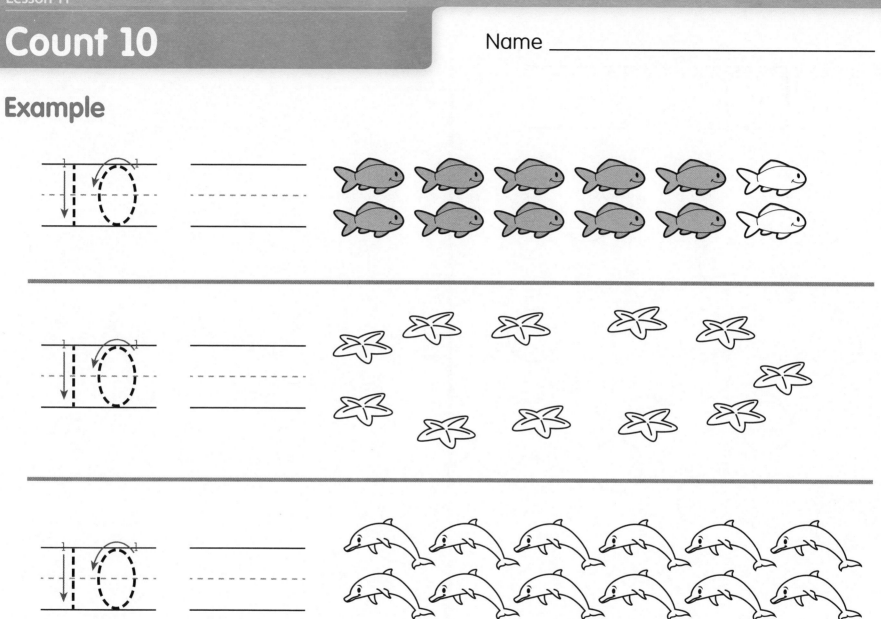

Have your child practice writing 10 and counting out 10 objects. Ask your child to trace and write the number 10. Then have your child color that number of objects.

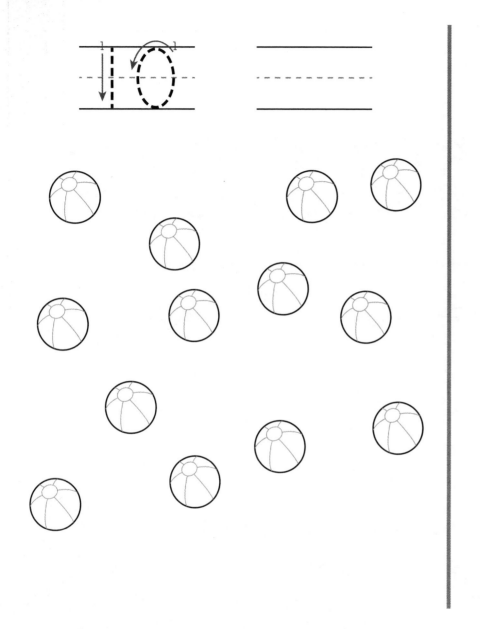

Have your child trace and write the number 10, count and color 10 objects, and then draw 10. On the left, have your child trace and write the number 10 and then color 10 objects. On the right, ask your child to write the number 10 and then draw a picture to show 10 objects.

Dear Family,

This week your child is learning to compare within 10.

The lesson includes comparing groups of up to 10 objects to find which group has more and which group has less. There are many strategies that can be used in comparing. When comparing objects in a picture, you can draw lines between the objects in the two groups, or cross out pairs of objects (one from each group) until one group has no more objects to cross out. If comparing actual objects, you may line them up in two rows to see which group has more and which has less.

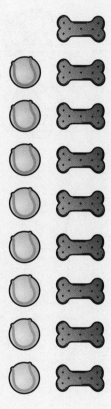

As your child begins to think more abstractly, he or she will start to recognize that 7 is more than 4, no matter what objects are being counted or how they are arranged.

Comparing groups of objects will help prepare your child for solving subtraction problems that involve finding how many more or how many fewer objects are in one group than another.

Invite your child to share what he or she knows about comparing within 10 by doing the following activity together.

Materials: 20 small objects of 2 different kinds (such as 10 crackers and 10 pretzels, 10 dried beans and 10 pasta shapes, or 10 buttons and 10 paper clips), 2 bowls

Do this activity to help your child practice comparing within 10.

• Place 10 objects of one kind in a bowl for your child. Place 10 objects of another kind in a bowl for yourself.

• You and your child each take a handful of objects and place them on the table. Your child compares the groups of objects using any strategy he or she prefers and says which group has more. For example, if there are 8 beans and 3 pasta shapes, your child should say, "8 is more than 3." (Sometimes the groups will have the same number of objects. If that is the case, add or remove one of your objects.)

• Return the objects to the bowls and repeat the activity several times. Then have your child compare the groups to find which shows less. For example, if there are 8 crackers and 3 pretzels, your child should say: "3 is less than 8."

In addition to doing the above activity, encourage your child to compare numbers of objects in his or her daily life. For example, ask your child to compare numbers of buttons and pockets, cups and plates, or swings and slides. Ask your child to compare pictures of objects in books.

Compare Within 10

Name _____

Have your child count and color the 8 dogs. Have your child color green a group that has less than 8. Have your child color brown a group that has more than 8. Then have your child color the rest of the picture.

Example

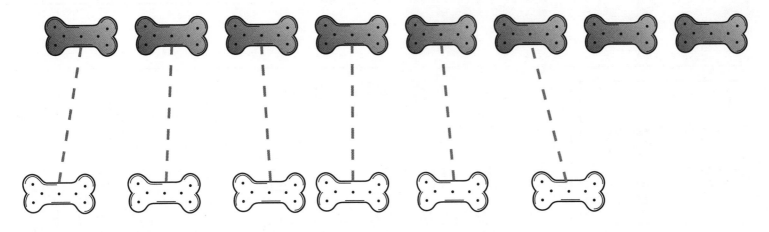

Have your child draw lines to match objects. On the top, have your child trace the lines and color the group with more biscuits. On the bottom, have your child draw lines and then color the group with fewer balls.

Compare Within 10

Name _____

Example

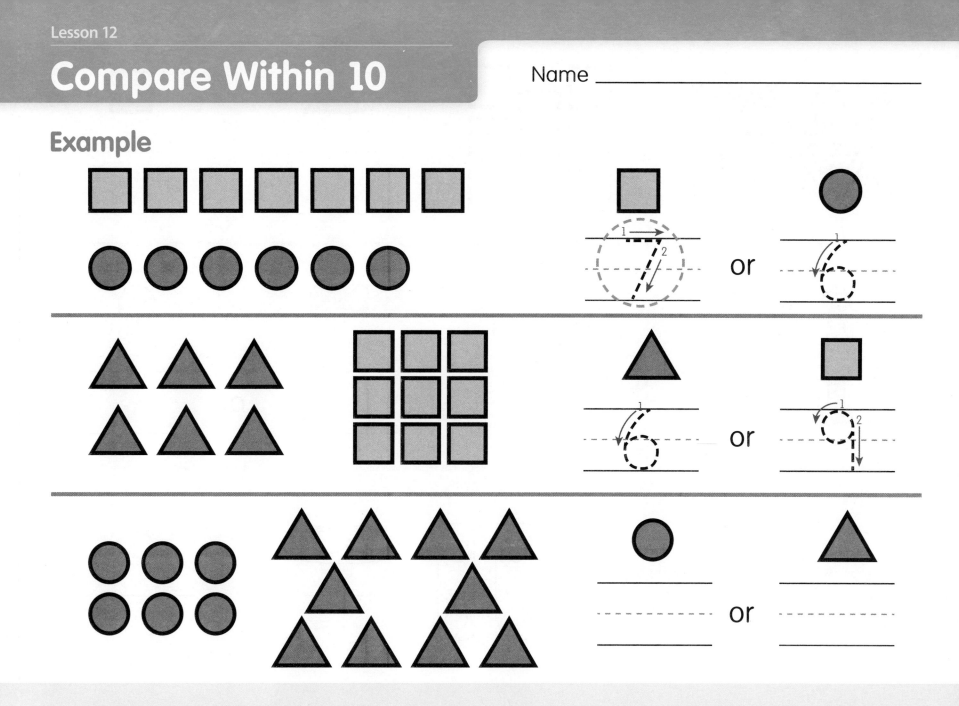

In each problem, guide your child to compare the numbers of objects. Have your child write how many are in each group and then circle the number that is more.

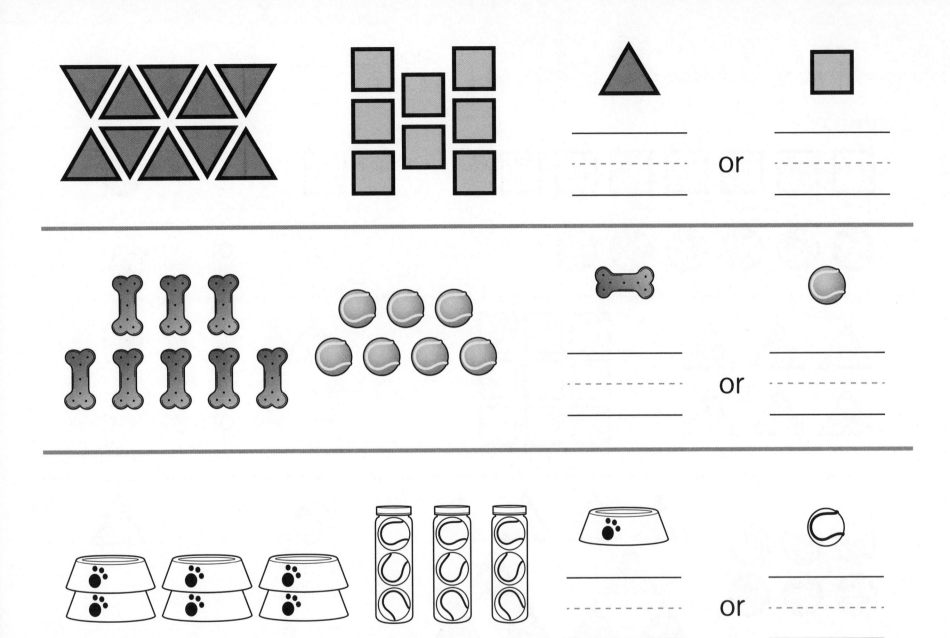

_____   or   _____

_____   _____

In each problem, guide your child to compare the numbers of objects. Have your child write how many are in each group and then circle the number that is more.

Compare Within 10

Name _____

Example

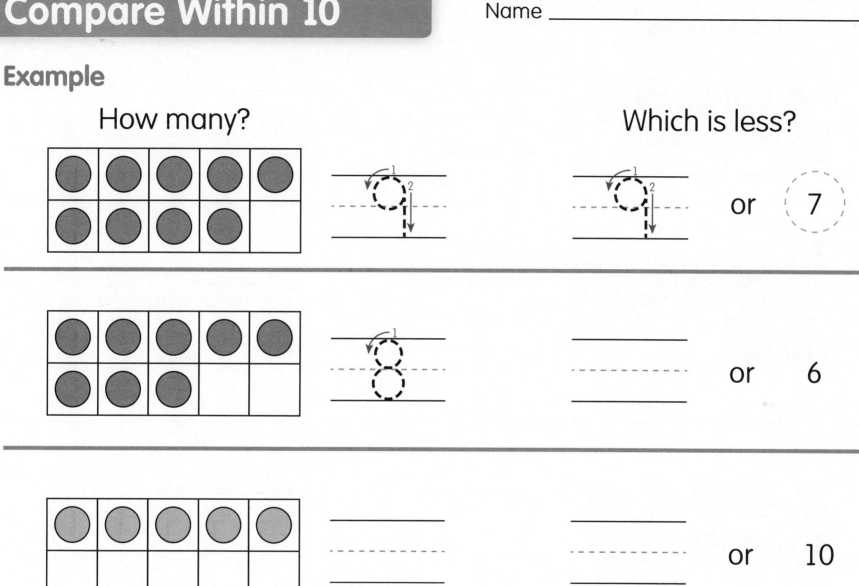

How many?

Which is less?

or ⟨ 7 ⟩

or 6

or 10

Guide your child to compare the number of counters in a 10-frame with a given number and tell which is less. Have your child count and write the number of counters in the 10-frame. Ask him or her to compare that number to the number shown on the right. Circle the number that is less.

How many?

Which is less?

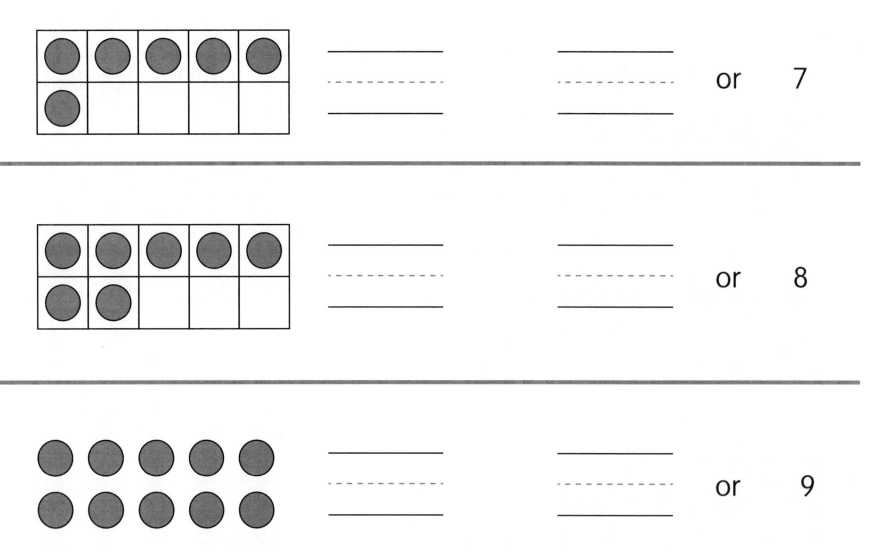

_____
- - - - - - - - - - - - - - -   or   7
_____

_____
- - - - - - - - - - - - - - -   or   8
_____

_____
- - - - - - - - - - - - - - -   or   9
_____

Guide your child to compare a number of counters with a given number and tell which is less. Have your child count, write the number of counters, and compare that number to the number shown on the right. Circle the number that is less.

Dear Family,

This week your child is learning find the numbers that make 10.

This lesson uses pictures, counters, and 10-frames to find the different combinations of numbers that make 10.

Using a 10-frame helps to visualize 10 as a quantity, as well as visualize the numbers that make 10. For example, by filling a 10-frame in different ways, you can see that 10 is made up of 4 and 6, 7 and 3, and other number pairs. The structure of a 10-frame, which has 2 rows of 5, can also help your child recognize that 10 is made up of 2 groups of 5. Knowing all the ways to make 10 will allow your child to use multiple strategies to add and subtract.

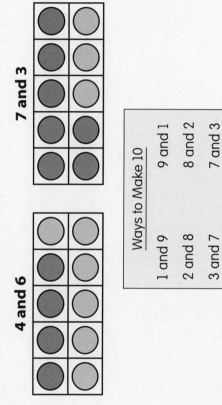

4 and 6

7 and 3

Ways to Make 10

1 and 9	9 and 1
2 and 8	8 and 2
3 and 7	7 and 3
4 and 6	6 and 4
5 and 5	

Invite your child to share what he or she knows about making 10 by doing the following activity together.

NEXT

Materials: egg carton, 18 small objects of 2 different colors or types to place in the egg carton (such as buttons in 2 different colors, small blocks in 2 different colors, or dried beans and pasta shapes)

Cut off two cups at one end of the egg carton. Now that the egg carton has 2 rows of 5 cups, help your child use it like a 10-frame to do the following activity. (If you prefer to not use an egg carton, you can draw a 10-frame instead or use the one on the back of the Family Letter for Lesson 10.)

- Put some objects of one color in the egg carton, placing them in the top row first and working from left to right.

- Have your child finish filling the egg carton with objects of a different color. Your child should say how the objects in the egg carton show a way to make 10, such as, "4 and 6 make 10." Repeat until you have found 5 different ways to make 10.

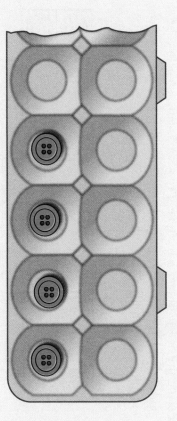

- You can also use the egg carton to review ways to make the numbers 3 through 9. Remind your child that the entire egg carton should not be filled for these numbers.

Make 10

Have your child use two colors to color a group of 10. Then have your child use two colors to color another group of 10, this time showing a different number pair. Have your child color the rest of the page.

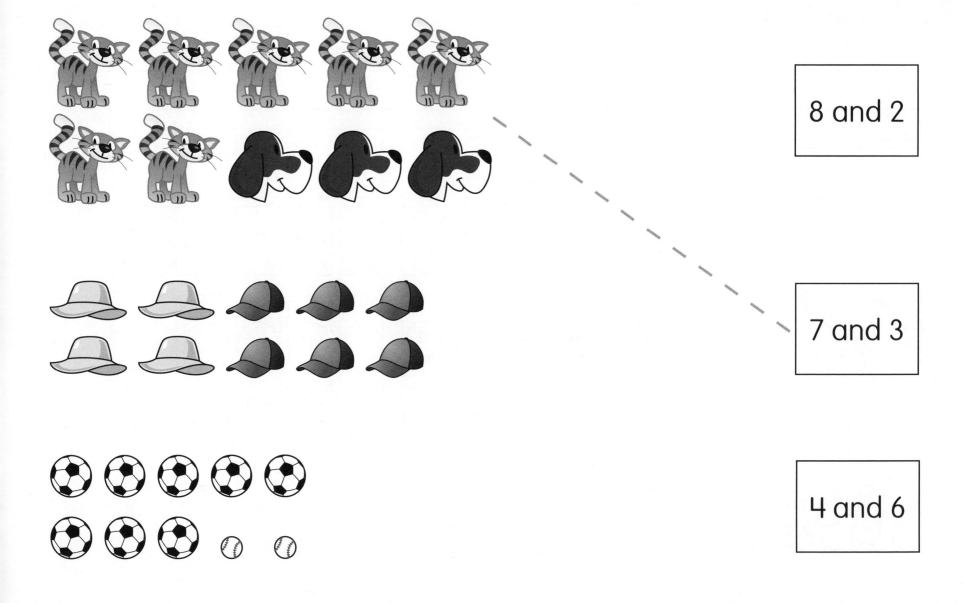

8 and 2

7 and 3

4 and 6

Have your child draw lines to match each group of 10 to the number pair that describes the group. Then have your child describe the group of 10. For example, your child might say, "This group of 10 is made of 7 cats and 3 dogs."

Make 10

Example

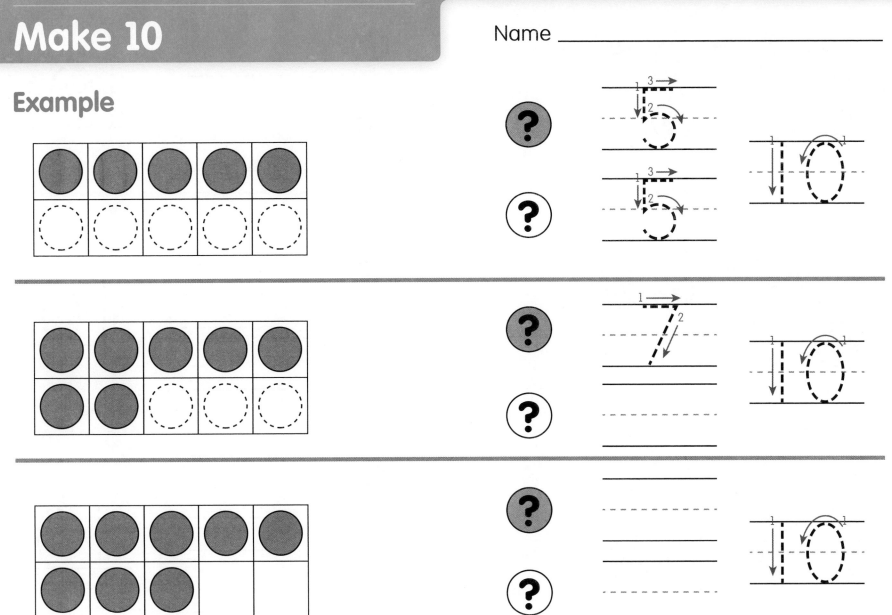

Guide your child to draw counters to finish each picture so that it shows 10. Have your child write the number of gray counters shown and the number of counters that he or she drew. Finally, have your child trace the number 10 to show the total.

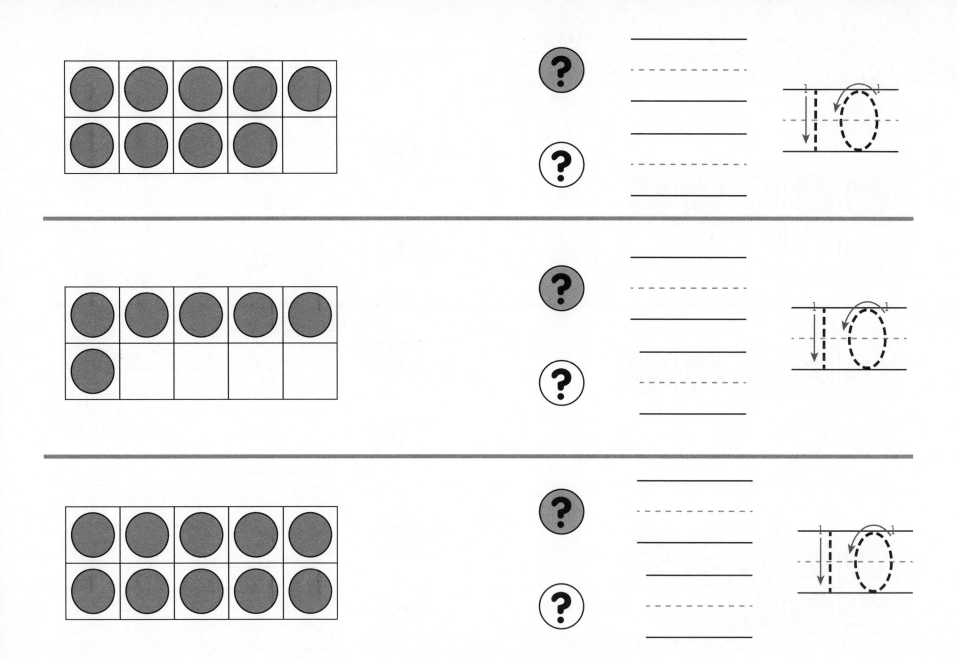

Guide your child to draw counters, if needed, to finish each picture so that it shows 10. Have your child write the number of gray counters shown and the number of counters that he or she drew. Finally, have your child trace the number 10 to show the total.

Make 10

Example

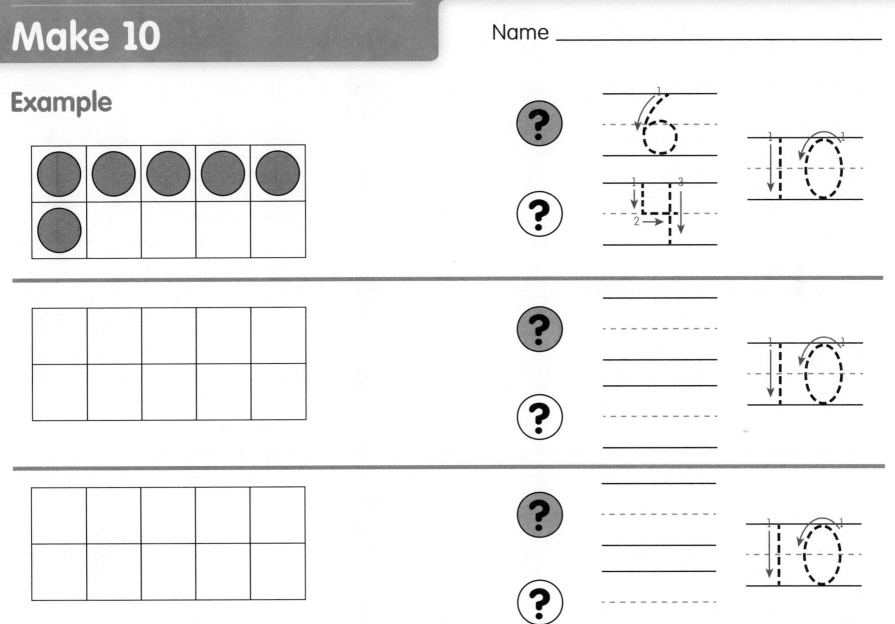

Guide your child to choose 3 different ways to complete the 10-frames by drawing gray and white counters to show a total of 10. In each problem, have your child count the number of each color, write the number pair, and trace the 10.

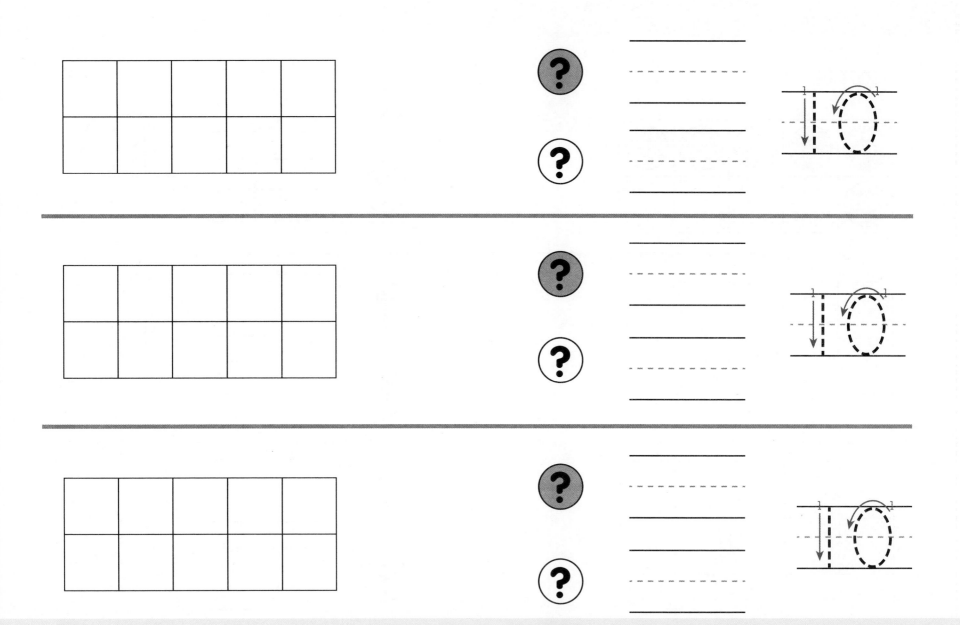

Guide your child to show 3 different ways to complete the 10-frames by drawing gray and white counters to make a total of 10. For the first two problems, encourage your child to show number pairs that are different from those on the previous page. For the last problem, have your child show 10 with only one color. In each problem, have your child count the number of each color, write the number pair, and trace the 10.

Numbers to 10

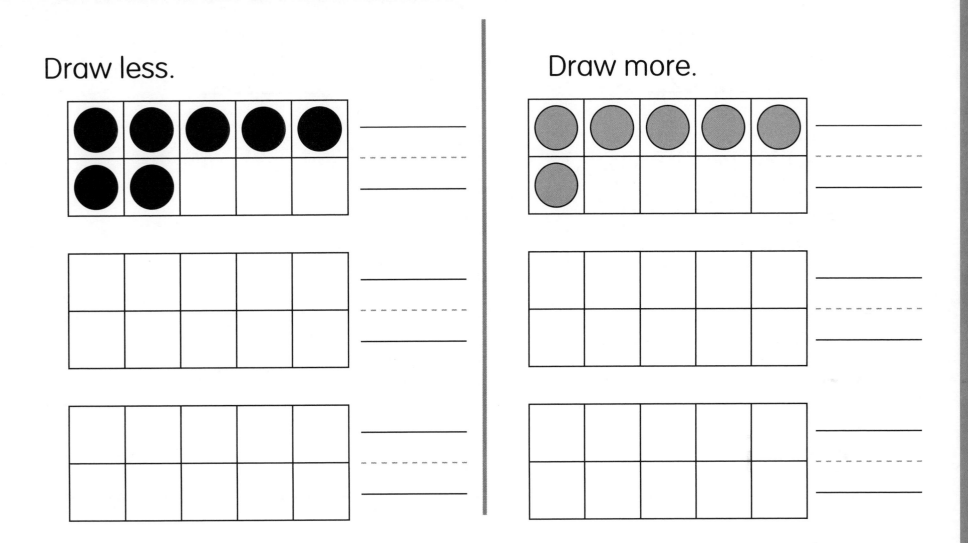

Draw less.

Draw more.

Have children draw less or more than a given number of counters. Have children count the number of black and gray counters and write the numbers to the right of the 10-frames. For the black counters, children draw counters and write numbers to show less than 7. For the gray counters, children draw counters and write numbers to show more than 6.

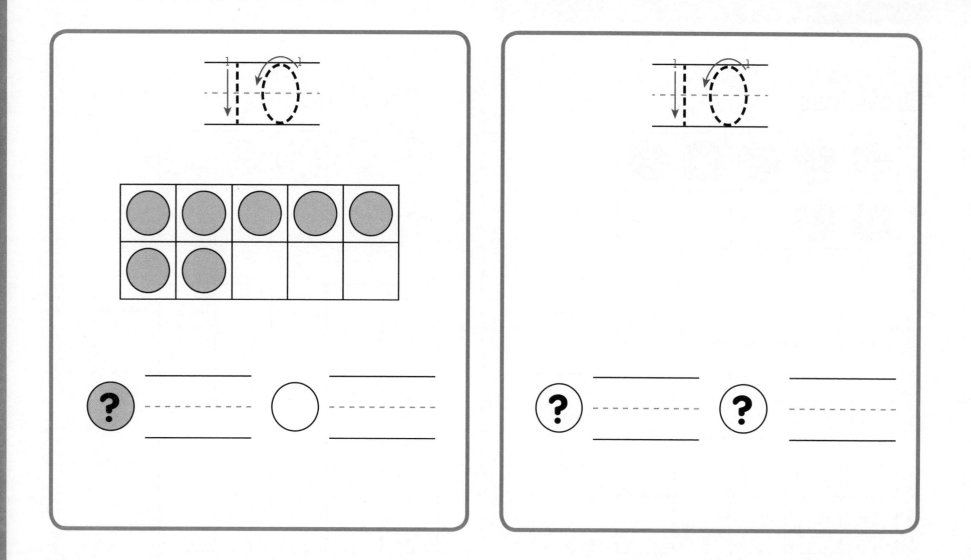

Have children use two colors to draw counters that show 10 two different ways and record the number pairs.

Make 10

Name _____

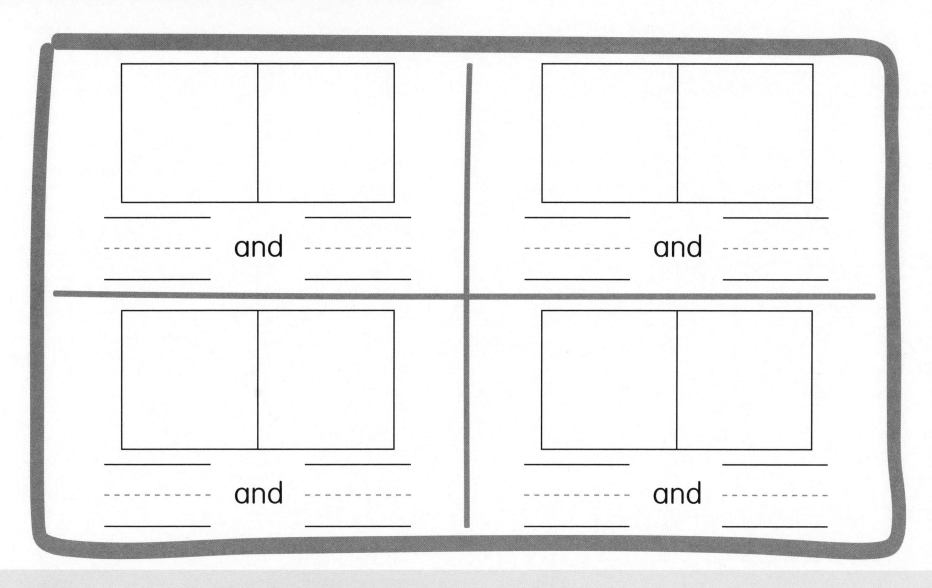

Materials For each pair: Dot Cards 1–9, bag; for each child: Make 10 Game Board
How to Play Take 1 dot card. Place it on any square. Your partner does the same. Try to make totals of 10. When you fill a pair of squares, write the numbers.
Skip a turn If you don't have a place for a card. The first player to fill all pairs of squares with totals of 10 wins.

Dear Family,

This week your child is learning about addition.

This lesson explores the idea of what it means to add. It also introduces the plus sign and the equal sign as a way to represent the joining together of two groups of objects into a single group. Your child will use connecting cubes as physical models and drawings as visual models to show adding two groups.

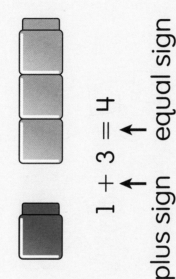

$$1 + 3 = 4$$

plus sign   equal sign

The lesson also introduces different problem situations.

Add To: *There are 2 birds in a tree. 3 more birds join them. How many birds are in the tree now?*

Put Together: *2 oranges and 3 apples are in a bowl. How many pieces of fruit are in the bowl!?*

Physically modeling addition, drawing pictures, and exploring different problem situations will help your child make connections to how addition is used in everyday life.

Invite your child to share what he or she knows about addition by doing the following activity together.

NEXT

Materials: 8 small objects of 2 different types or colors (such as pretzels and crackers, dried pasta pieces in 2 different shapes, or buttons in 2 different colors)

Do the following activity to help your child explore what it means to add.

- Give your child two groups of objects that have a combined total of 5 or less. For example, place snack items such as 3 pretzels and 2 crackers in two groups.

- Ask how many objects are in each group. After your child counts, ask an addition problem about the groups, such as: *There are 3 pretzels and 2 crackers. How many snacks are there in all?*

- Your child puts the groups together and counts to find the total. You might also ask your child to write a number sentence, for example 3 + 2 = 5.

- Ask your child addition problems about small groups of objects whenever you can. For example, have your child add apples and bananas, big spoons and small spoons, or yellow blocks and orange blocks.

Understand Addition

Name _____

What can you add?

Show 2 + 2.

Have your child draw a picture of objects he or she could add to show 2 + 2. You may want to give examples of adding, such as the following: *There are 2 cards on the table. I put 2 more cards on the table. How many cards are on the table now?* Or *There are 2 red apples and 2 green apples in a bag. How many apples are in the bag?* Encourage your child to tell a similar story about his or her drawing.

Why do you add?

Show 1 + 4.

Have your child draw a picture of objects he or she could add to show 1 + 4. For example, your child might add 1 large ball and 4 small balls. Have your child tell a story about the drawing. Encourage him or her to use the words *plus* and *add*.

Understand Addition

Name _____

Example

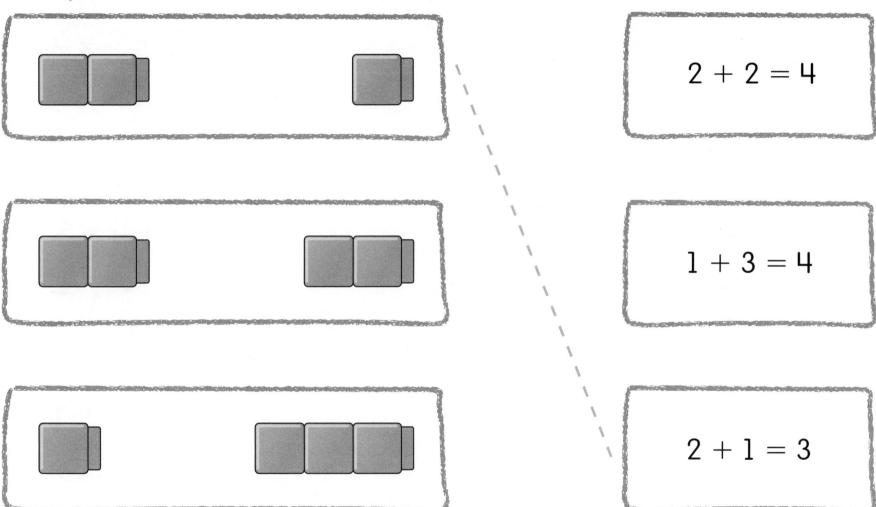

2 + 2 = 4

1 + 3 = 4

2 + 1 = 3

Guide your child to match pictures to addition sentences. Have your child describe how many cubes are being added in each picture. Read each number sentence aloud together and discuss the meaning of each. Then have your child draw lines to match each picture with its number sentence.

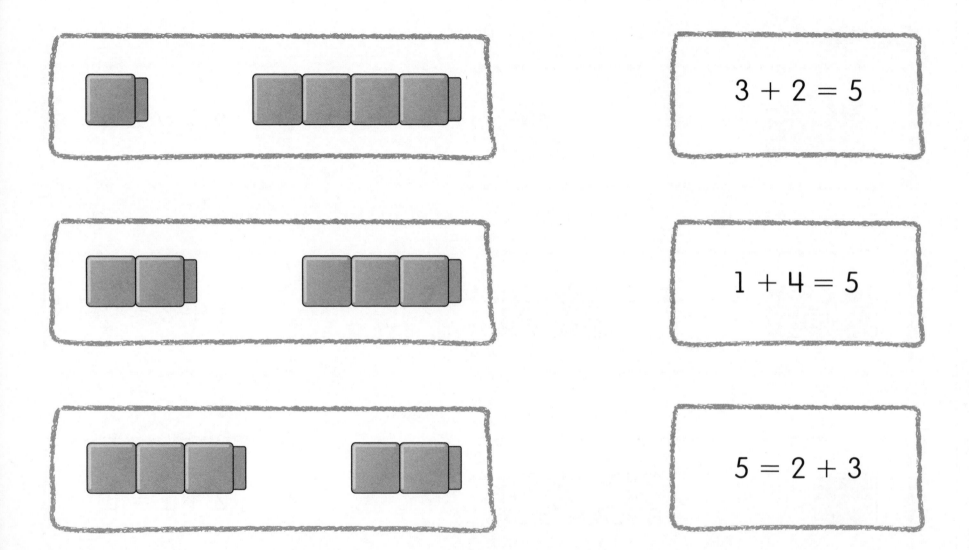

$$3 + 2 = 5$$

$$1 + 4 = 5$$

$$5 = 2 + 3$$

Guide your child to match pictures to addition sentences. Have your child describe how many cubes are being added in each picture. Read each number sentence aloud together and discuss the meaning of each. Then have your child draw lines to match each picture with its number sentence.

Understand Addition

Name _____

Example

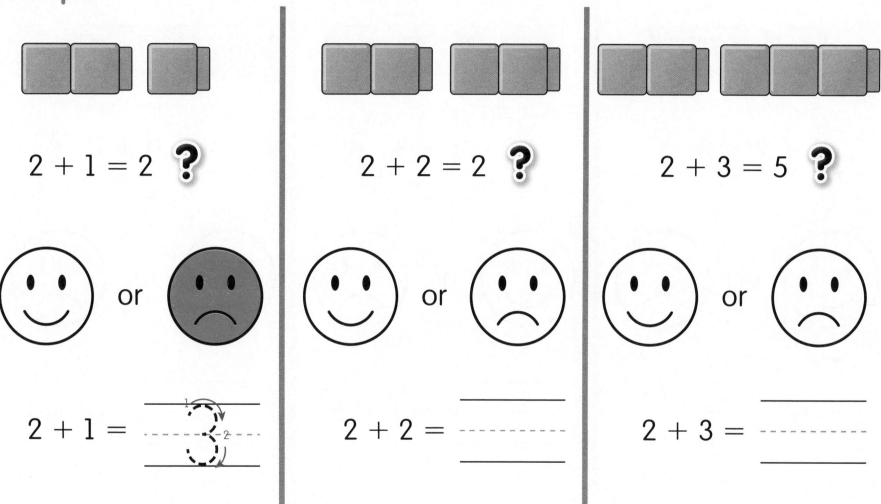

$2 + 1 = 2$ **?**	$2 + 2 = 2$ **?**	$2 + 3 = 5$ **?**
😊 or ☹	😊 or ☹	😊 or ☹
$2 + 1 = \ 3$	$2 + 2 = $ _____	$2 + 3 = $ _____

Guide your child to check whether the number sentence matches the cubes. First, discuss the number of cubes in each group and the total. Then decide if the number sentence matches the cubes. Have your child color the happy face if the number sentence and cubes match or the sad face if they do not match. Guide your child to complete the number sentence at the bottom of the problem.

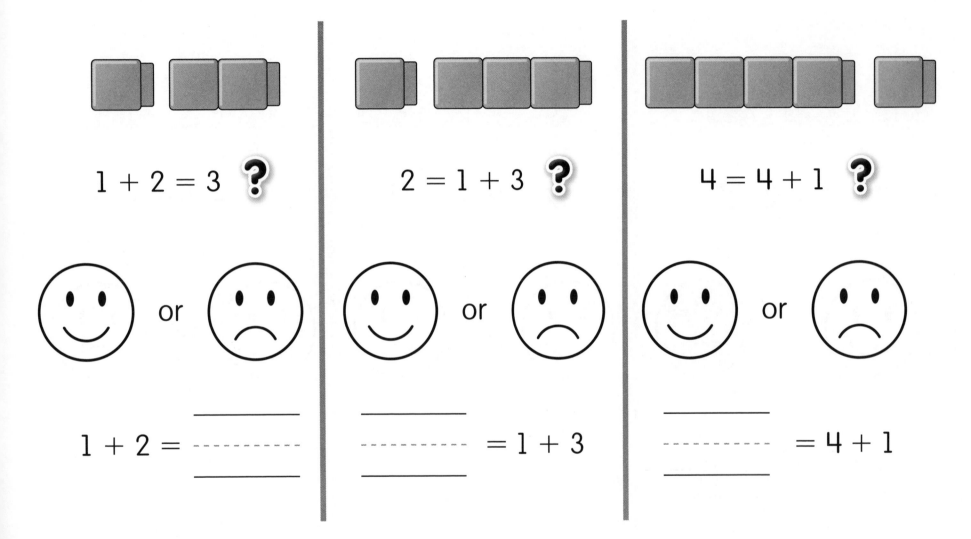

1 + 2 = 3 **?**

😊 or ☹

1 + 2 = _____

---

2 = 1 + 3 **?**

😊 or ☹

_____ = 1 + 3

---

4 = 4 + 1 **?**

😊 or ☹

_____ = 4 + 1

Guide your child to check whether the number sentence matches the cubes. First, discuss the number of cubes in each group and the total. Then decide if the number sentence matches the cubes. Have your child color the happy face if the number sentence and cubes match or the sad face if they do not match. Guide your child to complete the number sentence at the bottom of the problem.

Dear Family,

This week your child is learning to add within 5.

This lesson includes solving addition problems with totals up to 5. It also connects story problems to pictures, objects, 5-frames, and number sentences. This will provide your child with a strong foundation as he or she eventually moves from solving problems shown with pictures or models to solving problems shown only with numbers.

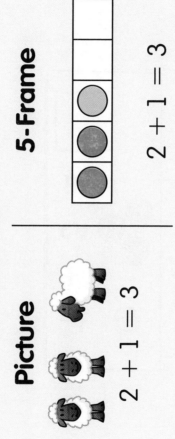

Picture

$2 + 1 = 3$

5-Frame

$2 + 1 = 3$

Story problems about numbers or objects being added are presented to connect math to the real world. Your child will create such story problems. This lesson introduces a new problem situation in which there is more than one possible answer.

Put Together, Both Addends Unknown: *Wes has 5 crackers. How many can he eat? How many can he share with a friend?* (The solution could be 0 and 5, 1 and 4, 2 and 3, 3 and 2, 4 and 1, or 5 and 0.)

Invite your child to share what he or she knows about adding within 5 by doing the following activity together.

NEXT

Materials: 8 small objects of 2 different colors or types (such buttons in 2 different colors or dried pasta pieces in 2 different shapes)

Do the following activity to help your child connect addition sentences to concrete objects.

- Fold a sheet of paper in half from top to bottom.

- Write an addition problem that has a total of 5 or less across the center of the half-sized page. Do not include the total.

- Show your child how to place a group of objects above each number.

- Have your child count how many objects there are in all and write the total after the equals sign.

- Write other addition problems for your child to solve on the three remaining sections of the folded paper. Each addition problem should have a total of 5 or less. Have your child solve the problems in a similar manner.

$$1 + 3 =$$

Add Within 5

Name _____

Have your child use red and yellow to color a group of animals or objects to show 3 + 1 and then tell the total. Then have your child use two other colors to color a group of animals or objects to show 2 + 2. Have your child color the rest of the picture.

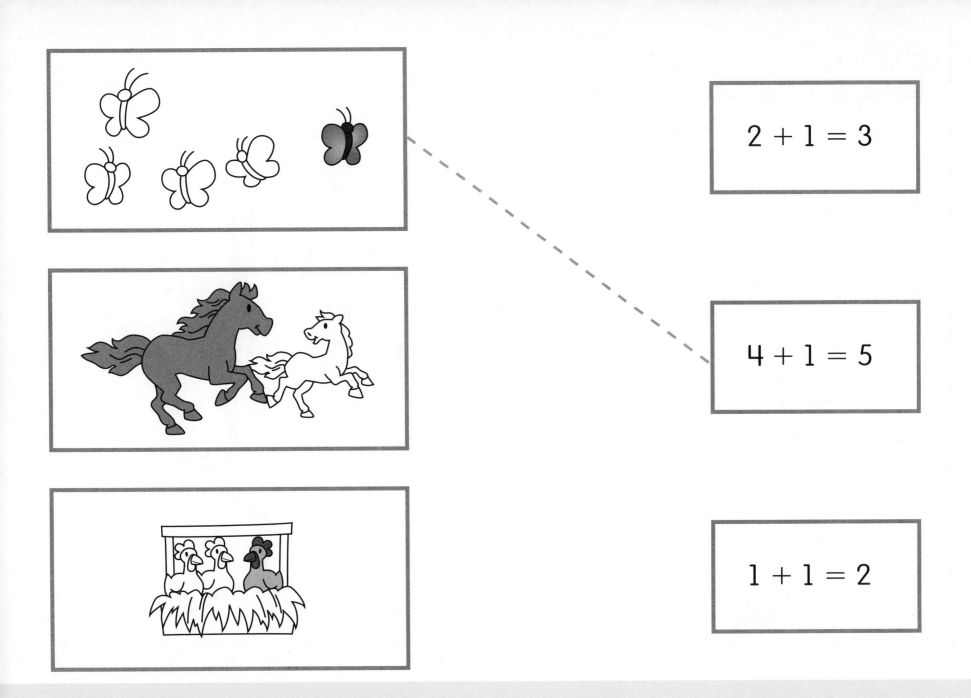

2 + 1 = 3

4 + 1 = 5

1 + 1 = 2

Have your child match pictures to addition sentences. Have your child tell the numbers of gray and white animals, as well as the total, in each picture. Read each addition sentence aloud together. Then have your child draw lines to match each picture to its addition sentence.

Add Within 5

Example

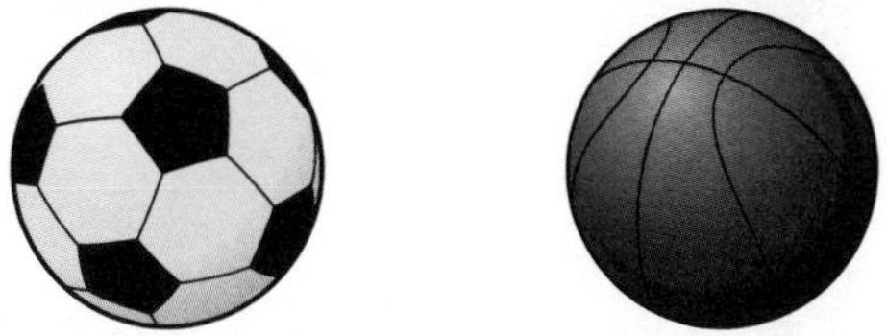

$1 + 1 = 2$

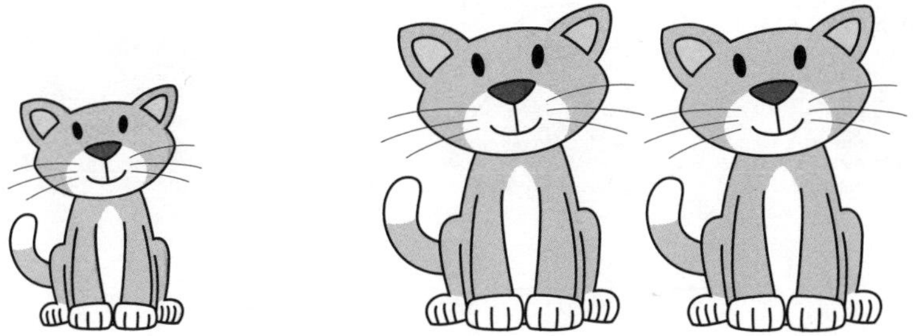

$1 + 2 = $ _____

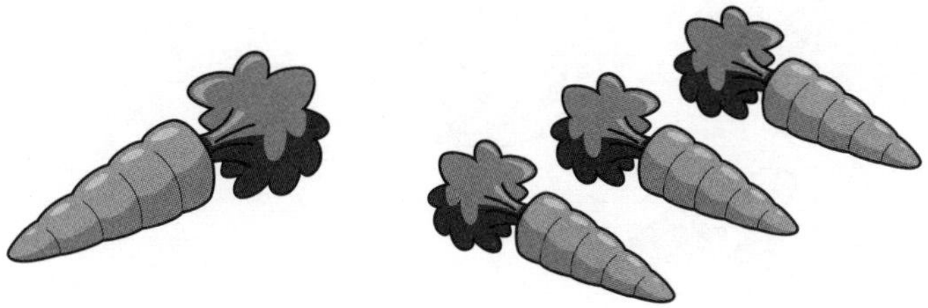

$1 + 3 = $ _____

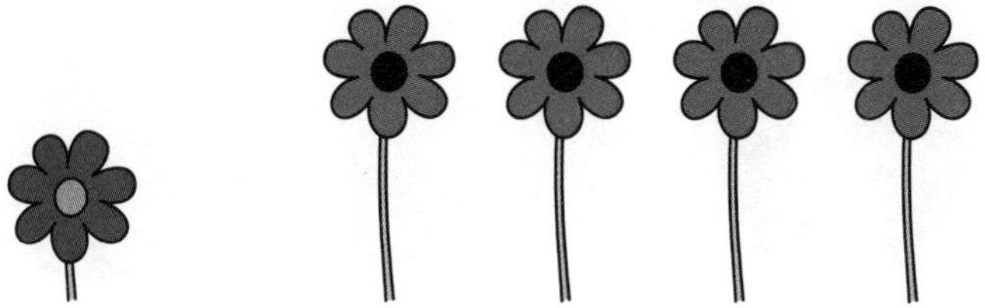

$1 + 4 = $ _____

Guide your child to compare each number sentence to the pictured addition problem and then count and write the total. Have your child read the completed number sentence aloud. Help him or her connect the written total with the number of objects shown.

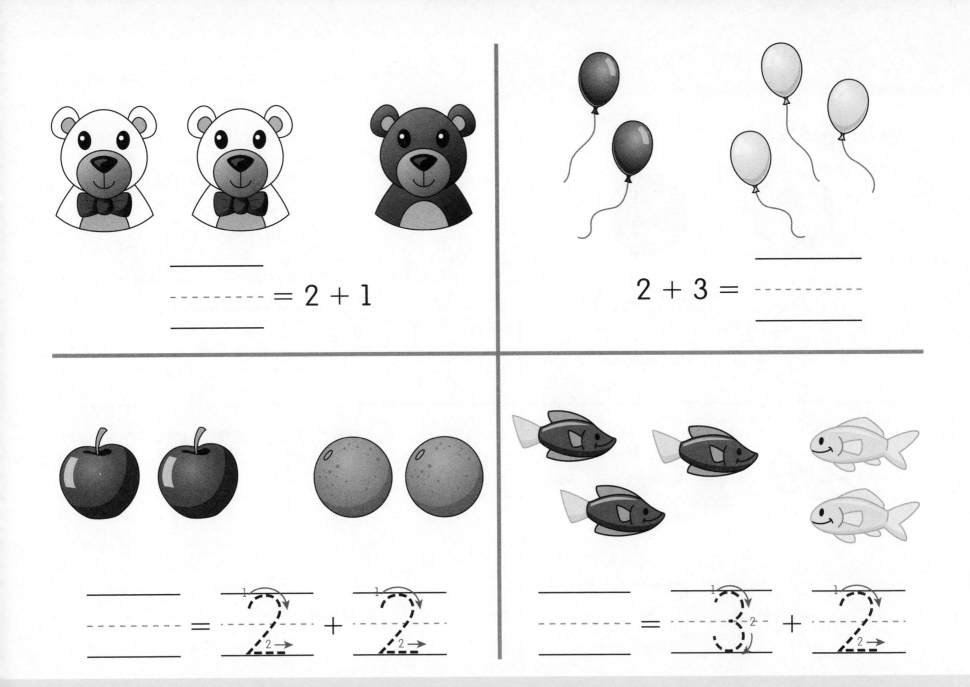

_____

---------- = 2 + 1

_____

_____

2 + 3 = ----------

_____

_____

---------- = 2 + 2

_____

_____

---------- = 3 + 2

_____

Guide your child to compare each number sentence to the pictured addition problem and then complete the number sentence. Have your child read the completed number sentence aloud. Help him or her connect the written total with the number of objects shown.

Add Within 5

Name _____

Example

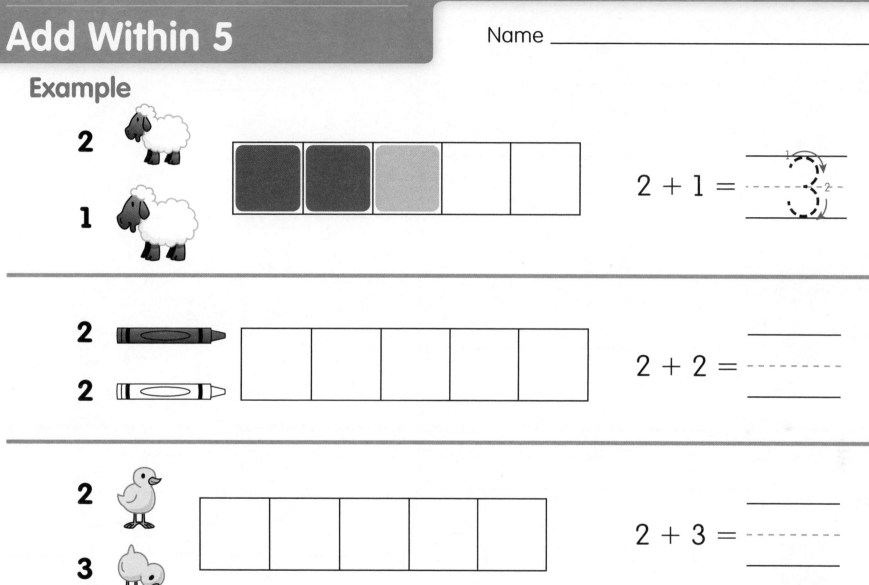

2

1

$2 + 1 = 3$

2

2

$2 + 2 = $ _____

2

3

$2 + 3 = $ _____

Guide your child to make up a story problem for each set of pictures, color the 5-frame using two colors to model the story, and then write the total. For example, to tell a story for the first problem, your child might say, "2 small sheep are in the barn. 1 big sheep joins them. Now 3 sheep are in the barn." In each problem, after your child colors the 5-frame and completes the number sentence, read the number sentence aloud together and connect it to the story problem.

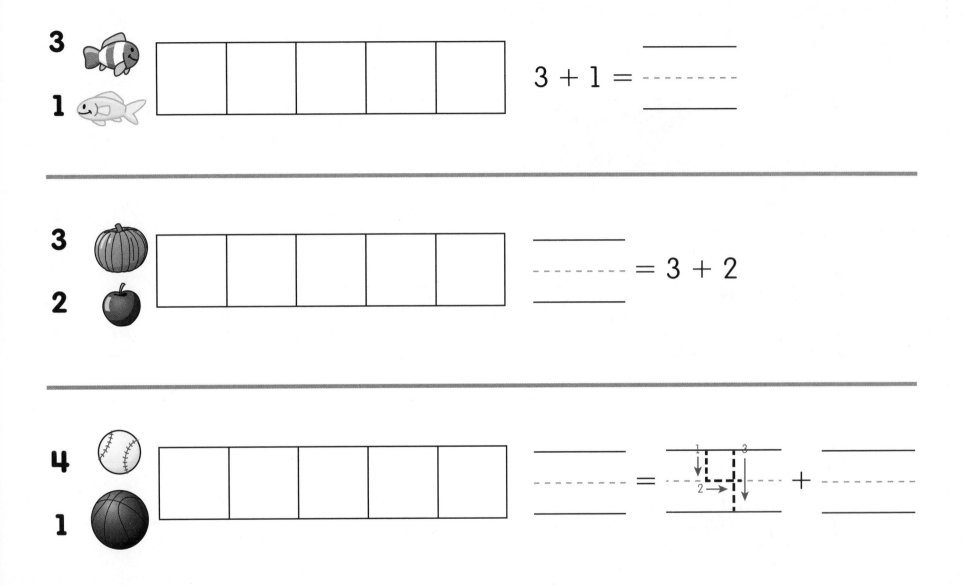

3 + **1** = _____

3 + **1** = - - - - - -

_____ = **3** + **2**

_____ = _____ + _____

Guide your child to make up a story problem for each set of pictures, color the 5-frame using two colors to model the story, and then complete the number sentence. Read the completed number sentence aloud with your child and connect it to the story problem.

Dear Family,

This week your child is learning about subtraction.

This lesson explores the idea of what it means to subtract and introduces the minus sign and the equal sign as a way to represent taking away objects from a group. Your child will use counters and/or connecting cubes as physical models and drawings as visual models to show taking away from a group.

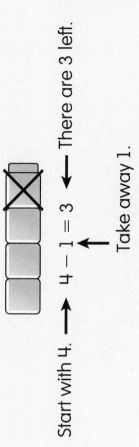

Start with 4. ➞ 4 − 1 = 3 ◀— There are 3 left.

←— Take away 1.

Modeling subtraction in these ways can help make connections to subtraction number sentences. For example, one side of a subtraction number sentence shows how many you start with and how many you take away. The other side shows how many are left.

This lesson also explores take away problem situations.

Take From Result Unknown: *There are 5 birds in a tree. 2 birds fly away. How many birds are in the tree now?*

Physically modeling subtraction, drawing pictures, and exploring subtraction problem situations will help your child make connections to how subtraction is used in daily life.

Invite your child to share what he or she knows about subtraction by doing the following activity together.

NEXT

Materials: 5 animal-shape crackers or animal toys (or any small objects such as buttons or blocks)

Show your child groups of 2 to 5 animals. Tell subtraction stories such as the one below. Help your child use the objects to act out each story and solve the problem.

Example:

- *4 ducks were in a pond.* (Have your child count the toy ducks.)
- *1 duck swam away.* (Remove 1 duck from the group.)
- *How many ducks are left?* (Have your child count and tell how many ducks are left.)

If you do not have small objects shaped like animals, you can use any small objects and explain that you will pretend they are ducks (or any animal that is your child's favorite).

Understand Subtraction

Name _____

Why do you subtract?

Show 4 − 1.

Have your child draw a picture that shows 4 take away 1. You may want to give an example of subtracting, such as the following: *There are 4 books on the shelf. I take 1 book. How many books are left on the shelf?* Encourage your child to tell a similar story about his or her drawing.

What can you subtract?

Show 3 − 2.

Understand Subtraction

Name _____

Example

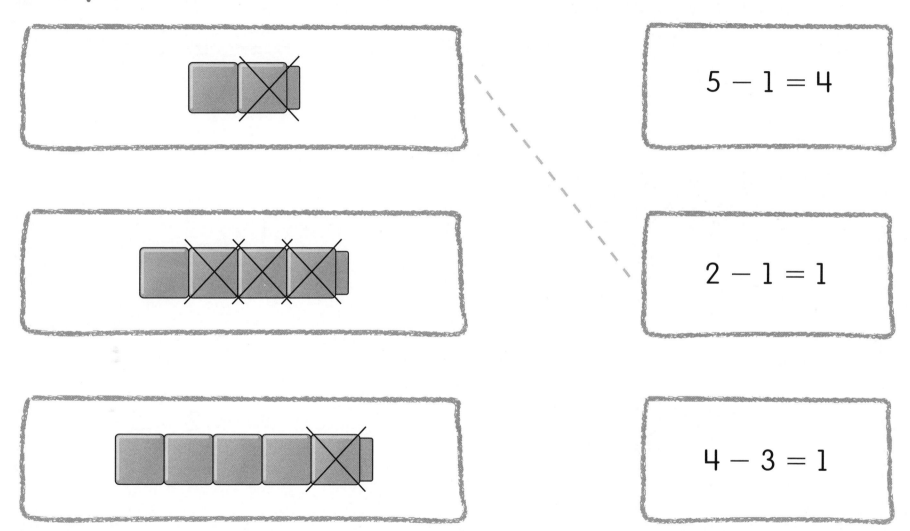

$$5 - 1 = 4$$

$$2 - 1 = 1$$

$$4 - 3 = 1$$

Guide your child to match pictures to subtraction sentences. Have your child describe the number of cubes in each picture and how many are taken away. Read each number sentence aloud together and discuss the meaning of each. Then have your child draw lines to match each picture with its number sentence.

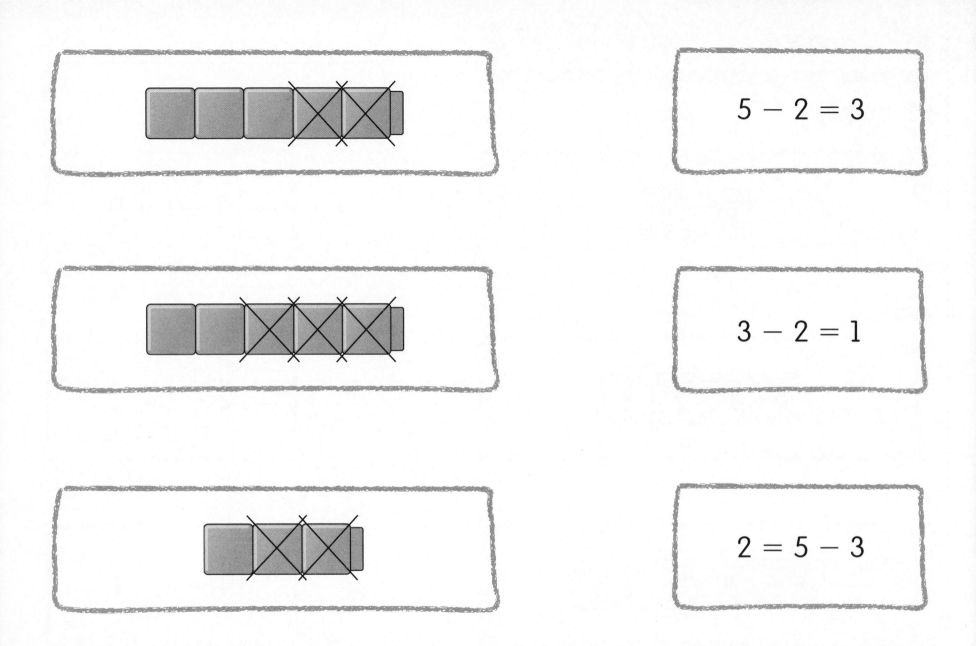

Understand Subtraction

Name _____

Example

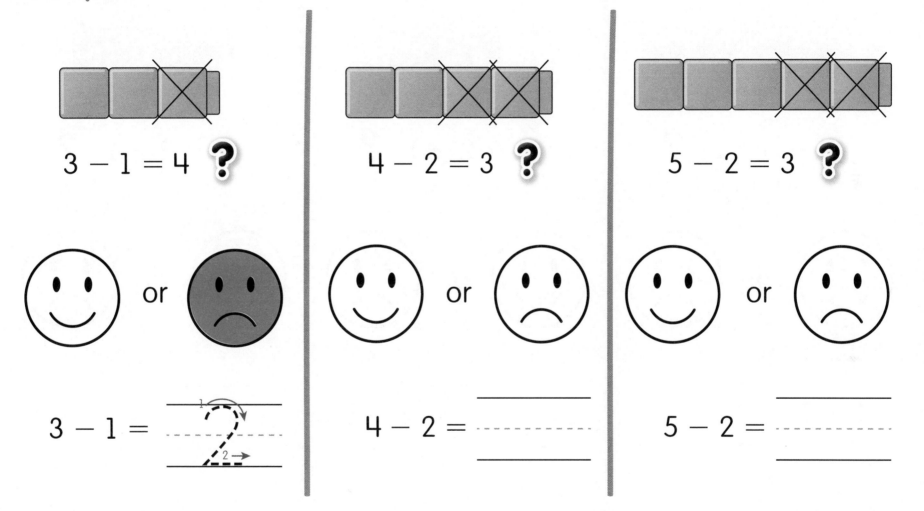

3 − 1 = 4 ❓

😊 or 🙁

3 − 1 = 2

4 − 2 = 3 ❓

😊 or 🙁

4 − 2 = _____

5 − 2 = 3 ❓

😊 or 🙁

5 − 2 = _____

Guide your child to check whether the number sentence matches the cubes. First, discuss the number of cubes in each group and the number being taken away. Have your child color the happy face if the number sentence and cubes match or the sad face if they do not match. Guide your child to complete the number sentence at the bottom of the problem.

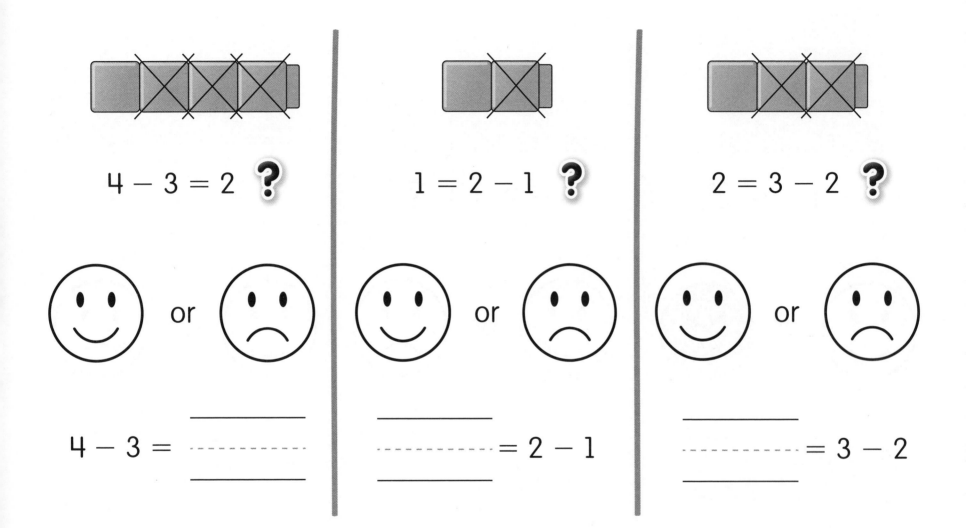

$4 - 3 = 2$ **?**

$1 = 2 - 1$ **?**

$2 = 3 - 2$ **?**

😊 or ☹

😊 or ☹

😊 or ☹

$4 - 3 = $ _____

_____ $= 2 - 1$

_____ $= 3 - 2$

Guide your child to check whether the number sentence matches the cubes. First, discuss the number of cubes in each group and the number being taken away. Have your child color the happy face if the number sentence and cubes match or the sad face if they do not match. Guide your child to complete the number sentence at the bottom of the problem.

Dear Family,

This week your child is learning to subtract within 5.

Subtraction problems in this lesson involve taking away part of a group of up to 5 objects and finding how many are left. In class, your child may use actual objects, connecting cubes, and/or counters on 5-frames to act out taking away part of a group.

When pictures of objects are shown with subtraction problems, you can cross out objects to show the action of taking away. The lesson starts by crossing out pictures of real-world objects such as cups or balloons. Then it ends by crossing out pictures of counters on 5-frames.

Connecting pictures, models, and subtraction stories to number sentences helps build a strong foundation for subtraction. Eventually your child will transition from solving problems shown with concrete objects or drawings to solving problems shown only with numbers.

Picture

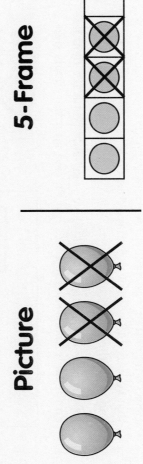

5-Frame

Invite your child to share what he or she knows about subtracting within 5 by doing the following activity together.

Subtracting Within 5 Activity

Materials: pencil, index cards or paper, 5 small objects (such as pennies, buttons, dried beans, or pasta shapes), cup

Do the following activity to help your child model and solve subtraction problems within 5.

- On an index card or paper, write 5 − 3 = ☐.

- Place the subtraction problem and 5 pennies on the table.

- Point to the number 5 and say: *There are 5 pennies. How many do we need to take away?*

- Help your child recognize that the minus sign and number 3 show that you need to take away 3. Have your child remove 3 pennies and place them in a cup.

- Ask: *How many pennies are left?* Have your child count the pennies on the table and write the answer in the box after the equals sign.

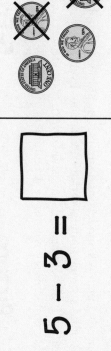

Repeat with other subtraction problems within 5, such as 3 − 1, 5 − 2, and 4 − 3.

During your daily routine, help your child use objects to model subtraction whenever you can. For example, when clearing the table, you might say: *There are 4 cups on the table. I'm taking away 1. How many cups are left?* Model subtraction with up to 5 crayons, blocks, spoons, raisins, crackers, or other objects.

Subtract Within 5

Name _____

Have your child color the 5 plates and 3 pieces of cake and tell a subtraction story about this part of the picture. Then have your child color a part of the picture that shows 5 take away 1 and tell a story about that. Have your child color the rest of the picture.

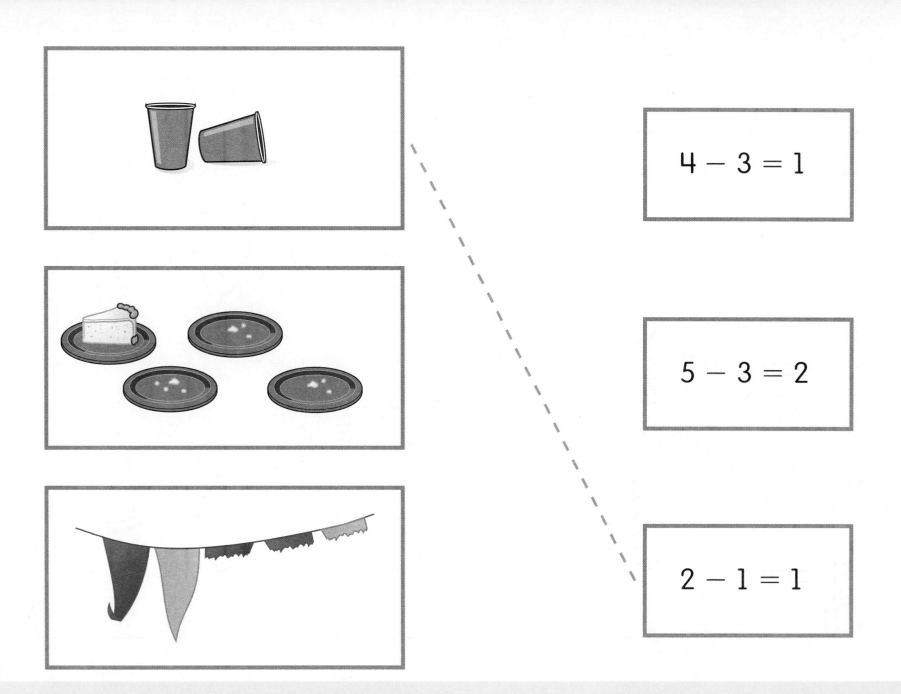

$$4 - 3 = 1$$

$$5 - 3 = 2$$

$$2 - 1 = 1$$

Have your child match pictures to subtraction sentences. Have your child tell a subtraction story for each picture. Read each number sentence aloud together. Then have your child draw lines to match each picture to its subtraction sentence.

Subtract Within 5

Example

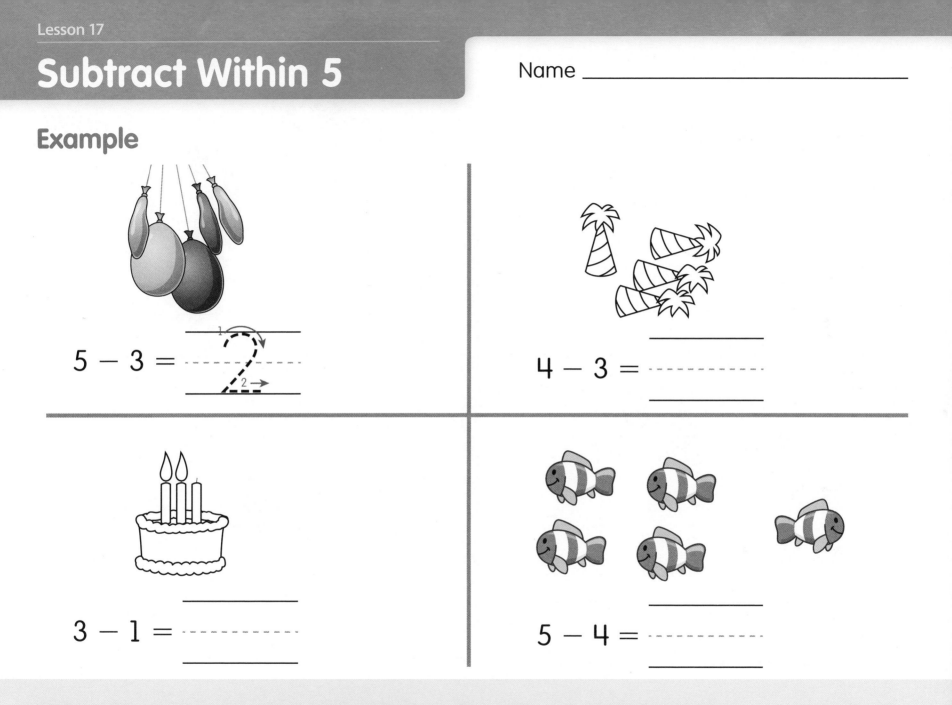

$5 - 3 =$ **2**

$4 - 3 =$ _____

$3 - 1 =$ _____

$5 - 4 =$ _____

Guide your child to compare each subtraction picture to the number sentence and then count and write the number left. Have your child read the completed number sentence aloud. Help him or her connect the written numbers with the number of objects shown.

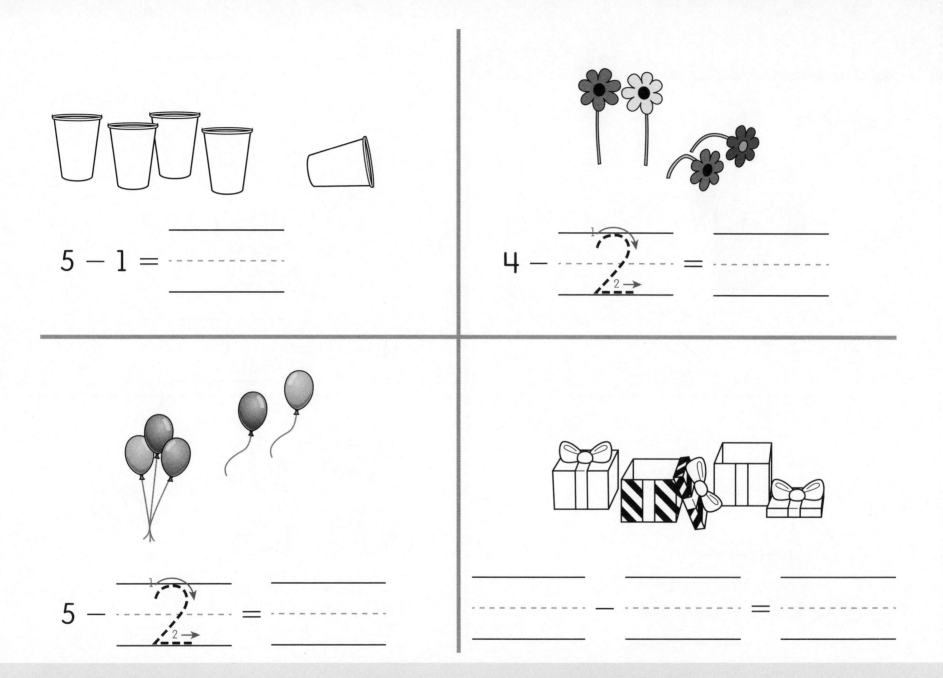

5 − 1 = _____

4 − 2 = _____

5 − 2 = _____

____ − ____ = ____

Subtract Within 5

Name _____

Example

$5 - 1 =$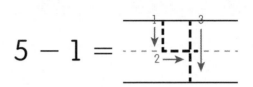

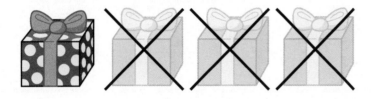

$4 - 3 =$ _____

$3 - 2 =$ _____

Guide your child to make up a story problem for each set of pictures. Then have him or her count and write the number left. Have your child read the completed number sentence aloud and connect it with the story problem.

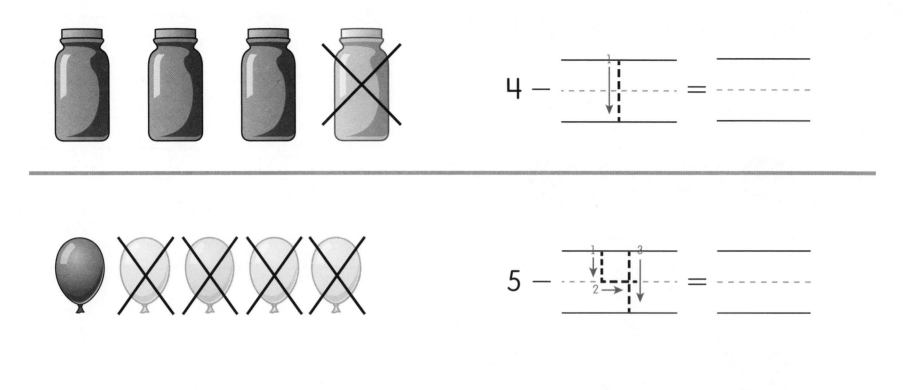

$$4 - \underline{\hspace{3em}} = \underline{\hspace{3em}}$$

$$5 - \underline{\hspace{3em}} = \underline{\hspace{3em}}$$

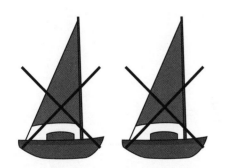

$$\underline{\hspace{3em}} - \underline{\hspace{3em}} = \underline{\hspace{3em}}$$

Guide your child to make up a story problem for each set of pictures. Then have him or her complete the number sentence. Have your child read the completed number sentence aloud and connect it with the story problem.

Dear Family,

This week your child is learning to add within 10.

This lesson includes addition problems with totals from 6 to 10 and continues to connect story problems to pictures, objects, models, and number sentences. In class, your child may also model addition problems with fingers, which are useful and easily available tools for adding.

Your child will find two numbers that add up to a given total using counters on 10-frames. He or she will also add two numbers that have a sum up to 10. Repeated work with 10-frames leads to the ability to quickly visualize numbers as amounts, which is important for building addition skills. Also, because a 10-frame is made up of 10 boxes arranged in 2 rows of 5, it can help your child see how the numbers being added and the total relate to both 5 and 10—a useful understanding for later work with greater numbers.

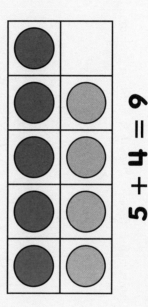

5 + 4 = 9

Invite your child to share what he or she knows about adding within 10 by doing the following activity together.

Have your child use fingers to solve the addition problems below and tell you each total. You may want to present the problems in a story context. Your child may add with fingers in any way he or she prefers.

If your child needs assistance, have him or her mirror you as you use your fingers to find 5 + 4.

• Say: *There are 5 cups in the sink and 4 cups on the counter. How many cups are there in all?* Show 5 fingers on one hand.

• Say: *Now let's add 5 and 4.* Hold up 4 fingers on the other hand.

• Ask: *How many fingers are up now?* Have your child count the 9 fingers that are up.

Follow a similar procedure to solve the other addition problems below.

5   +   4

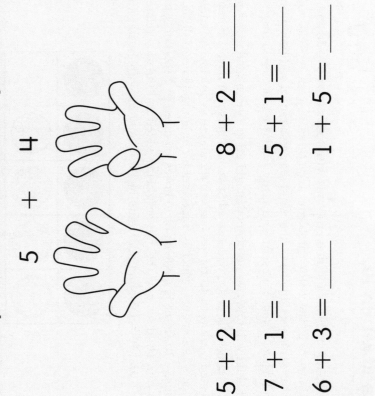

5 + 2 = ___   8 + 2 = ___

7 + 1 = ___   5 + 1 = ___

6 + 3 = ___   1 + 5 = ___

Add Within 10

Name _____

Have your child use red and yellow to color a group of related objects and describe an addition problem. For example, he or she might color the 4 large collars red and the 6 small collars yellow and demonstrate that 4 + 6 = 10. Then have your child use two other colors to color another group of related objects and describe an addition problem. Have your child color the rest of the picture.

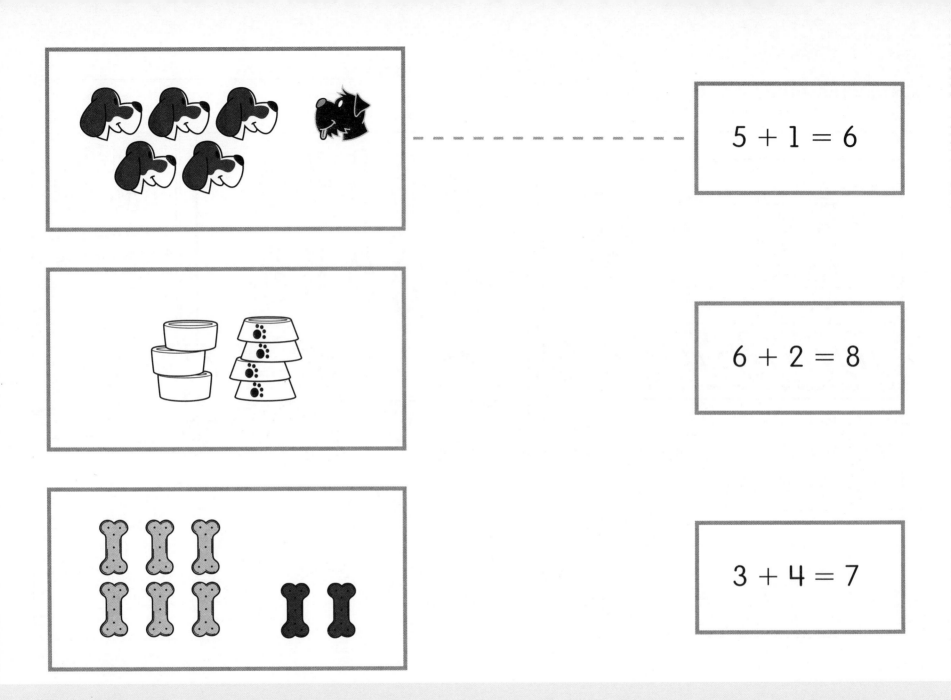

$5 + 1 = 6$

$6 + 2 = 8$

$3 + 4 = 7$

Have your child match pictures to addition sentences. Have your child describe the two groups and the total in each picture. Read each number sentence aloud together. Then have your child draw lines to match each picture to its addition sentence.

Add Within 10

Example

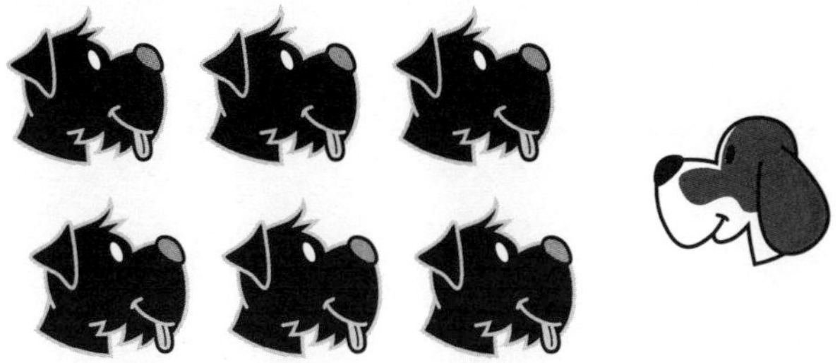

$6 + 1 = 7$

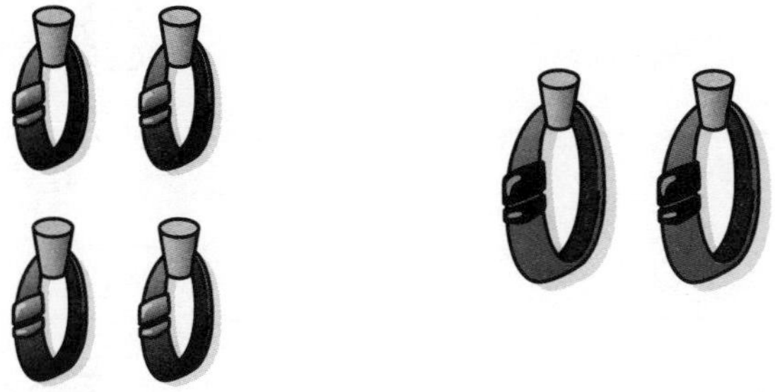

$4 + 2 =$ _____

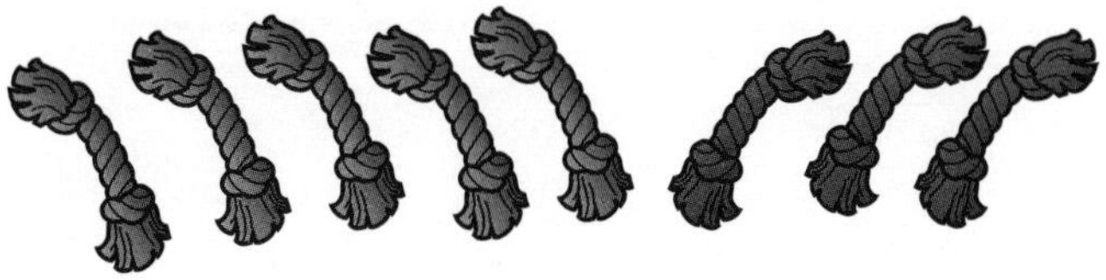

$5 + 3 =$ _____

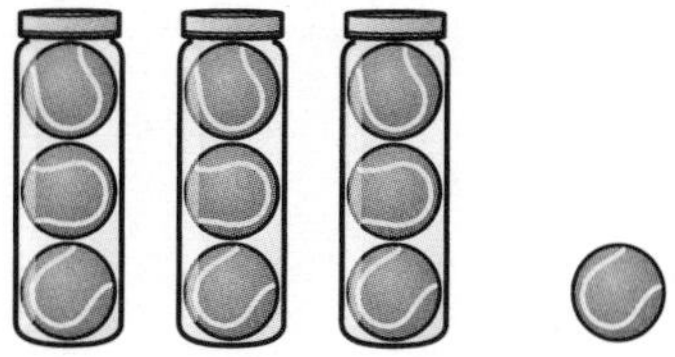

$9 + 1 =$ _____

Guide your child to compare each picture to the addition sentence and then count and write the total. Have your child read the completed number sentence aloud. Help him or her connect the written total with the total number of objects shown.

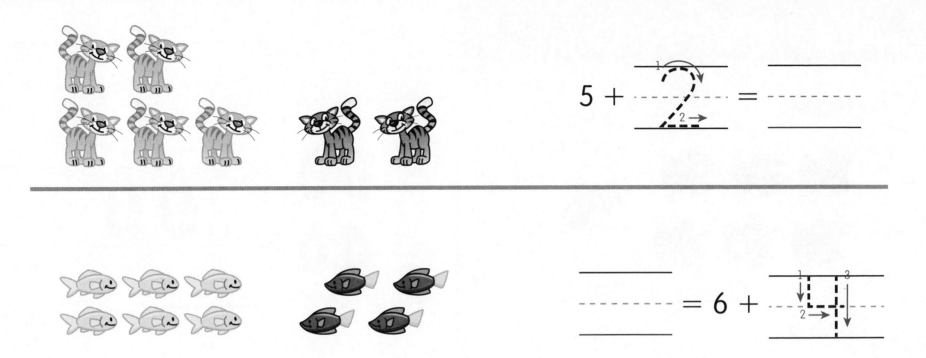

$$5 + 2 = $$

_____ = 6 + 4

_____ = 3 + _____

Guide your child to compare each picture to the addition sentence and then complete the number sentence. Have your child read the completed number sentence aloud. Help him or her connect the written total with the total number of animals shown.

Add Within 10

Example

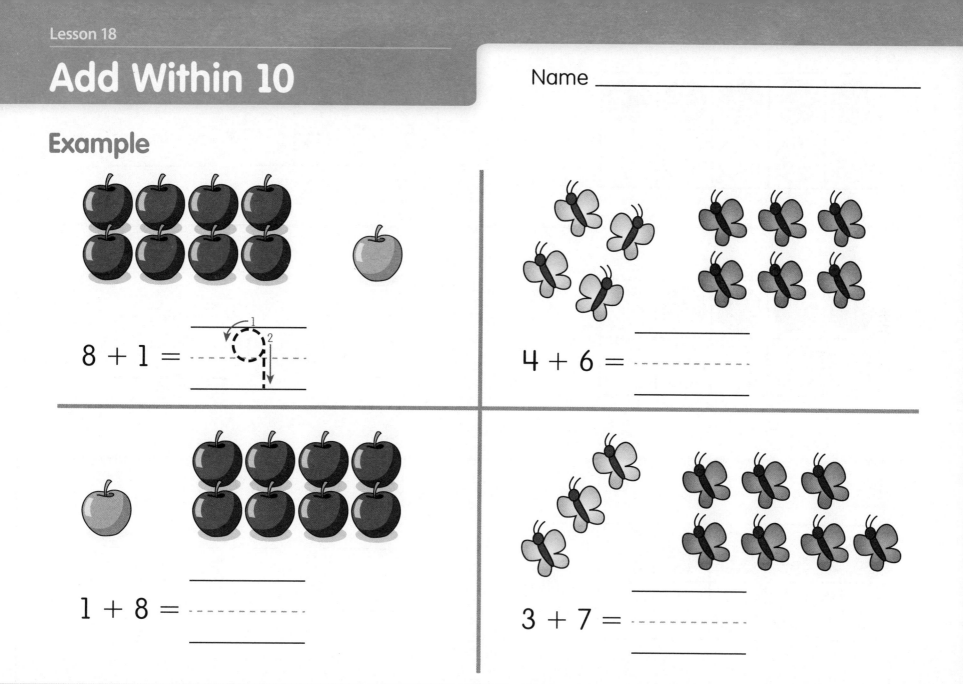

$8 + 1 =$ _____

$4 + 6 =$ _____

$1 + 8 =$ _____

$3 + 7 =$ _____

Guide your child to compare each picture to the addition sentence and then count and write the total. Have your child read the completed number sentence aloud. Help him or her connect the written total with the total number of objects shown.

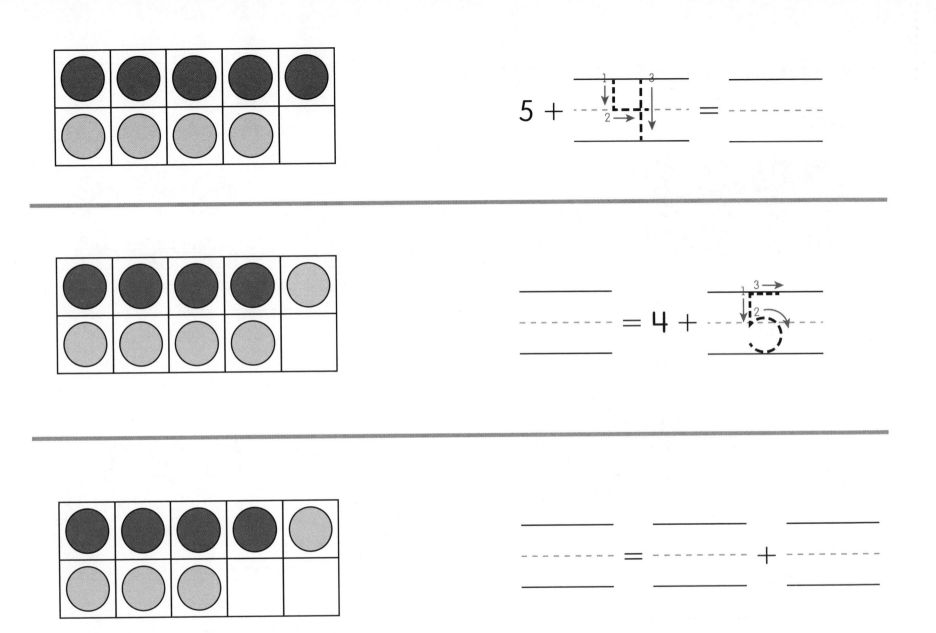

$5 + \underline{} = \underline{}$

$\underline{} = 4 + \underline{}$

$\underline{} = \underline{} + \underline{}$

Guide your child to compare each picture to the addition sentence and then complete the number sentence. Have your child read the completed number sentence aloud. Help him or her connect the written total with the total number of counters shown.

Dear Family,

This week your child is learning to subtract within 10.

This lesson includes subtraction problems that involve taking away part of a group of up to 10 objects and finding how much is left. There is a continued focus on connecting story problems about subtraction to pictures, objects, models, and number sentences.

Your child will also examine pictures of hands as models for subtracting and may practice modeling subtraction problems with fingers. Counters on 10-frames will be used to model and solve subtraction problems. Exploring these various models will allow your child to continue developing a strong understanding of what it means to subtract. These models also emphasize the relationship between the numbers in each subtraction problem to 5 and 10. This is useful for both subtraction within 10 and for subtraction with greater numbers.

Start with 8 counters. Then take away 3.

8 − 3 = 5

Invite your child to share what he or she knows about subtracting within 10 by doing the following activity together.

NEXT

Have your child use fingers to solve the subtraction problems below and tell you the answer. You may want to present the problems in a story context. Your child may subtract with fingers in any way he or she prefers.

If your child needs assistance have him or her mirror you as you use fingers to solve 8 − 3.

- Say: *I had 8 grapes and I ate 3 of them. How many grapes are left?* Show 8 with 5 fingers on one hand and 3 fingers on the other hand.

- Say: *Now let's take away 3.* Fold down 3 fingers.

- Ask: *How many fingers are still up?* Have your child count the 5 fingers that are up.

Show 8.   Take away 3.

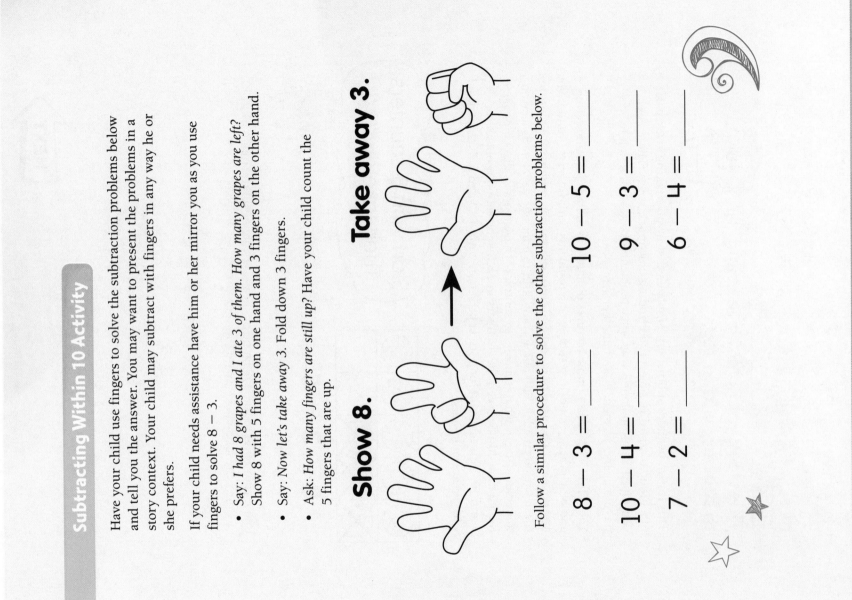

Follow a similar procedure to solve the other subtraction problems below.

8 − 3 = _____   10 − 5 = _____

10 − 4 = _____   9 − 3 = _____

7 − 2 = _____   6 − 4 = _____

Subtract Within 10

Name _____

Have your child color the 4 standing flowers and the 2 drooping flowers and then tell a subtraction story about this part of the picture. Then have your child color a part of the picture that shows 10 take away 1 and tell a story about that. For example, *The boy had 10 balloons. One balloon floated away. How many balloons does the boy have now?* Have your child color the rest of the picture.

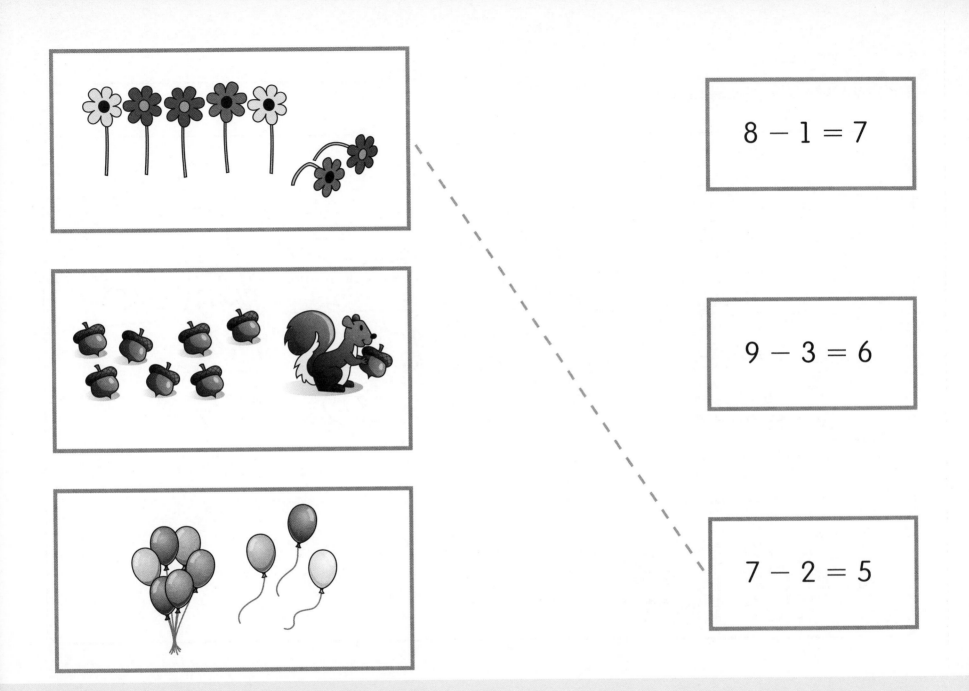

Have your child match pictures to subtraction sentences. Ask your child to tell the total number of objects in each picture and then describe how many are being subtracted. Guide your child to find the number sentence that matches each picture and read it aloud together while looking at the picture. Then have your child draw a line to show the match.

Subtract Within 10

Name _____

Example

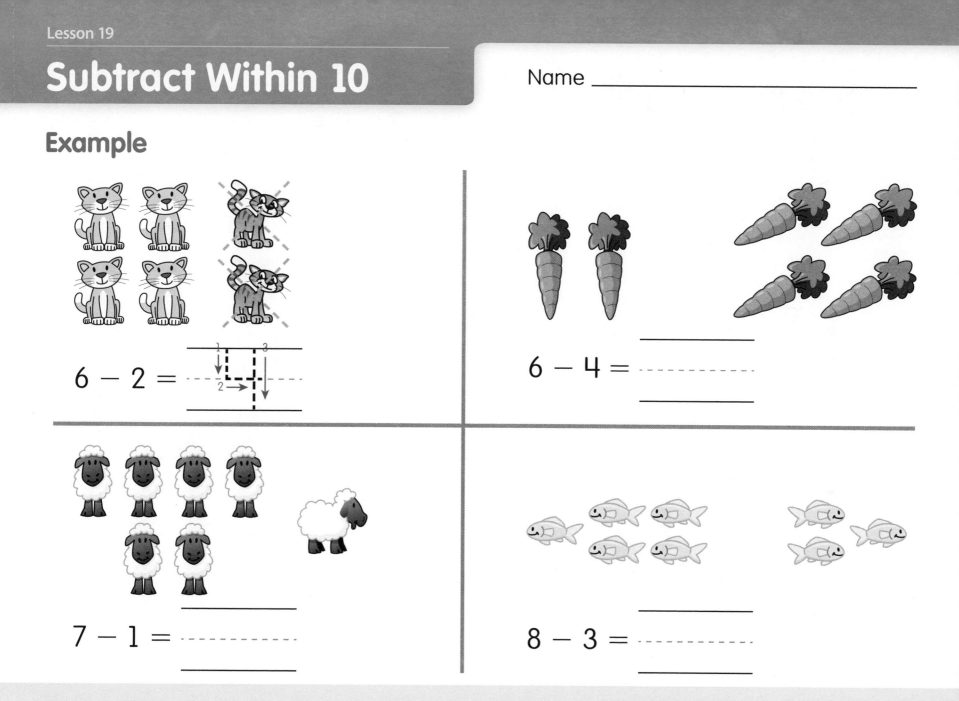

6 − 2 = _____

6 − 4 = _____

7 − 1 = _____

8 − 3 = _____

Guide your child to compare each picture to the number sentence and then complete the subtraction sentence. Have your child put an X on the animals or objects being taken away. Then have your child complete the number sentence. Read each number sentence aloud together.

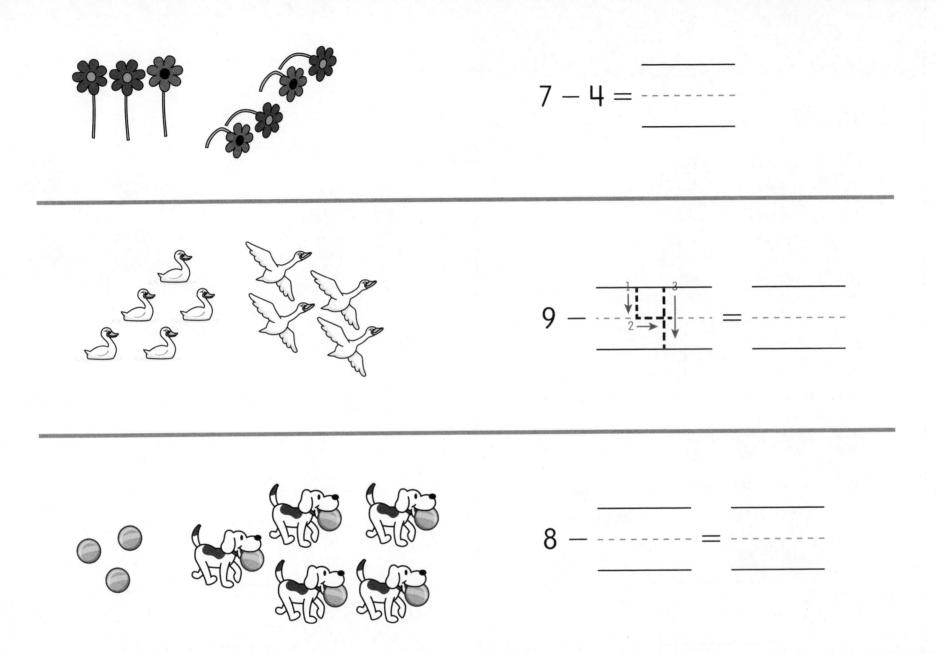

$7 - 4 =$ _____

$9 -$ _____ $=$ _____

$8 -$ _____ $=$ _____

Guide your child to compare each picture to the number sentence and then complete the number sentence. Have your child put an X on the animals or objects being taken away. Then have your child complete the number sentence. Read each number sentence aloud together.

Subtract Within 10

Name _____

Example

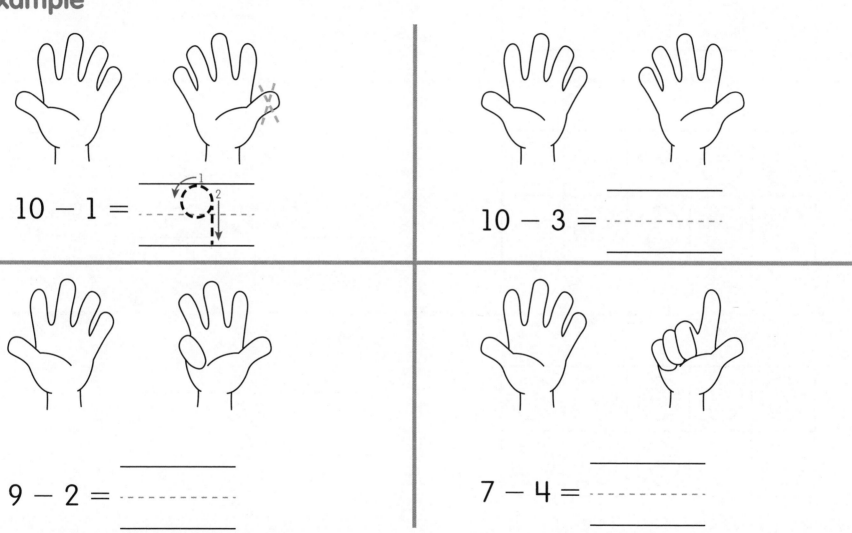

$10 - 1 =$ _____

$10 - 3 =$ _____

$9 - 2 =$ _____

$7 - 4 =$ _____

Guide your child to compare the finger pictures to the number sentence. Have your child put an X over fingers being taken away. Then guide your child to complete each number sentence. Read each number sentence aloud together.

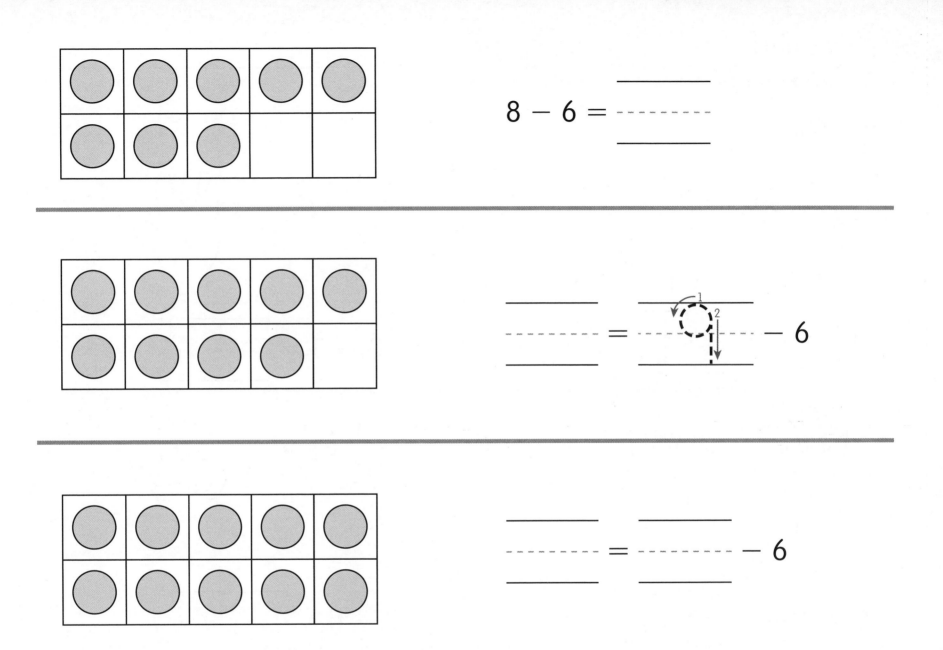

$$8 - 6 = \rule{2cm}{0.4pt}$$

$$\rule{2cm}{0.4pt} = \rule{2cm}{0.4pt} - 6$$

$$\rule{2cm}{0.4pt} = \rule{2cm}{0.4pt} - 6$$

Guide your child to compare each picture to the number sentence. Have your child put an X over counters being taken away. Then guide your child to complete each number sentence. Read each number sentence aloud together.

Dear Family,

This week your child is reviewing both addition and subtraction facts within 5 and moving from problems shown with pictures to problems shown only with numbers.

This lesson begins to show how addition and subtraction facts relate to each other. For example, knowing that $3 + 1 = 4$ can help you find that $4 - 1 = 3$. And knowing that $3 + 2 = 5$ can help you find that $5 - 2 = 3$. Focusing on the relationships between math facts will help your child build strong problem-solving skills, as well as solve addition and subtraction problems more quickly and accurately.

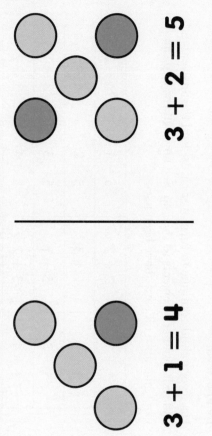

$$3 + 1 = 4 \qquad 3 + 2 = 5$$

This week's lesson progresses from solving problems shown with pictures to solving problems shown only with numbers. Even with numbers-only problems your child will be encouraged to use any strategy he or she likes for solving, such as modeling with fingers.

Invite your child to share what he or she knows about practicing addition and subtraction facts to 5 by doing the following activity together.

NEXT

Addition and Subtraction Facts to 5 Activity

Materials: 20 index cards or pieces of paper, a small cup and about 60 small objects (such as pennies, dried beans, or pasta shapes)

Help your child practice addition and subtraction facts to 5 by doing this activity.

- Write the addition and subtraction facts below on index cards or pieces of paper. Mix the cards and place them facedown in a pile.

- Your child turns over the top card and uses any strategy (such as modeling with fingers or objects) to find the answer. Then he or she counts out the same number of objects as the answer and places them in a cup.

- Have your child continue to turn over cards, find the answer, and add that number of objects to the cup. See how full the cup can get! Continue until all cards have been used.

1 + 1	2 + 2	5 − 1	4 − 2
1 + 2	2 + 3	5 − 2	4 − 3
1 + 3	3 + 1	5 − 3	3 − 1
1 + 4	3 + 2	5 − 4	3 − 2
2 + 1	4 + 1	4 − 1	2 − 1

Practice Facts to 5

Name _____

Have your child color the 5 children in the picture. Then have him or her tell an addition story and a subtraction story about the 5 children. For example, *Two girls and 3 boys are at the beach. How many children are at the beach?* and *There are 5 friends playing. One friend leaves. How many friends are playing now?* As your child colors the rest of the picture, encourage him or her to share an addition story and a subtraction story for each group of objects.

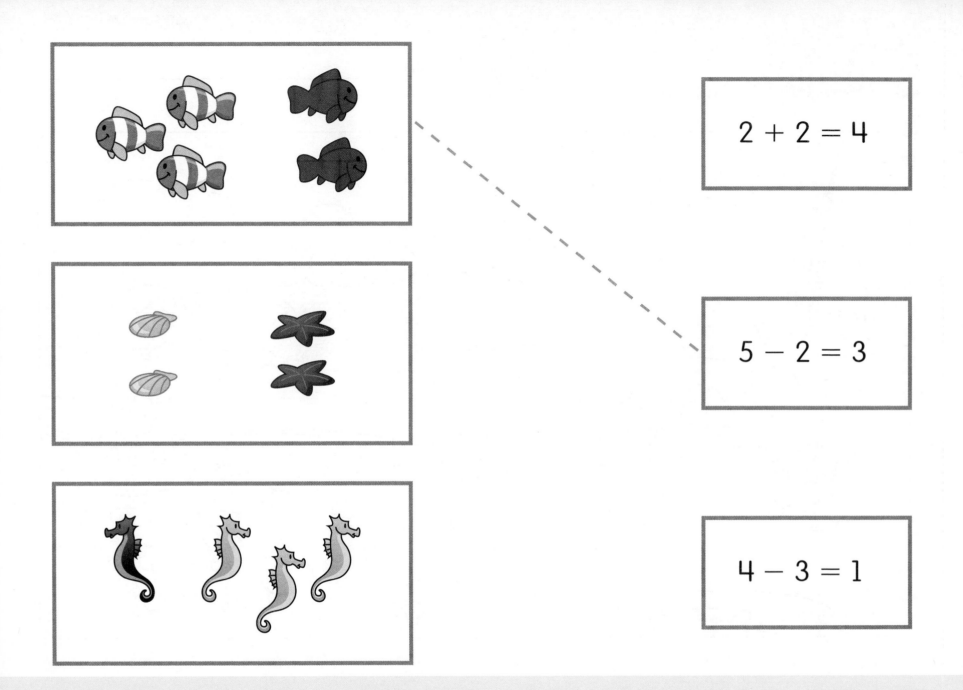

Have your child match pictures to number sentences. Read each number sentence aloud together. Then have your child draw lines to connect each picture to a matching number sentence. In the top and bottom pictures, you may wish to have your child put an X on the animals being taken away.

Practice Facts to 5

Name _____

Example

2 + 1 = ____ 3 ____

2 + 2 = _____

3 − 1 = _____

4 − 2 = _____

Guide your child to use the picture to help complete each number sentence. Read each number sentence aloud together. Guide your child to look for patterns as he or she compares the number sentences. For example, 2 + 1 is 3, so if you start with 3 and take away 1, you have 2 left.

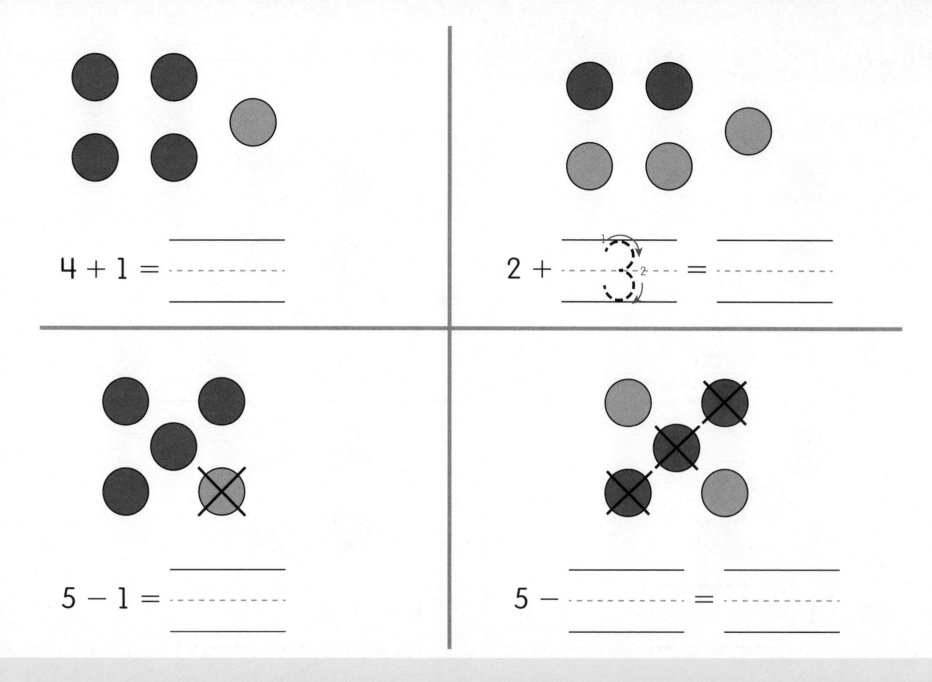

4 + 1 = _____

2 + 3 = _____

5 − 1 = _____

5 − _____ = _____

Guide your child to use the picture to help complete each number sentence. Read each number sentence aloud together. Guide your child to look for patterns as he or she compares the number sentences. For example, 4 + 1 is 5, so if you start with 5 and take away 1, you have 4 left.

Practice Facts to 5

Name _____

1 = orange   2 = green   3 = yellow   4 = red   5 = purple

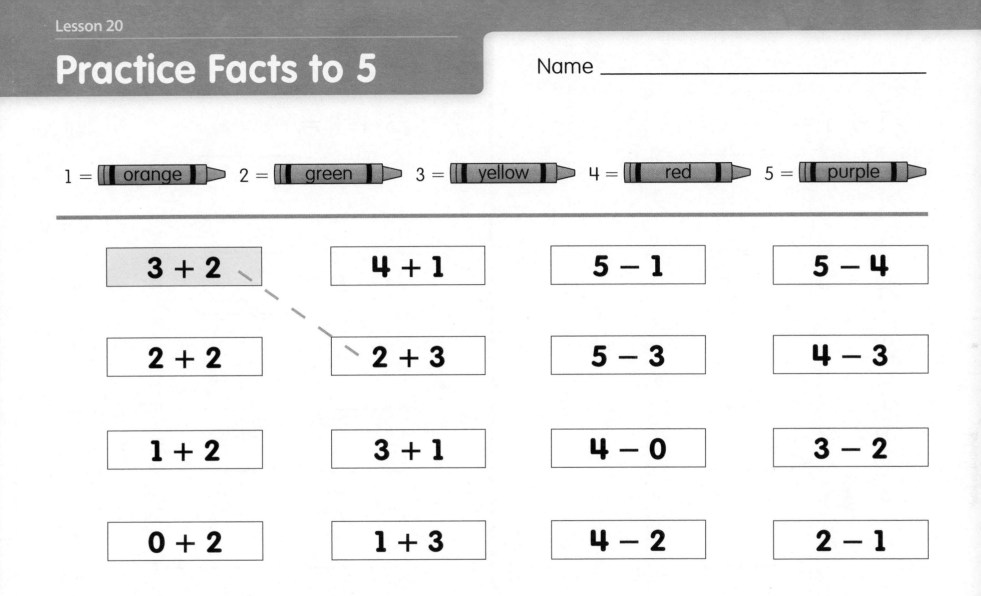

3 + 2	4 + 1	5 − 1	5 − 4
2 + 2	2 + 3	5 − 3	4 − 3
1 + 2	3 + 1	4 − 0	3 − 2
0 + 2	1 + 3	4 − 2	2 − 1

Have your child color the facts based on the color of the answer shown at the top of the page. Discuss any number patterns in the rows and columns. Have your child draw lines to connect the facts that have the same addends but in a different order.

$1 + 1 =$ _____

$5 - 3 =$ _____

$4 - 2 =$ _____

$3 - 1 =$ _____

$3 + 1 =$ _____

$4 - 0 =$ _____

_____ $+$ _____ $= 4$

_____ $-$ _____ $= 4$

Have your child complete each fact. Guide your child to complete each fact in the first column. Discuss any patterns your child notices. Then have your child complete the first two facts in the second column. Discuss patterns he or she notices. Then have your child write one addition and one subtraction fact that equals 4 and is different from those above.

Add and Subtract

Name _____

? **?**

_____   _____

- - - - - - - - - **+** - - - - - - - - - **= 4**

_____   _____

? **?**

_____   _____

- - - - - - - - - **+** - - - - - - - - - **= 5**

_____   _____

? **?**

_____   _____

- - - - - - - - - **+** - - - - - - - - - **= 10**

_____   _____

Have children find two numbers to make a given total. Have children color each 10-frame with two different colors to show their numbers. Explain that there are many correct answers for each problem. Then have them write their numbers to complete the number sentence.

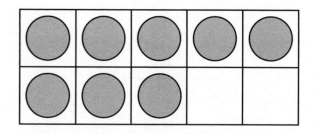

$8 - 4 =$ _____

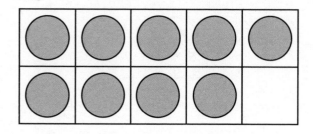

$9 - 4 =$ _____

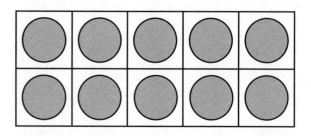

$10 - 4 =$ _____

For each problem, have children cross out the number of counters being taken away and complete the number sentence.

Last One Wins

Name _____

Materials For each pair: 10 counters; for each child: Last One Wins Game Board

How to Play Take turns putting 1 or 2 counters on the board. On your turn, tell how many counters are on the board. Then add 1 or 2 counters. Tell how many you added and tell the new total. For example, "There are 3 counters. I added 2 more, and now there are 5." The player who fills the last square wins.

Dear Family,

This week your child is exploring teen numbers.

Teen numbers are the numbers 11 to 19. As your child explores groups of 11 to 19 objects, he or she will learn to recognize that teen numbers are made up of a ten and some more. For example, 16 can be thought of as 10 and 6 more.

This understanding helps make the connection between teen numbers and the amounts they represent, which is important for future work with greater numbers in our place-value system.

In class, your child may model teen numbers with connecting cubes and/or 10-frames. When modeling with connecting cubes, teen numbers can be shown as a group of 10 connected cubes and some extra single cubes. When modeling with 10-frames, teen numbers are shown by filling one 10-frame with counters and then placing the extra counters in a second 10-frame to show 10 and more.

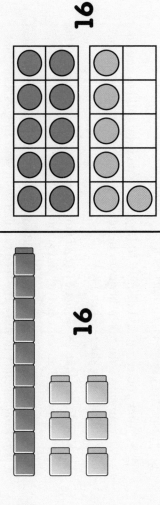

Invite your child to share what he or she knows about teen numbers by doing the following activity together.

Materials: 8 index cards or small pieces of paper

Make teen number cards for this activity by writing the numbers 11 to 19 on index cards or small pieces of paper. (You may want to keep these cards to reuse with Lesson 23.) Place the cards facedown in a pile.

Tell your child that you will work together to show teen numbers with the fingers on your hands and your child's hands.

- Say: *Let's show 14. I'll start by using my fingers to count 10.*

- After you count and display 10 fingers, guide your child to continue counting with his or her own fingers, raising one finger at a time until he or she reaches 14.

- Ask: *To make 14, we need 10 and how many more?* Your child should respond that you need 10 and 4 more to make 14.

Repeat the activity, having your child turn over the top number card and working together to show the teen number with your fingers. Continue until all the number cards have been used.

10

12 13 14

11

Understand Teen Numbers

Name _____

What are teen numbers?

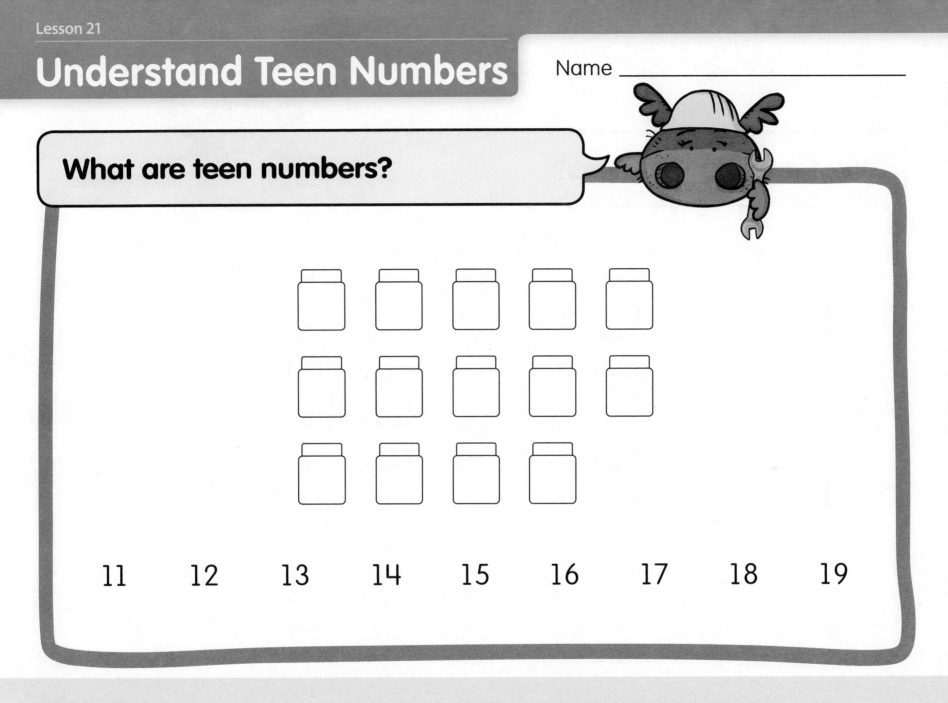

11   12   13   14   15   16   17   18   19

Have your child color the first 10 cubes red. Then have your child color 3 more cubes blue and circle the total number of colored cubes.

What are teen numbers?

11   12   13   14   15   16   17   18   19

Have your child color the first 10 cubes red. Then have your child color the "extras" a different color. Have your child circle the total number of colored cubes.

Lesson 21 *Understand* Teen Numbers

Understand Teen Numbers

Name _____

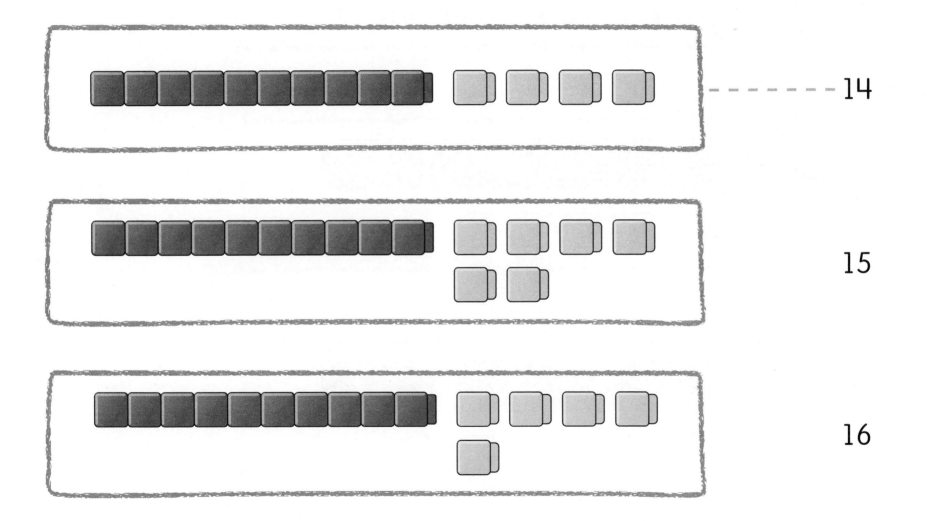

Guide your child to match groups of cubes to teen numbers. Have your child describe the cubes in each group as 10 and some number of extras. For example, to describe the cubes in the top box, your child might say, "There are 10 cubes and 4 extras." Then have your child draw lines to match the pictures to the numbers.

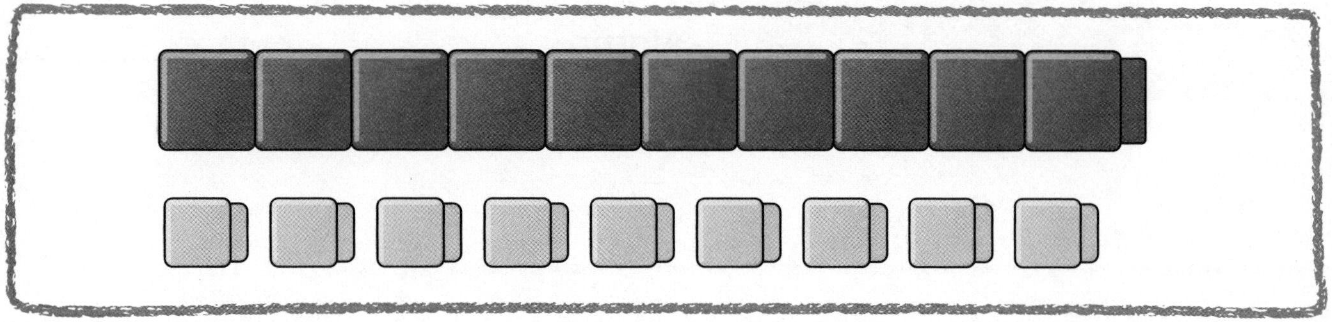

18

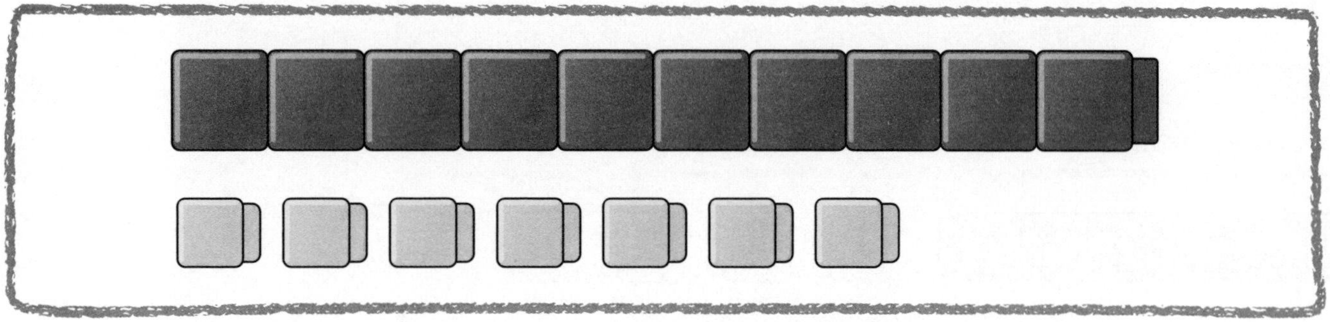

17

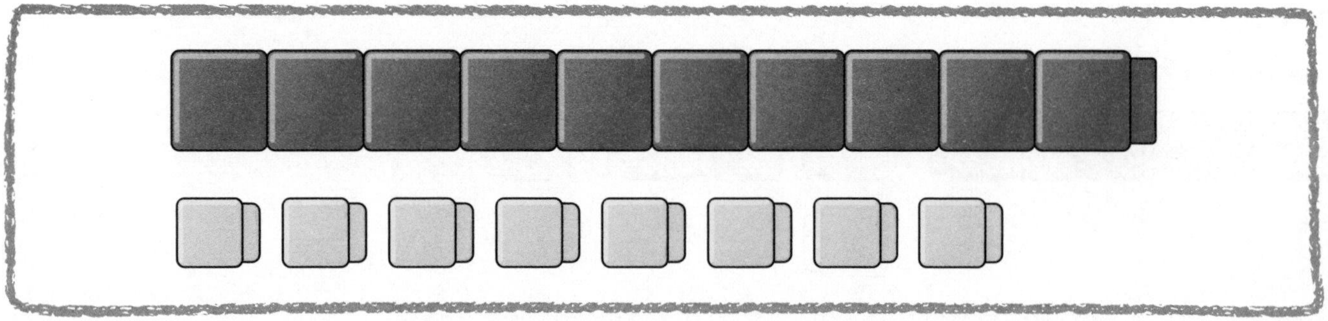

19

Guide your child to match groups of cubes to teen numbers. Have your child describe the cubes in each group as 10 and some number of extras. Then have your child draw lines to match the pictures to the numbers.

Understand Teen Numbers

Name _____

Example

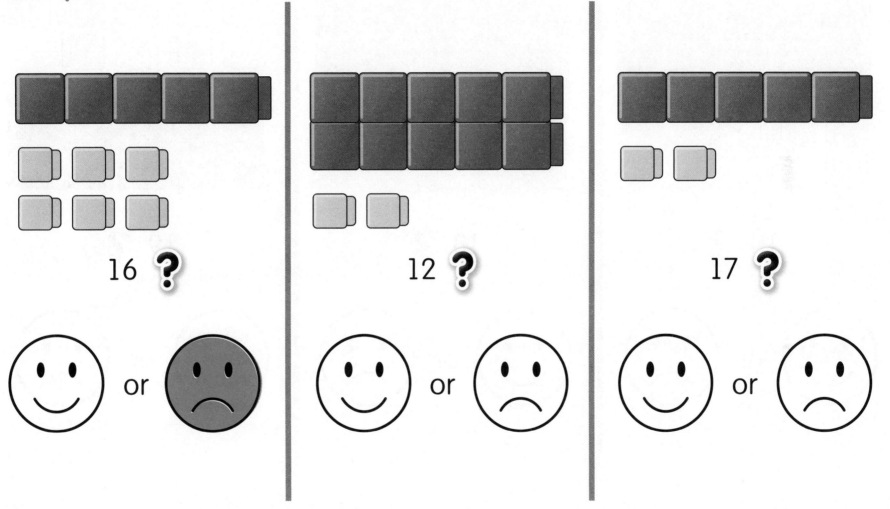

16 ❓

😊 or 🙁

12 ❓

😊 or 🙁

17 ❓

😊 or 🙁

Guide your child to check whether the teen number matches the model. Remind him or her that teen numbers are 10 and some more. Have your child color the happy face if the number and the model match or the sad face if they do not match.

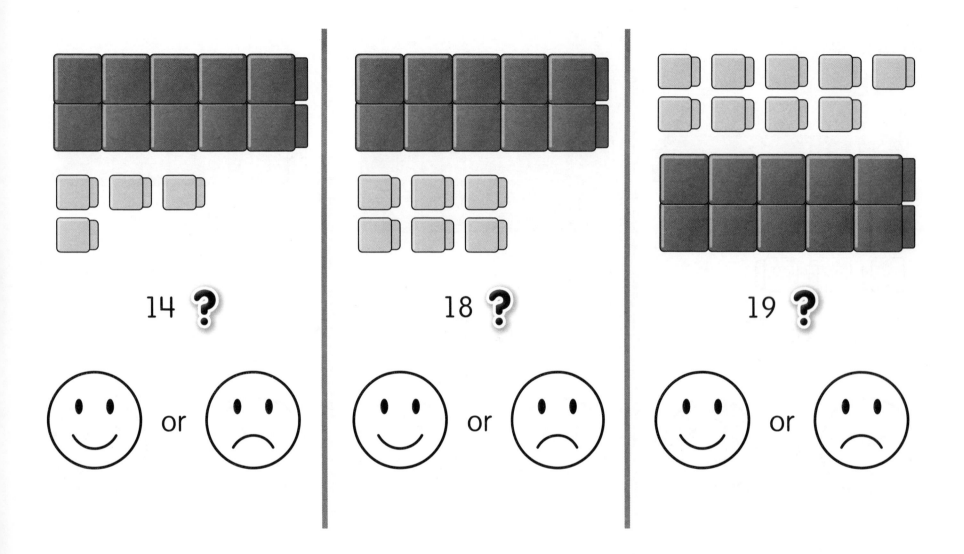

14 **?**

😊 or 🙁

18 **?**

😊 or 🙁

19 **?**

😊 or 🙁

Guide your child to check whether the teen number matches the model. Remind him or her that teen numbers are 10 and some more. Have your child color the happy face if the number and the model match or the sad face if they do not match.

Dear Family,

This week your child is building counting skills with teen numbers and the number 20.

The lesson provides practice counting groups of 11 to 20 objects using a variety of strategies for keeping track of what has been counted. For example, your child may point to or move each object as it is counted or mark each object in a picture as it is counted.

There will also continue to be a focus on understanding teen numbers as 10 and some more. For example, you can count pictures of objects by circling a group of 10 objects first and then counting the "extras" beyond 10 to find how many more there are.

10

11 12 13

Organizing teen numbers this way when counting them will help your child prepare for work with numbers beyond 20 which can be represented as groups of tens and ones.

This lesson also includes practice with writing teen numbers and the number 20.

Invite your child to share what he or she knows about teen numbers and the number 20 by doing the following activity together.

NEXT

Counting Teen Numbers Activity

Materials: shallow plastic container with lid or shallow metal baking pan, $\frac{1}{2}$ to 1 cup of salt or sugar, colored paper (optional)

Your child will use his or her finger to practice writing the numbers 11 to 20 in a layer of salt or sugar.

- Pour $\frac{1}{2}$ to 1 cup of salt or sugar into a shallow plastic container or shallow metal pan. Spread out the salt or sugar info a fairly thin layer.

- Have your child use his or her finger to practice writing the numbers 11 to 20 in the salt or sugar. (Note: If you are working on a white table, you may wish to place a sheet of colored paper under the container so that the numbers are easier to see.)

- Show your child how to wipe a hand across the salt or sugar each time he or she is ready to write a new number.

In addition to doing the above activity, practice counting 11 to 20 objects with your child whenever you can. For example, encourage your child to count eggs in a carton, raisins on a plate, or crayons in a box.

Count Teen Numbers

Name _____

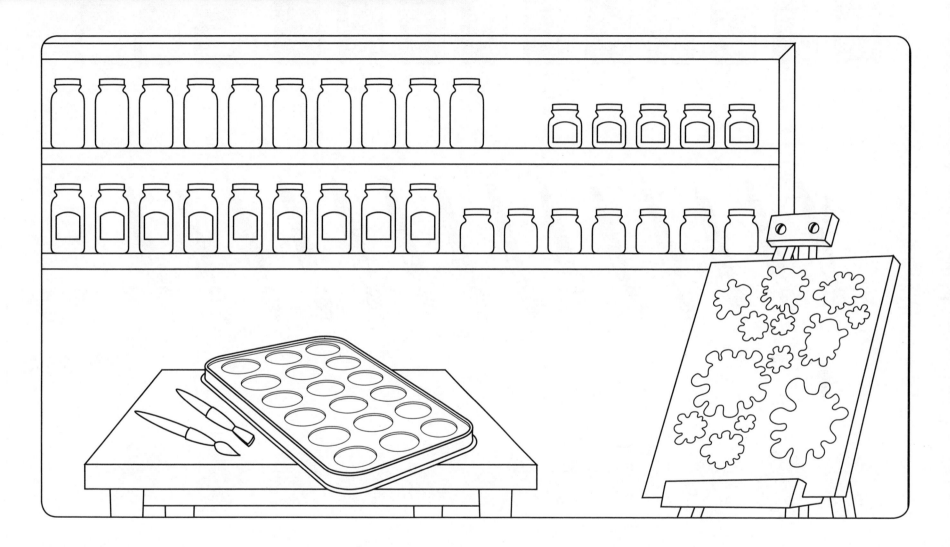

Have your child color a group of 15 paint jars, using green for 10 of them and orange for the extras. Tell your child to color a group of 12 watercolors in the tray, using green for 10 of them and purple for the extras. Have your child color the rest of the picture.

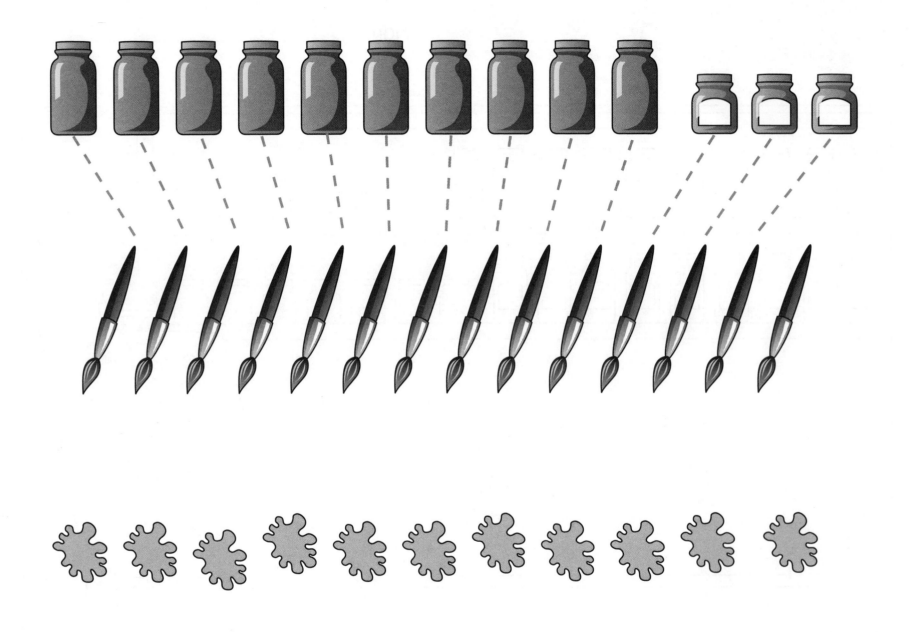

Have your child count and draw lines to match objects. Have your child count as he or she traces lines to connect paint jars to brushes. Ask your child to tell the total number of jars and total number of brushes. Then have your child connect brushes to paint blots, counting aloud as he or she draws lines.

Count Teen Numbers

Name _____

Example

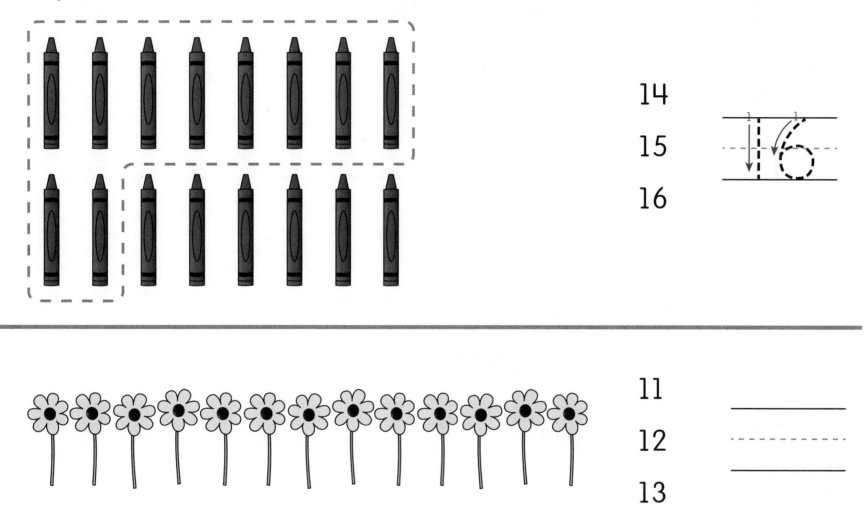

14

15

16

11

12

13

Guide your child to count teen numbers. Have your child count the objects in each problem. Then have him or her write the number counted. Have your child check his or her answer by circling a group of 10 objects and then counting the "extras."

14

15

- - - - - - - - - -

16

17

18

- - - - - - - - - -

19

Guide your child to count teen numbers. Have your child count the objects in each problem. Then have him or her write the number counted. Have your child check his or her answer by circling a group of 10 objects and then counting the "extras."

Count Teen Numbers

Name _____

Example

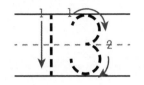

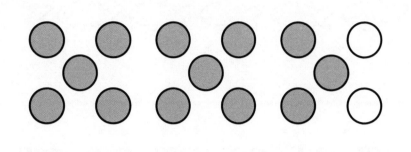

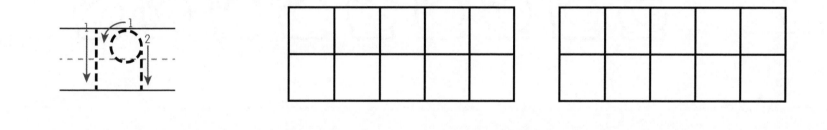

Guide your child to trace each teen number and then count out that number of shapes. Guide your child to lightly mark each shape as he or she counts to keep track of what has been counted. Then have your child count again, coloring the shapes.

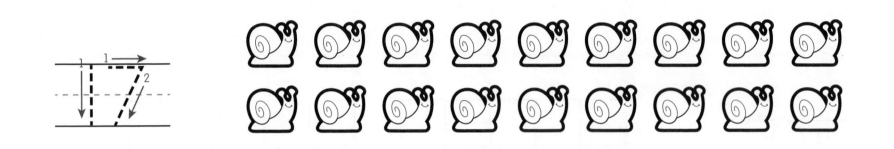

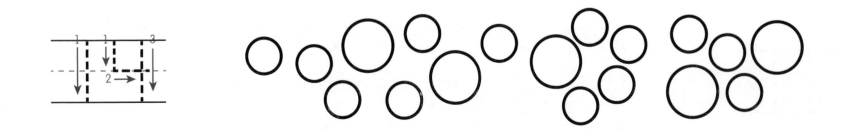

Guide your child to trace each teen number and then count out that number of objects. Guide your child to lightly mark each object as he or she counts to keep track of what has been counted. Then have your child count again, coloring the objects.

Dear Family,

This week your child is learning to make teen numbers by combining a group of 10 and some more.

The lesson uses pictures, 10-frames, and number bonds to show the numbers 11 to 19 as a group of 10 and some extras. For example, the teen number 16 can be shown on 10-frames by placing 10 counters on one frame and 6 counters on the other.

10-Frames

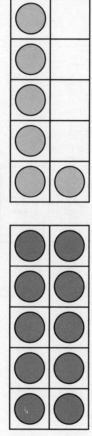

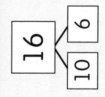

The group of 10 and group of 6 that make 16 can also be represented on a number bond. A **number bond** is a model showing the parts that make up a number. Using number bonds will help your child think about how to build and break apart numbers, which will be important for future work with addition and subtraction. The number bond below shows that 10 and 6 are parts of 16.

Number Bond

16

10   6

Invite your child to share what he or she knows about making teen numbers by doing the following activity together.

NEXT

Making Teen Numbers Activity

Materials: 8 index cards or small pieces of paper, 19 small objects (such as cereal pieces, pasta shapes, or pennies), full-sized paper and pencil

Make teen number cards by writing the numbers 11 to 19 on index cards or small pieces of paper, or use the cards from the Lesson 21 activity. Place the cards facedown in a pile.

Draw a large number bond that covers a full sheet of paper. Help your child complete each of the following steps to practice showing teen numbers as 10 and some more.

- Turn over a teen number card. Count out that number of objects and place them in the top box of the number bond.

- Move 10 of the objects from the top box of the number bond into the bottom left box of the number bond.

- Move the rest of the objects from the top box into the bottom right box.

- Place the number card in the top box of the number bond.

- Encourage your child to describe the number bond in terms of 10 and some more. For example, "10 and 4 more make 14."

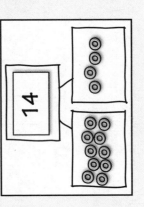

Make Teen Numbers

Name _____

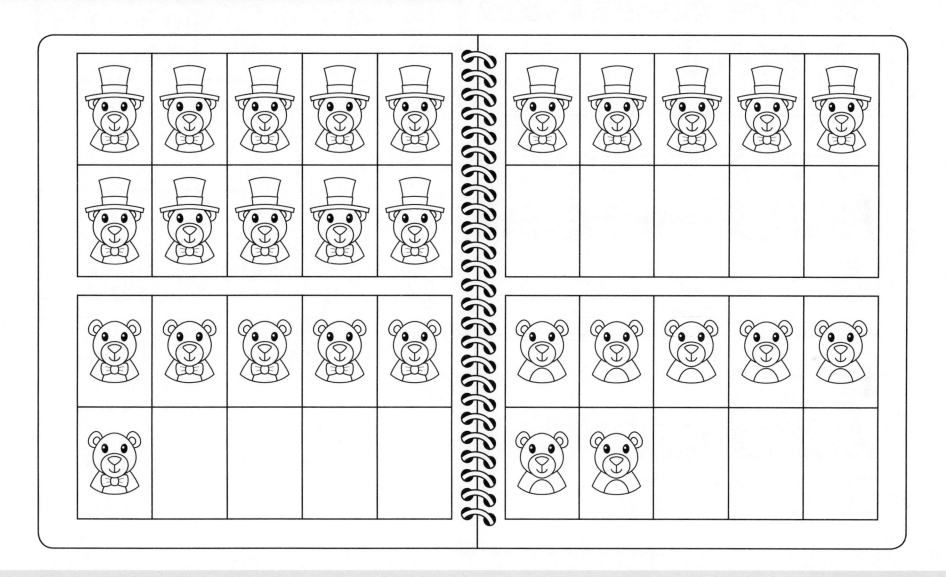

Have your child color the bears in the top left 10-frame brown. Then have your child color a second group of bears brown to make a total of 15 brown bears. Have your child color the other two sets of bears with different colors.

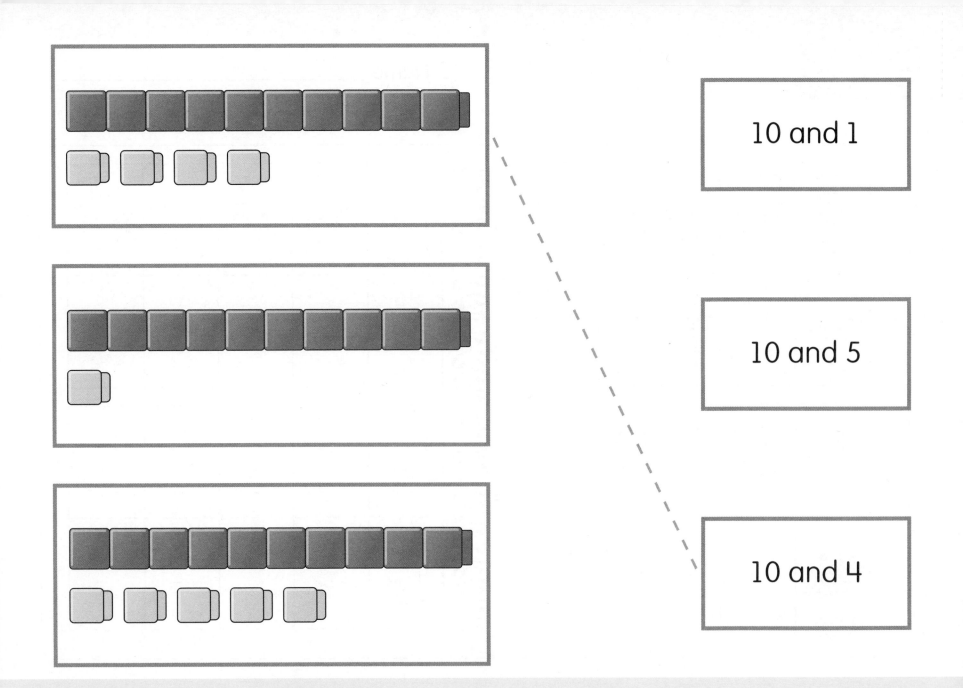

Have your child draw lines to match each group of cubes to the number pair that describes the group. Then have your child describe the cubes as 10 and some extras, and say the teen number. For example, your child might say, "10 cubes and 4 extras make 14."

Make Teen Numbers

Name _____

Example

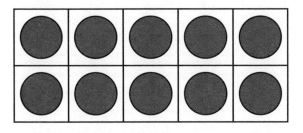 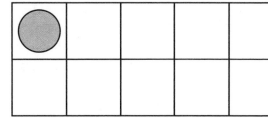 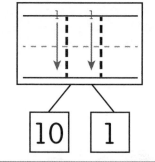

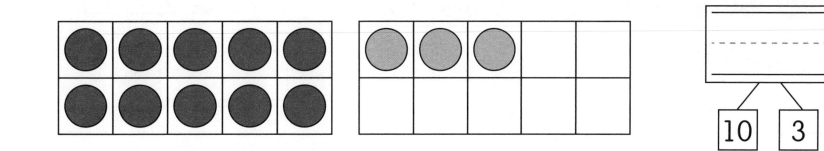

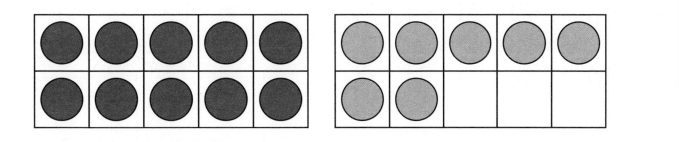 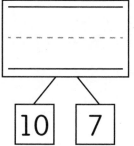

Guide your child to use 10-frames and number bonds to show teen numbers. Have your child look at the number of dark gray and light gray counters and write the total number of counters at the top of the number bond. Guide your child to describe the number as 10 and some extras. For example, to describe 11, your child might say, "11 is 10 and 1 extra."

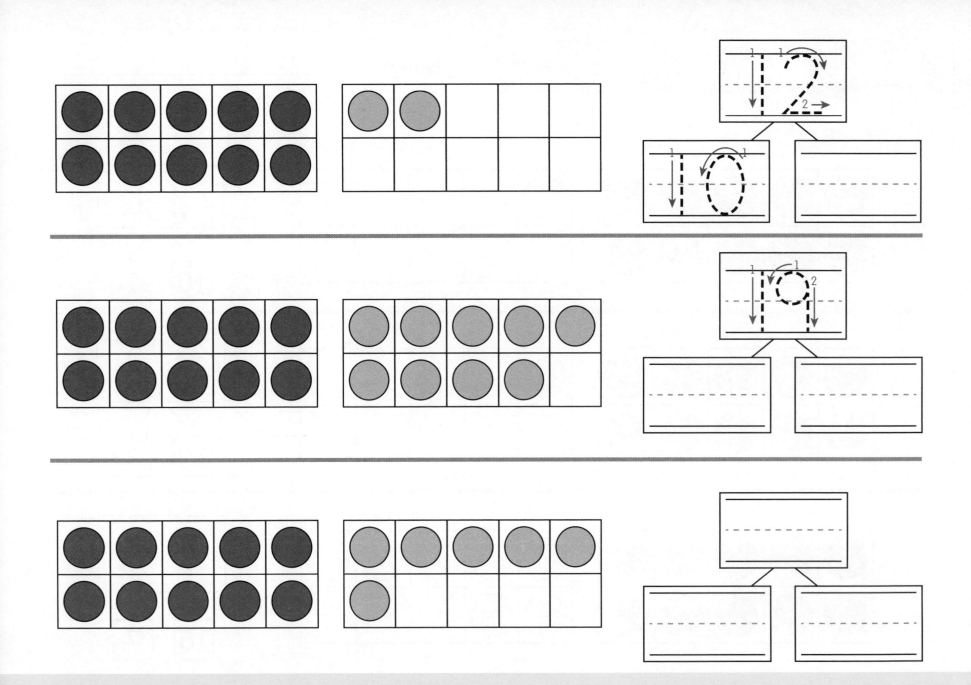

Guide your child to use 10-frames and number bonds to show teen numbers. Have your child write the total number of counters at the top of the number bond and the number of counters in each frame below. Guide your child to express the number as 10 and some extras.

Make Teen Numbers

Example

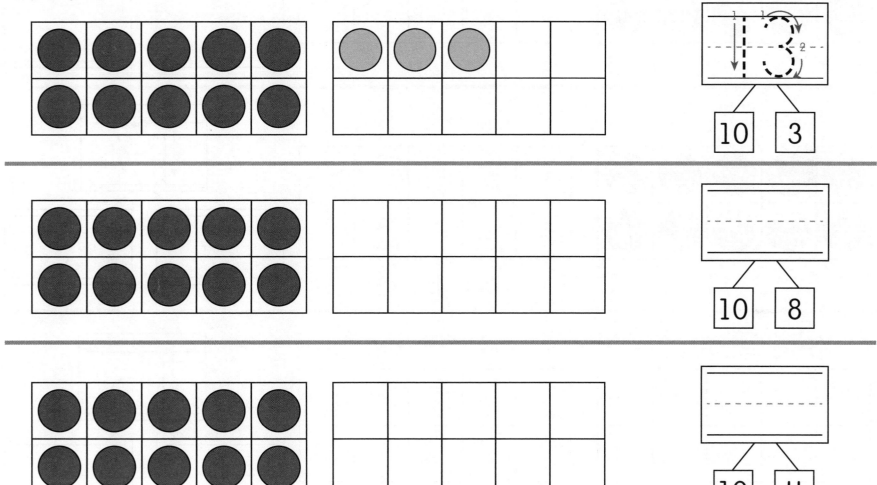

Guide your child to complete 10-frames and number bonds to show teen numbers. Have your child draw the number of counters needed to match the number bond. Then guide your child to write the total to complete the number bond.

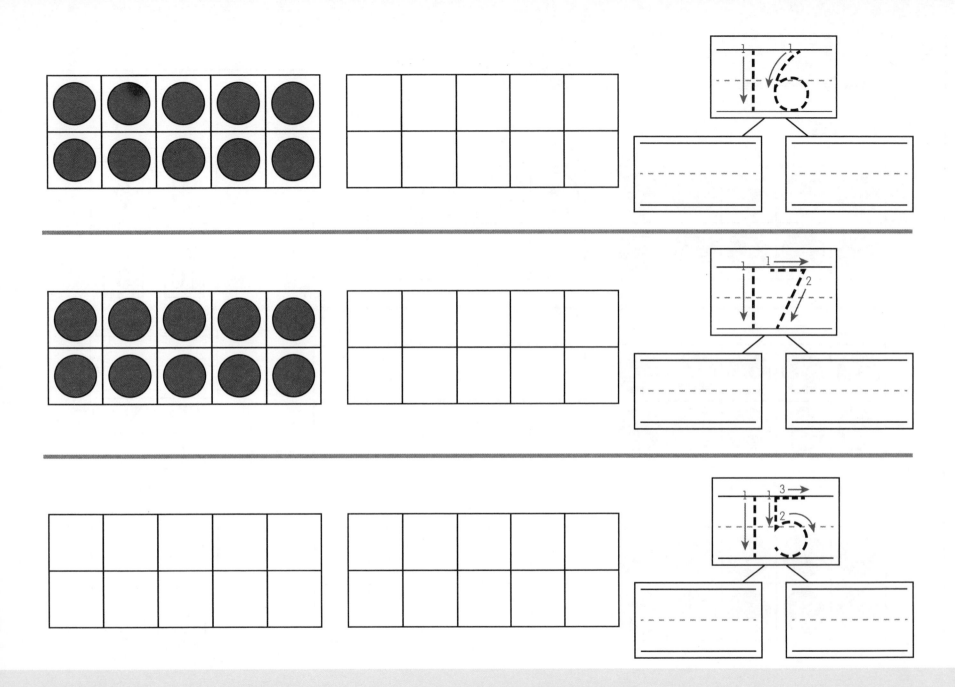

Guide your child to complete 10-frames and number bonds to show teen numbers. Have your child draw the number of counters needed to make the total shown in the number bond. Then guide your child to trace the total and write the parts to complete the number bond.

Dear Family,

This week your child is learning to count to 100 by tens.

Counting by tens involves reciting the decade numbers (10, 20, 30, 40, etc.) to 100. Learning to count by tens will help prepare your child for counting by ones across the decade numbers. For example, being able to recite "10, 20, 30" will help your child later count "19, 20, 21" and "29, 30, 31."

Counting objects organized into groups of 10 helps to emphasize that each decade number is 10 more than the the previous decade number.

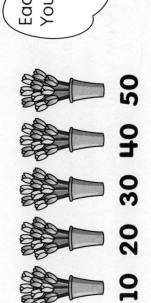

Each pot has 10 flowers. You can count by tens to find there are 50 flowers in all.

10 20 30 40 50

Your child will also practice counting by tens without objects or pictures.

Invite your child to share what he or she knows about counting to 100 by tens by doing the following activity together.

NEXT

Lesson 24 Count to 100 by Tens   201

Practice counting by tens with your child whenever you can: 10, 20, 30, 40, 50, 60, 70, 80, 90, 100! To help your child learn the sequence of decade numbers and to make practicing more fun, you can add motions as you count, such as clapping, marching, or tapping your toes as you say each number. You may want to have you and your child take turns choosing a motion to do.

If your child needs an extra challenge, count by tens in a four-number sequence and clap instead of saying one of the numbers. Then your child says the number that is missing. For example, say, "30, 40, [clap], 60." Your child should say that 50 is the missing number.

10, 20, 30, 40, 50, 60, 70, 80, 90, 100

There are many ways to practice counting by tens. You can clap, march, or tap your toes while you count!

Count to 100 by Tens

Name _____

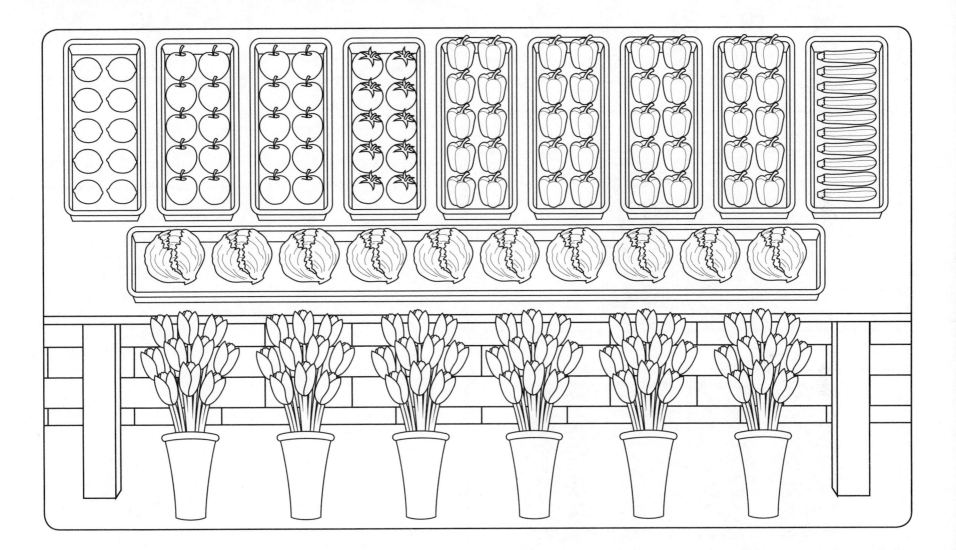

Have your child color 3 groups of 10 flowers and then count by tens to find how many he or she colored. Have your child color 7 groups of 10 fruits and/or vegetables and count them by tens. Have your child color the rest of the picture.

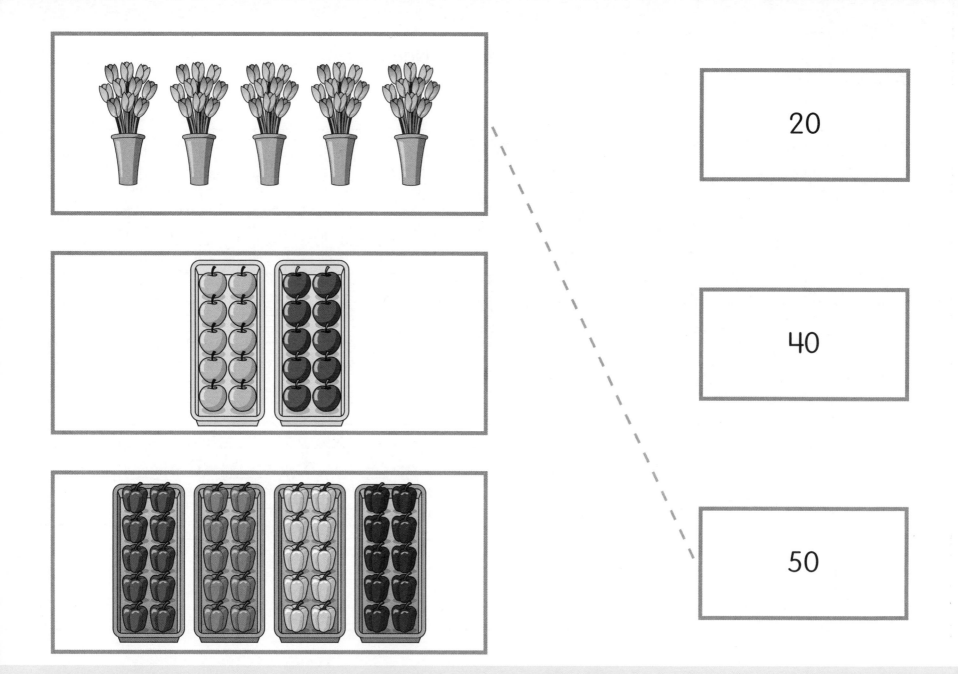

Have your child draw lines to match each group of objects to the number that tells how many. Tell your child that each vase or basket has 10 objects in it. Guide your child to count by tens to find how many objects are in each group and then draw lines to the matching totals.

Count to 100 by Tens

Name _____

Example

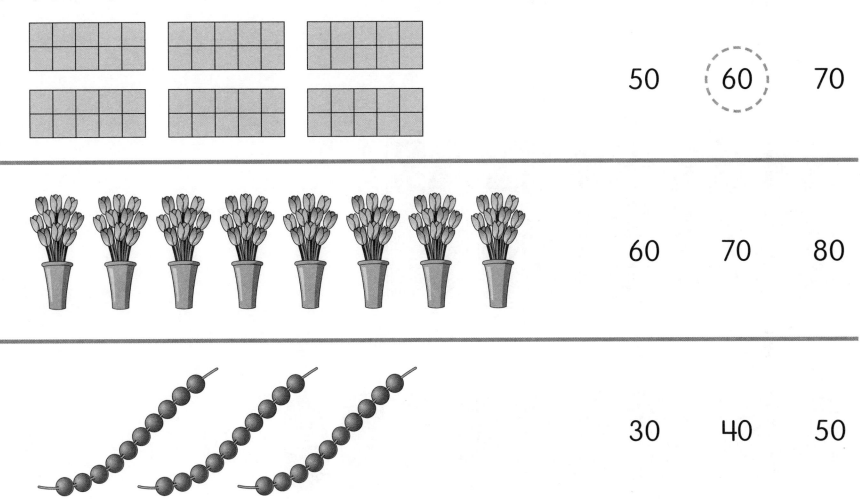

50   (60)   70

60   70   80

30   40   50

Guide your child to count objects by tens. Explain that there are 10 objects in each group. Have your child count aloud by tens to find the total number of objects in each problem. Then have your child circle the total number.

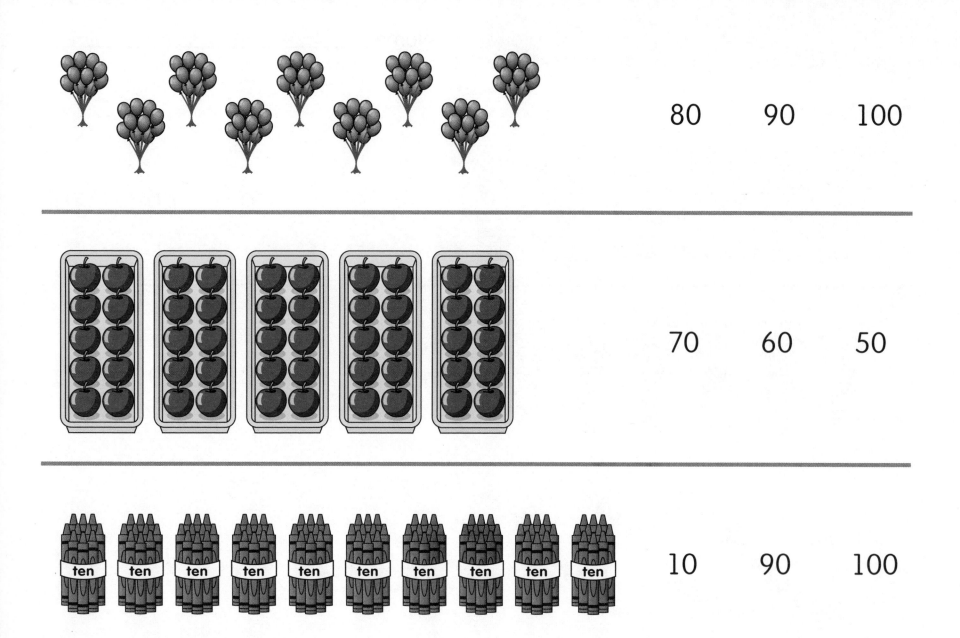

80   90   100

70   60   50

10   90   100

Guide your child to count objects by tens. Explain that there are 10 objects in each group. Have your child count aloud by tens to find the total number of objects in each problem. Then have your child circle the total number.

Count to 100 by Tens

Name _____

1	2	3	4	5	6	7	8	9	
11	12	13	14	15	16	17	18	19	20
21	22	23	24	25	26	27	28	29	
31	32	33	34	35	36	37	38	39	40
41	42	43	44	45	46	47	48	49	50
51	52	53	54	55	56	57	58	59	60
61	62	63	64	65	66	67	68	69	
71	72	73	74	75	76	77	78	79	80
81	82	83	84	85	86	87	88	89	
91	92	93	94	95	96	97	98	99	100

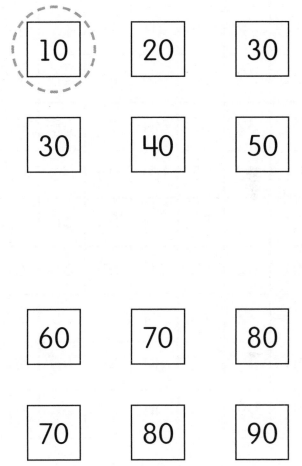

10   20   30

30   40   50

60   70   80

70   80   90

For each row on the hundreds chart with a missing number, guide your child to circle the number to the right that completes that row. Have your child count aloud to 10 by ones to find which number completes the first row. Then guide your child to focus on the last column and count together by tens, having your child circle the numbers that complete the chart.

1	2	3	4	5	6	7	8	9	10
11	12	13	14	15	16	17	18	19	
21	22	23	24	25	26	27	28	29	30
31	32	33	34	35	36	37	38	39	
41	42	43	44	45	46	47	48	49	50
51	52	53	54	55	56	57	58	59	
61	62	63	64	65	66	67	68	69	70
71	72	73	74	75	76	77	78	79	80
81	82	83	84	85	86	87	88	89	
91	92	93	94	95	96	97	98	99	

10	20	30
30	40	50
60	70	80
80	90	100
80	90	100

For each row on the hundreds chart with a missing number, guide your child to circle the number to the right that completes that row. Have your child focus on the last column. Count together by tens, having your child circle the numbers that complete the chart.

Dear Family,

This week your child is learning to count to 100 by ones.

It is important to practice counting to 100 by ones, starting at 1 or any other number. The focus is on learning to say the numbers in order, rather than on counting objects or writing numbers. In class, your child may do various movement activities while counting, such as clapping or passing a ball in a group.

This lesson also involves working with a hundreds chart, which is a chart that shows the numbers 1 to 100 in ten rows and ten columns. The hundreds chart helps to reinforce the sequence of numbers and shows patterns in our number system.

Hundreds Chart

1	2	3	4	5	6	7	8	9	10
11	12	13	14	15	16	17	18	19	20
21	22	23	24	25	26	27	28	29	30
31	32	33	34	35	36	37	38	39	40
41	42	43	44	45	46	47	48	49	50
51	52	53	54	55	56	57	58	59	60
61	62	63	64	65	66	67	68	69	70
71	72	73	74	75	76	77	78	79	80
81	82	83	84	85	86	87	88	89	90
91	92	93	94	95	96	97	98	99	100

Invite your child to share what he or she knows about counting to 100 by ones by doing the following activities together.

NEXT

Help your child practice counting from 1 to 100 whenever you can, and do the following activities together.

Ask your child to predict how far you can walk by taking 100 steps. For example, the prediction might be that it will take 100 steps to walk from your front door to the mailbox or from the playground swings to the slide. Then walk with your child, counting each step together, to find how many steps it takes.

Practice counting from numbers other than 1. For example, start counting at 32. After your child joins in to count with you, continue for at least 10 more numbers. For an extra challenge, say just one or two numbers and have your child continue counting on his or her own.

Play a stop and start counting game. Count aloud with your child starting from different numbers. Raise your hand to show when to stop counting and lower your hand to show when to continue counting where you left off. For an extra challenge, have your child count aloud alone as you raise and lower your hand to show when to stop and when to start counting.

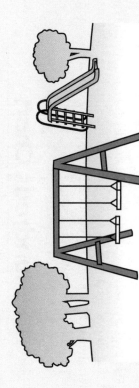

Count to 100 by Ones

Name _____

Have your child use one color to color the first 10 spaces on the game board. Then have your child color each group of 10 spaces a different color. Have your child move a counter along the board and count aloud by ones to 100.

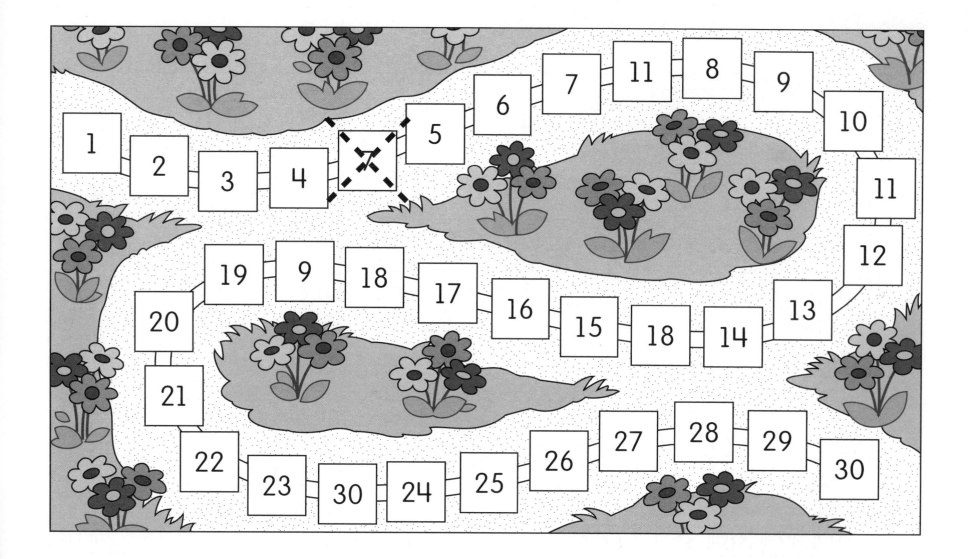

Have your child count from 1 to 30, color the numbers he or she says, and cross out the numbers that do not belong. Then have your child count from 1 to 30 again, pointing to each colored number as it is said.

Count to 100 by Ones

Name _____

1	2	3	4	5	6	7	8	9	10
11	12	13	14	15	16	17	18	19	20
21	22	23	24		26	27	28	29	30
31	32	33	34	35	36	37	38	39	40
41	42		44	45	46	47	48	49	50
	52	53	54	55	56	57	58	59	60
61	62	63	64	65	66	67	68	69	70
71	72	73	74	75	76	77	78	79	
81	82	83	84	85	86		88	89	90
91	92	93	94	95	96	97	98	99	100

(25)   26   35

42   43   44
51   60   61

60   70   80
87   88   96

For each row on the hundreds chart with a missing number, guide your child to circle the number to the right that completes that row. Count aloud by ones together until you get to the first empty box. Help your child find the missing number to the right of the hundreds chart and circle it. Count on together until you reach the next empty box, and repeat the process.

1	2	3	4	5	6	7	8	9	10
11	12	13	14	15	16	17	18	19	20
21	22	23	24	25	26	27		29	30
31	32	33	34	35	36	37	38	39	40
41	42	43	44	45	46	47	48	49	50
51		53	54	55	56	57	58	59	60
61	62	63	64	65		67	68	69	70
71	72	73	74	75	76	77	78	79	80
81	82	83	84	85	86	87	88	89	
	92	93	94	95	96	97	98	99	100

8	26	28

52	53	62
66	70	75

80	90	91
82	90	91

For each row on the hundreds chart with a missing number, guide your child to circle the number to the right that completes that row. Count aloud by ones together until you get to the first empty box. Help your child find the missing number to the right of the hundreds chart and circle it. Count on together until you reach the next empty box, and repeat the process.

Count to 100 by Ones

Name _____

Example

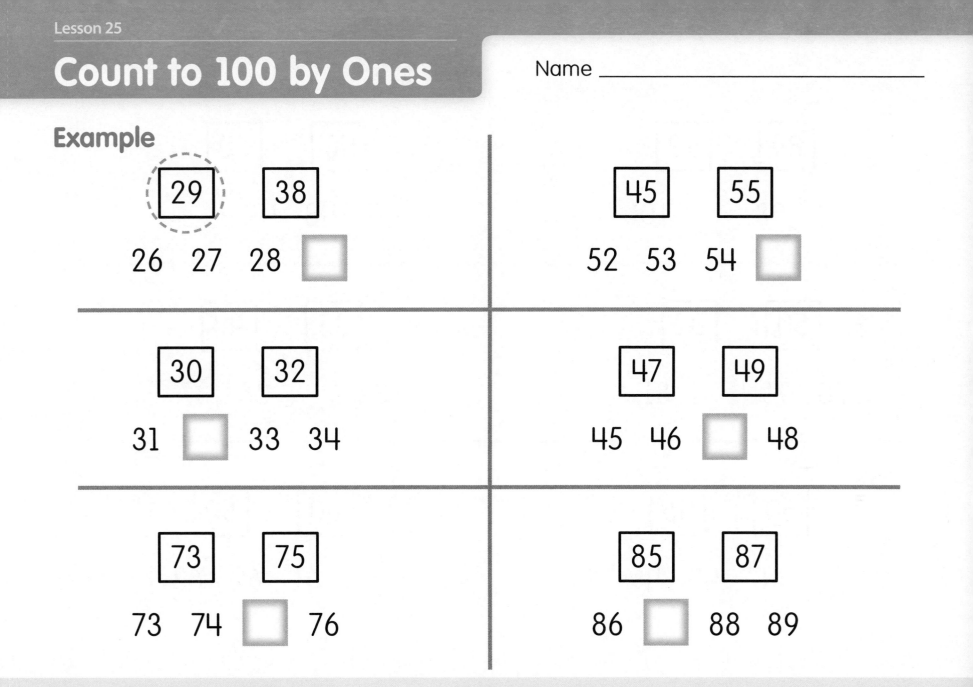

(29) 38	45 55
26 27 28 ☐	52 53 54 ☐
30 32	47 49
31 ☐ 33 34	45 46 ☐ 48
73 75	85 87
73 74 ☐ 76	86 ☐ 88 89

Guide your child to circle the correct number to complete each list. Have your child read aloud the list of numbers in the bottom row of each problem, decide what the missing number is, and circle that number above. Then have your child read the completed list of numbers to check his or her answer.

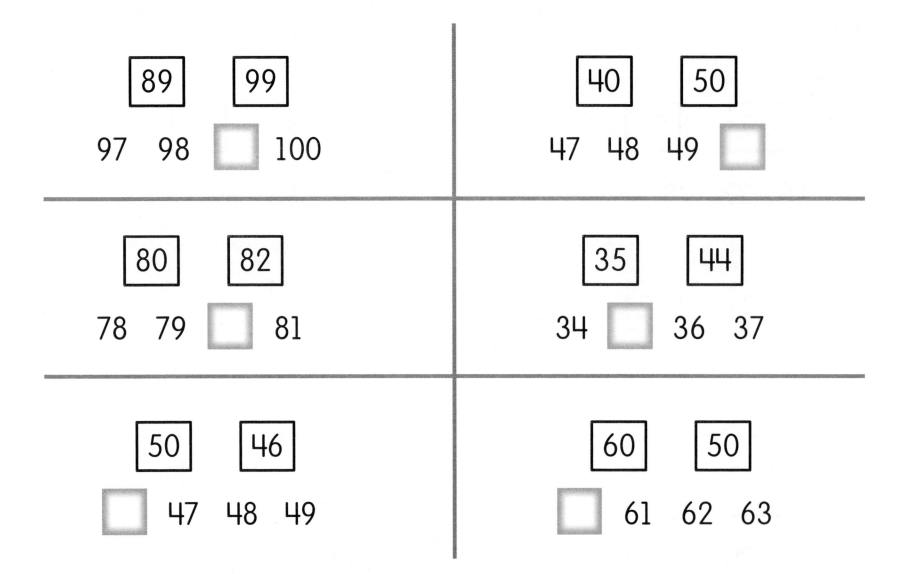

89　99

97　98　☐　100

40　50

47　48　49　☐

80　82

78　79　☐　81

35　44

34　☐　36　37

50　46

☐　47　48　49

60　50

☐　61　62　63

Guide your child to circle the correct number to complete each list. Have your child read aloud the list of numbers in the bottom row of each problem, decide what the missing number is, and circle that number above. Then have your child read the completed list of numbers to check his or her answer.

Numbers 11 to 100

Name _____

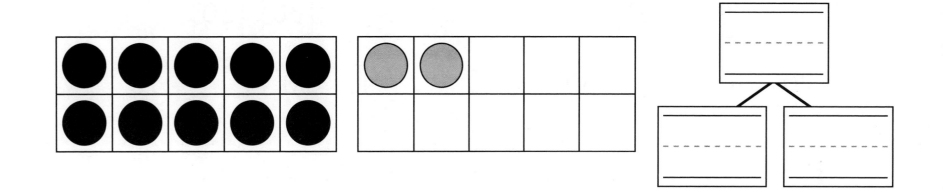

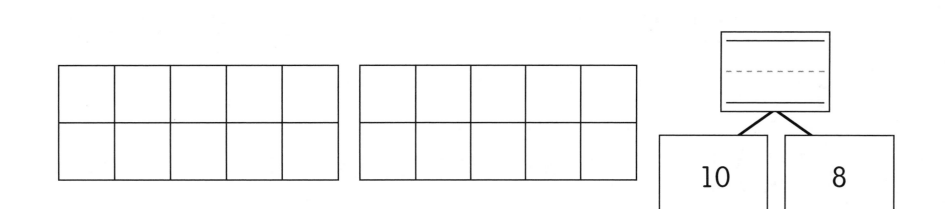

Have children complete 10-frames and number bonds to model teen numbers. In the first problem, children use the picture to complete the number bond. In the last problem, children draw counters to match the number bond, then write the total.

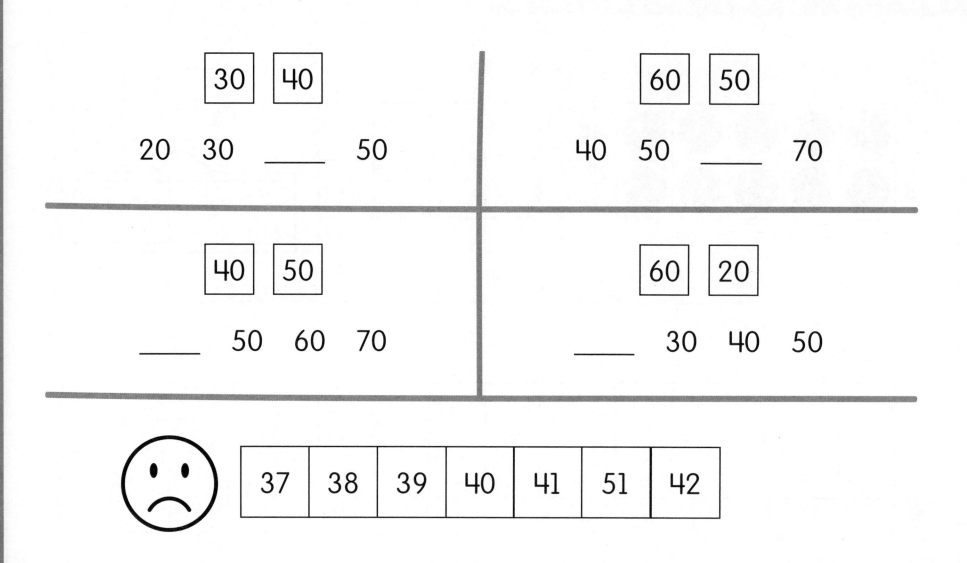

| 30 | 40 |

20   30   ____   50

| 60 | 50 |

40   50   ____   70

| 40 | 50 |

____   50   60   70

| 60 | 20 |

____   30   40   50

| 37 | 38 | 39 | 40 | 41 | 51 | 42 |

Have children count by tens, then by ones. For the first four problems, ask children to circle the number that completes the lists as they count by tens. For the last problem, have children cross out the box that shows the incorrect number as they count by ones.

Teen Number Cover-Up

Name _____

11	**12**	**13**
14	**15**	**16**
17	**18**	**19**

Materials For each pair: Teen Number Picture Cards; for each child: Teen Number Cover-Up Game Board
How to Play Take a card and tell the number it shows. Put it on a matching number square on the game board. If the card does not show a teen number, do not cover a square. If the number is already covered, skip a turn. The first player to cover all the squares wins.

Dear Family,

This week your child is learning to compare objects by length and by height.

You can compare two objects by length or by height to find which object is longer, taller, or shorter. Your child will compare the lengths and heights of objects in pictures as well as actual objects. When comparing the lengths or heights of actual objects it is important to line up the objects at one end to see which object extends farther up (for height) or farther left or right (for length).

Learning to recognize and understand the attributes of length and height will help your child prepare to do other measurement activities in later grades, including using measuring tools (such as rulers and tape measures) and measuring with standard units (such as inches and centimeters).

The striped ribbon is longer than the solid ribbon.

The white flower is shorter than the purple flower.

Invite your child to share what he or she knows about comparing length and comparing height by doing the following activities together.

NEXT

Comparing Lengths and Comparing Heights Activities

Materials: spoon and other household objects for comparing length

Tell your child that you are going on a length hunt together.

- Explain that you will look for 3 objects around your home that are longer than a spoon and 3 objects that are shorter than a spoon.

- As your child compares household objects to a spoon, encourage him or her to line up one end of the spoon with one end of the object whose length is being compared.

- Some examples of objects that might be longer than a spoon are a book, a table, and a shoe. Some items that might be shorter than a spoon are a key, a toy car, or a paper clip.

In addition to doing the above activity, ask your child to compare lengths or heights whenever you have the opportunity. For example, at the dinner table, you might ask, "Which is longer, the fork or the spoon? Which is shorter?"

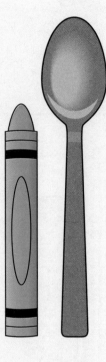

Compare Length

Name _____

Have your child use red to color the taller tree, the taller flowers, the longer bench, and the longer bat. Ask your child what word he or she could use to describe the other tree, flowers, bench, and bat. Then have your child color the rest of the picture.

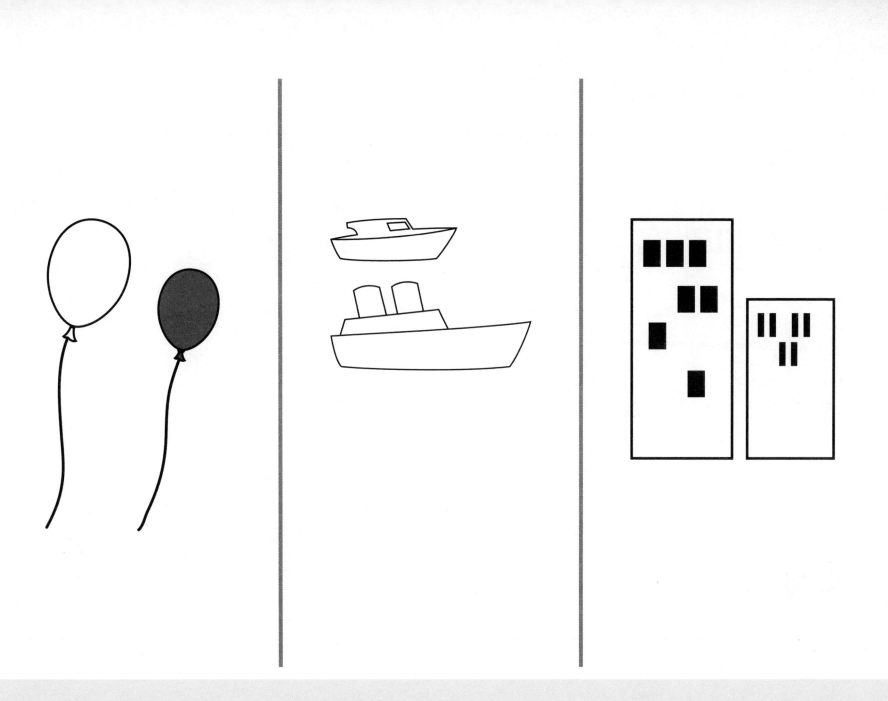

Have your child compare the heights or lengths of the objects. Guide your child to compare the heights of the balloons, the lengths of the boats, and the heights of the buildings. Have him or her color the shorter object in each pair.

Compare Length

Name _____

Example

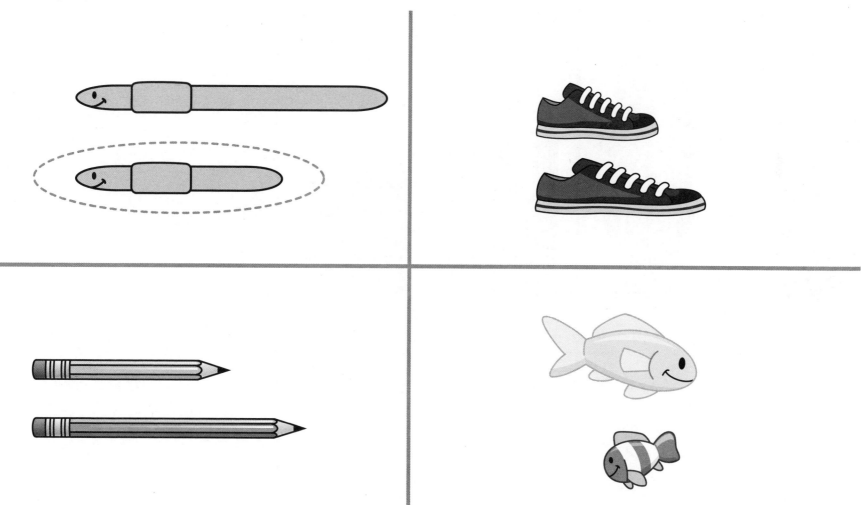

Guide your child to identify which objects are longer and which are shorter. Have your child circle the shorter object in each pair. Ask your child to explain how he or she decided which object is shorter.

Guide your child to identify which objects are taller and which are shorter. Have your child circle the shorter object in each pair. Ask your child to explain how he or she decided which object is shorter.

Compare Length

Example

Guide your child to identify which objects are longer and which are shorter. Have your child circle the longer object in each pair. Ask your child to explain how he or she decided which object is longer.

Guide your child to identify which objects are taller and which are shorter. Have your child circle the taller object in each pair. Ask your child to explain how he or she decided which object is taller.

Dear Family,

This week your child is learning to compare objects by weight.

Comparing two objects by weight involves finding which object is heavier or lighter. Your child will compare the weights of actual objects as well as the weights of objects shown in pictures. To compare weights, it may be helpful to think of a heavier object as harder to lift and a lighter object as easier to lift.

There will be some focus on recognizing that larger objects are not necessarily heavier than smaller objects. For example, even if a balloon is larger than a basketball, the balloon will be lighter than the basketball. This focus emphasizes that weight and size are different attributes. Understanding and comparing weights will help prepare your child for other later work with measurement units.

Invite your child to share what he or she knows about comparing weight by doing the following activity together.

NEXT

Comparing Weights Activity

Tell your child that you are going to play an imagination game involving weights of objects. Then ask several questions about which imaginary bag full of objects would be heavier or which would be lighter. For example:

- *Which do you think would be heavier, a bag full of feathers or a bag full of rocks?*

- *Which do you think would be lighter, a bag full of popcorn or a bag full of potatoes?*

- *Which do you think would be heavier, a bag full of bricks or a bag full of balloons?*

If your child needs guidance with the terms *heavier* and *lighter*, ask which bag would be easier or harder to pick up and connect this to the ideas of heavier and lighter. After you have asked several of these questions, encourage your child to ask you a question about which of two bags would be heavier or lighter. Take turns asking each other questions and use your imagination!

Ask your child to compare objects by weight whenever you have the chance. For example, at the dinner table, you might ask, "Which is heavier, your spoon or your cup of milk? Which is lighter?" When your child is getting ready for school, you might ask, "Which is lighter, your lunchbox or your backpack? Which is heavier?"

Compare Weight

Name _____

Have your child color the can of soup. Next, have your child use green to color two objects that are heavier than the can of soup. Using a different color, have your child color one object that is lighter than the can of soup. Have your child color the rest of the picture.

Have your child circle the box of cereal. Have your child look for objects that are heavier than a box of cereal and color them red. Then have your child look for objects that are lighter than a box of cereal and color them blue.

Compare Weight

Name _____

Example

Guide your child to identify which objects are heavier. Have your child circle the heavier object in each pair. Ask your child to explain how he or she knows that the object circled is heavier than the other object.

Compare Weight

Name _____

Example

Guide your child to identify which objects are lighter. Have your child circle the lighter object in each pair. Ask your child to explain how he or she decided which object is lighter.

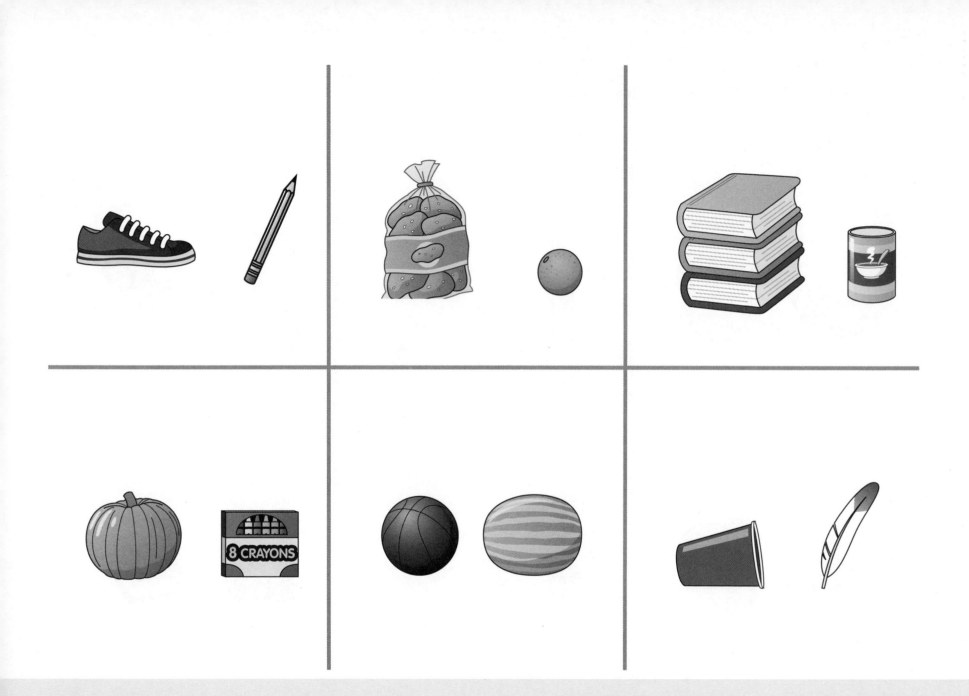

Guide your child to identify which objects are lighter. Have your child circle the lighter object in each pair. Ask your child to explain how he or she decided which object is lighter.

Dear Family,

This week your child is learning to sort objects.

Actual objects and pictures of objects can be sorted by attributes such as color, shape, size, and weight. After sorting objects into different categories, your child will count how many are in each group and compare the groups using language such as *same, equal, more than, fewer than,* and *less than.*

For example, the fish in the picture below can be sorted into the following categories: big and small, striped and solid, swimming left and swimming right. Also, there are more solid fish than striped fish and there are fewer big fish than small fish.

Sorting objects into groups, as well as counting and comparing the numbers of objects in each group, will help your child prepare to work with charts and graphs in later grades.

Invite your child to share what he or she knows about sorting objects by doing the following activity together.

Materials: 8 to 10 objects that can be sorted by size, color, shape, and/or other attributes (such as buttons, beads, blocks, coins, or dried beans)

Give your child 8 to 10 objects of at least 2 different shapes, colors, and/or sizes. They should be able to be sorted 2 different ways, such as by size and then by color.

Ask your child to sort some or all of the objects into 2 groups. If needed, you can suggest sorting by shape, color, or size. Encourage your child tell you about the groups. Then ask your child to sort some or all of the objects into 2 groups in a different way. For example, if the objects are first sorted by color, they can then be sorted by size. Discuss what the new groups look like. For an additional challenge, add objects of a different shape, color, or size and ask your child to sort the objects into 3 groups.

Big Beads

Small Beads

Sort Objects

Name _____

Have your child color the striped fish red and the rest of the fish yellow. Then have your child color the big rocks one color and the small rocks a different color. Have your child color the rest of the picture.

Have your child sort objects based on feature. Discuss with your child how the objects shown are similar and different. Guide your child to see that some objects can be eaten while others cannot. Have your child color all the objects that can be eaten. Then have your child count the objects he or she colored and compare that number to the number of objects that are not colored.

Sort Objects

Name _____

Example

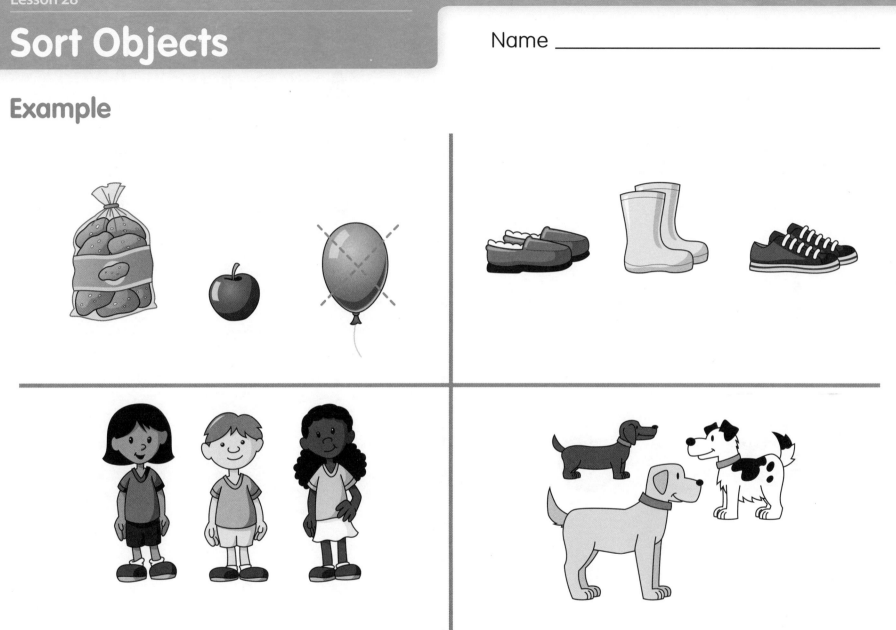

Guide your child to identify one object that does not belong with the others. Explain that there may be more than one correct answer. Have your child cross out one object he or she sees as different. Then have your child share the reasons for crossing out each object.

Guide your child to identify one object that does not belong with the others. Explain that there may be more than one correct answer. Have your child cross out one object he or she sees as different. Then have your child share the reasons for crossing out each object.

Sort Objects

Example

Guide your child to sort the objects. Guide your child to realize that the two given groups are balls and other sport items. Have your child draw a line from each object at the bottom of the page to the group to which it belongs.

Have your child sort the animals. Guide your child to realize that the two given groups are big animals and small animals. Have your child draw a line from each animal at the bottom of the page to the group to which it belongs.

Compare and Sort

Name _____

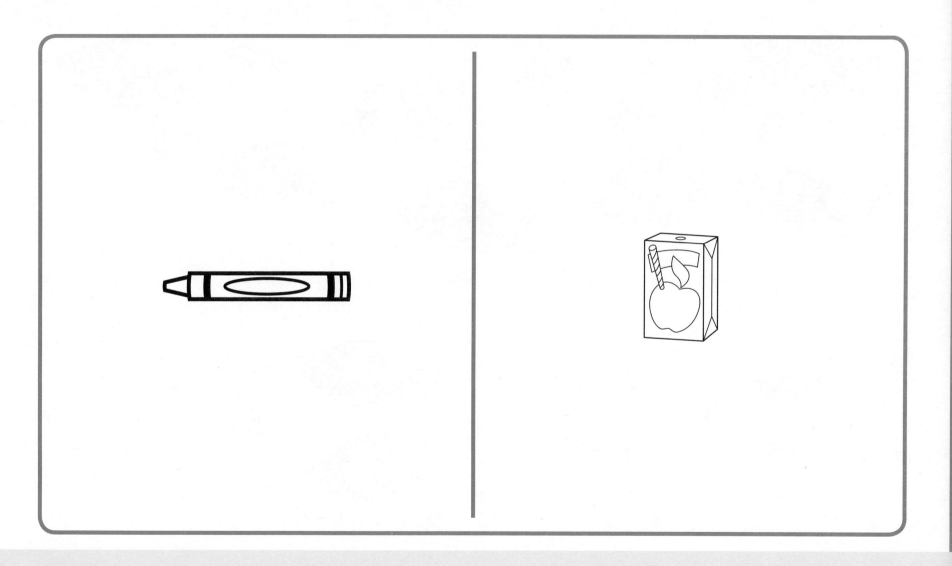

Have children draw pictures to show "longer" and "heavier." Have children draw a crayon that is longer than the one shown. Then have children draw an object that is heavier than a juice box.

Have children sort the fish by size. Have children find all the small fish and write how many. Then have them find all the big fish and write how many.

Shorter and Longer

Name _____

Shorter

Same

Longer

Materials For each pair: 2 dot cubes (1–6); for each child: Shorter and Longer Game Board, 50 connecting cubes
How to Play Roll 2 dot cubes. Count the dots and build a train with that many cubes. If the train is shorter than the crayon, put it in the "shorter" box. If the train is longer, put it in the "longer" box. If it is the same length, put it in the "same" box. The first person to get 1 shorter train and 1 longer train wins.

Dear Family,

This week your child is learning to recognize the position and shape of objects.

Position language such as *above, below, beside, in front of, behind,* and *next to* are used to describe the location of objects.

There are many different shapes that can be seen within real-world objects. Recognizing shapes in his or her environment will help your child prepare for upcoming geometry lessons about shape attributes such as sides and corners.

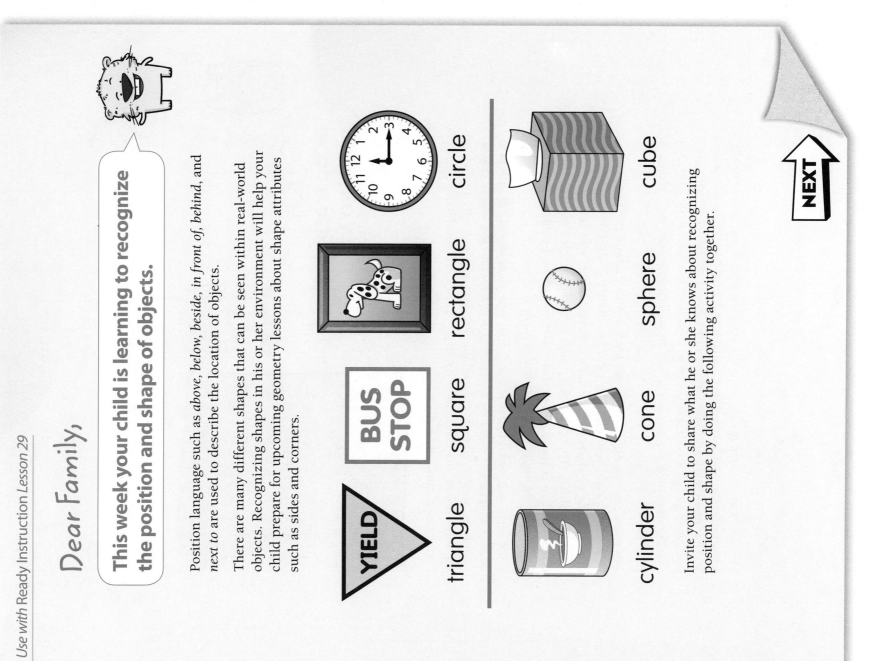

circle

rectangle

square

triangle

cube

sphere

cone

cylinder

Invite your child to share what he or she knows about recognizing position and shape by doing the following activity together.

NEXT

Seeing Position and Shape Activity

Play an "I Spy" game focusing on the position and shape of household objects. Describe where you see a shape and have your child try to find it. You might walk around to different rooms in the house or you may choose to gather a collection of objects to display together in ways that demonstrate position words such as *above, below, beside, in front of, behind,* and *next to.*

For example, you might say "I spy a circle above a bookshelf" to describe a clock. Your child looks around to try to find the circle you are thinking of. If the guess is for a different circle, you can say something like, "That is a circle, but it is not the circle I picked. The circle I picked is above a bookshelf." Have your child continue to guess until he or she finds the object you described.

Take turns asking and answering "I Spy" questions about household objects shaped like squares, rectangles, triangles, circles, cubes, cones, cylinders, and/or spheres. Household objects you might refer to include napkins, doors, shapes on food packages, plates, toy blocks, ice cream cones, soup cans, and balls.

I spy a cylinder next to a paper bag.

See Position and Shape

Name _____

Observe as you ask your child to color different objects on the page. Have your child color the child with the book, the child in front of him, and the window above the child with the book. Then have your child color the child next to the squirrel, the leaves below the safety cone, and one object above the bus. Tell your child to color the rest of the picture.

Guide your child to circle the flowers beside the bench and color the flower below the tree purple. Have your child color the object in front of a bench red and the boat behind the sailboat blue. You may wish to then allow your child to color the rest of the picture.

See Position and Shape

Name _____

Example

Guide your child to identify objects that are next to, above, behind, or below. Have your child circle the object that is next to the apple and the trash can with the leaf above it. Then have your child circle the animal that is behind the dog and the acorn that is below the bench.

Guide your child to identify objects that are above, behind, in front of, or beside. Have your child circle the animal above the squirrel and the object behind the milk. Then have your child circle the object in front of the bus and the object beside the tree.

See Position and Shape

Name _____

Example

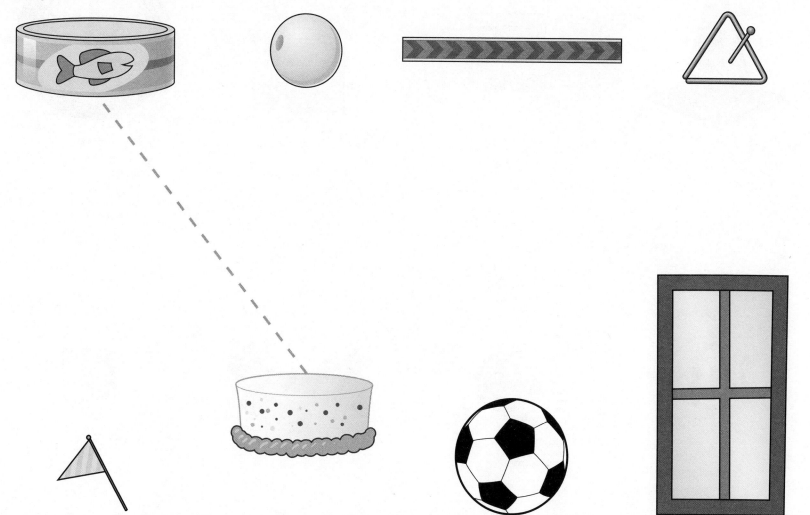

Dear Family,

This week your child is learning to name shapes.

He or she will also learn some of the ways to describe shapes. For example, triangles, hexagons, rectangles, and squares have corners and straight sides. A hexagon has 6 sides and a square has 4 equal sides. Circles, cylinders, spheres, and cones have curves. Learning some of the ways to describe shapes will help your child identify and distinguish between different shapes in geometry lessons and in the real world.

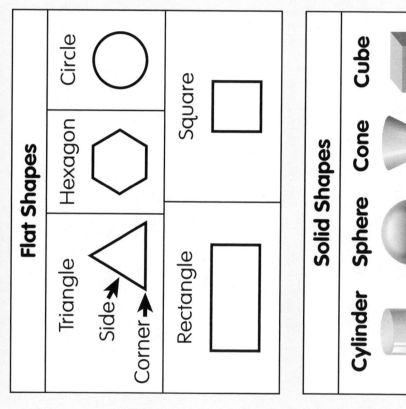

Invite your child to share what he or she knows about naming shapes by doing the following activity together.

Naming Shapes Activity

Tell your child that you are going on a shape hunt.

- Together, look around your home and neighborhood for objects shaped like rectangles, squares, triangles, hexagons, and circles. In addition, look for objects shaped like cylinders, spheres, cones, and cubes. You may wish to bring this letter so that you can use the shapes on the other side as a reference.

- Encourage your child to name the shapes you both find.

- You can also make a chart to keep track of how many objects you find of each shape.

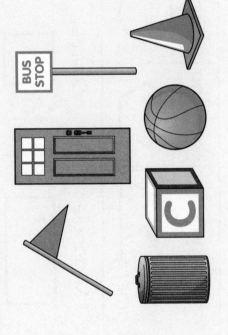

Name Shapes

Name _____

Observe as you ask your child to color different shapes on the page. Have your child color a square, a rectangle, a circle, a triangle, and a hexagon. Then have your child color a sphere, a cube, a cone, and a cylinder. Have your child color the rest of the picture.

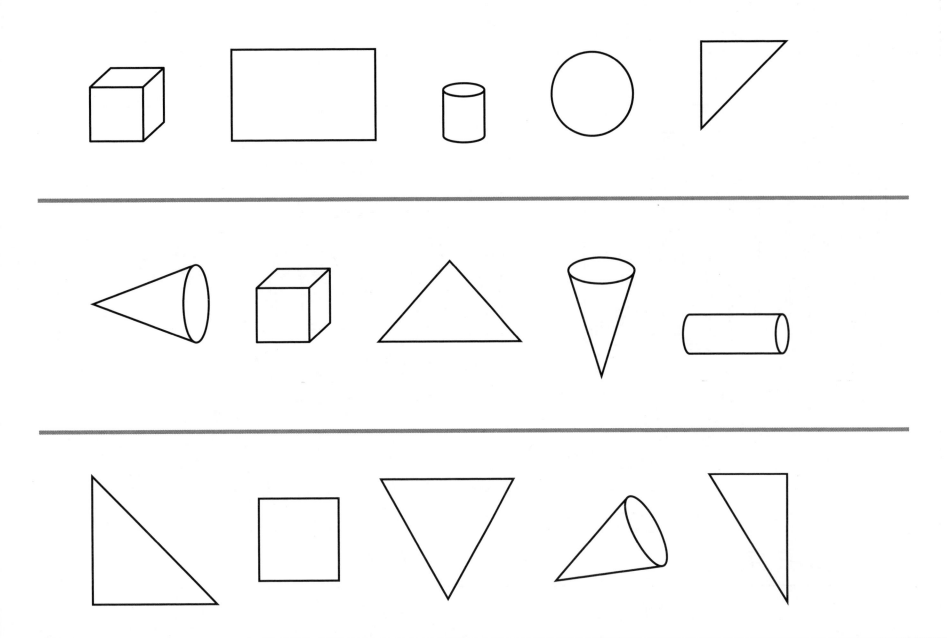

Guide your child to identify and sort shapes into categories. Have your child color all the flat shapes in the top row and all the solid shapes in the middle row. Then have your child color all the triangles in the bottom row.

Name Shapes

Name _____

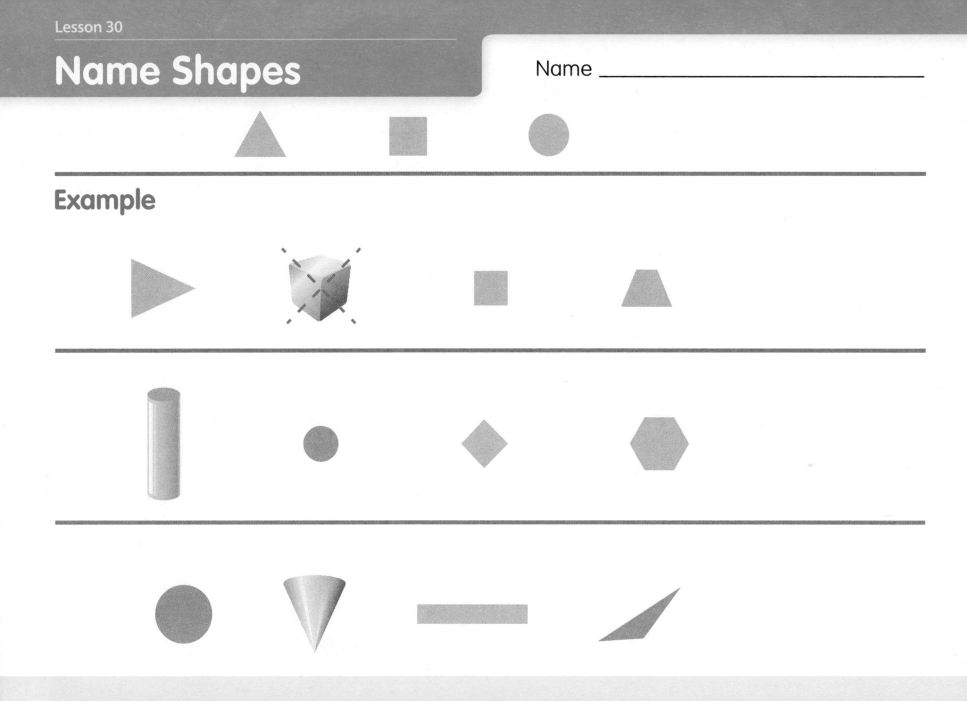

Example

Guide your child to distinguish flat shapes from solid shapes and then identify the flat shapes. Have your child mark all the solid shapes with an X. Then have your child ring (circle) the triangle at the top of the page red, the square green, and the circle blue. Have your child use those colors to ring the other triangles, squares, and circles.

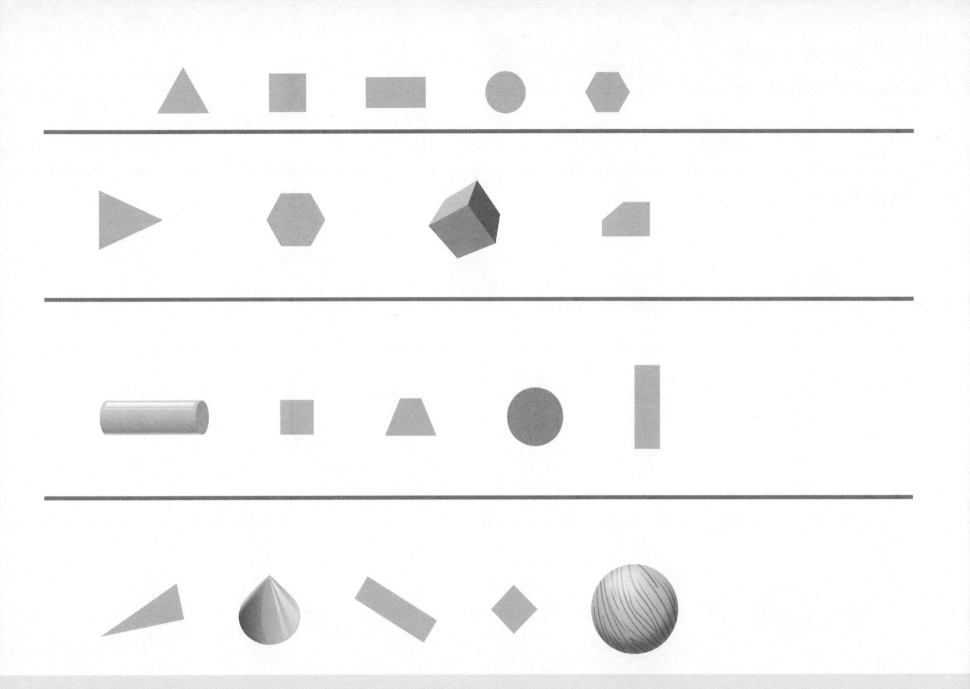

Guide your child to distinguish flat shapes from solid shapes and then identify the flat shapes. Have your child mark all the solid shapes with an X. Then have your child ring (circle) the triangle at the top of the page red, the square green, the rectangle purple, the circle blue, and the hexagon yellow. Have your child use those colors to ring the other triangles, squares, rectangles, circles, and hexagons.

Name Shapes

Name _____

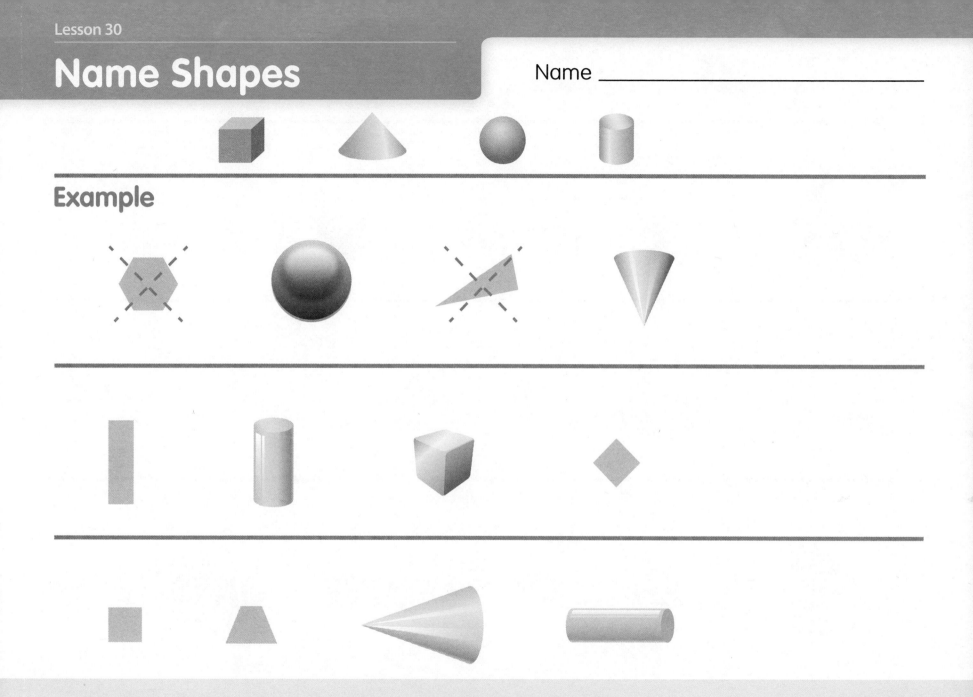

Example

Guide your child to distinguish flat shapes from solid shapes and then identify the solid shapes. Have your child mark all the flat shapes with an X. Then have your child ring (circle) the cube at the top of the page purple, the cone red, the sphere green, and the cylinder blue. Have your child use those colors to ring the other cubes, cones, spheres, and cylinders.

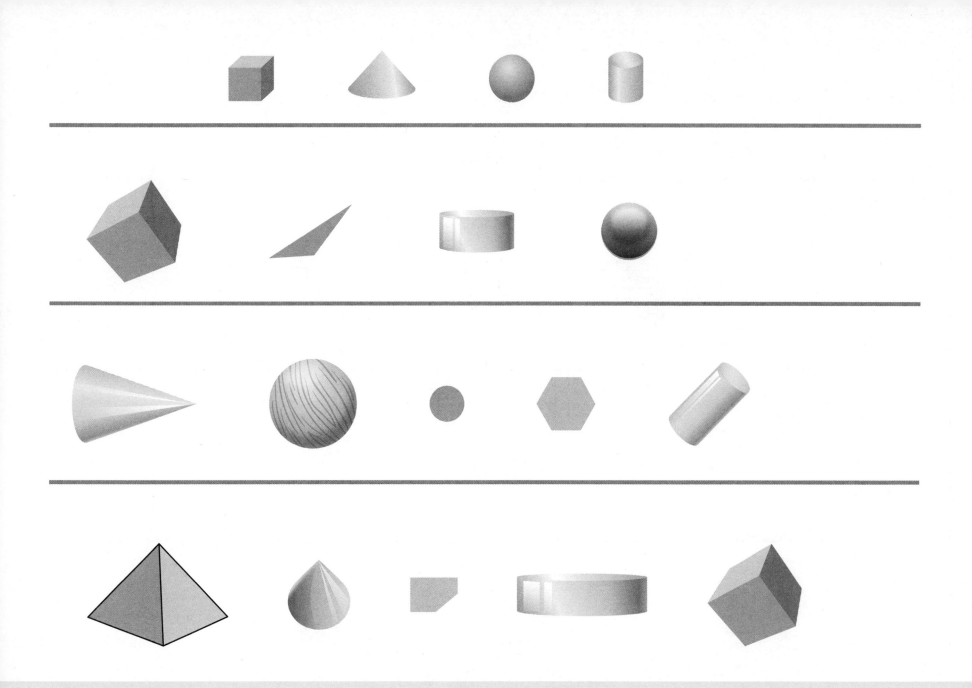

Guide your child to distinguish flat shapes from solid shapes and then identify the solid shapes. Have your child mark all the flat shapes with an X. Then have your child ring (circle) the cube at the top of the page purple, the cone red, the sphere green, and the cylinder blue. Have your child use those colors to ring the other cubes, cones, spheres, and cylinders.

Dear Family,

This week your child is learning to compare shapes.

In order to compare shapes you need to think about their attributes. For example, the cylinders, cones, and spheres below are alike because they are solid shapes that can roll.

Some solid shapes are alike because they can stack, such as the 3 shapes below. The first and third shapes, which are cubes, are most alike because they each have 6 square faces. A flat surface of a solid shape is called a **face**.

face → 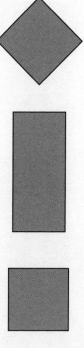 ← face

When comparing flat shapes, such as the those below, you can compare the number of sides and the lengths of sides. For example, each shape below has 4 sides. But only the first and third shapes, which are squares, have all sides of equal length.

Invite your child to share what he or she knows about comparing shapes by doing the following activity together.

NEXT

Materials: 1 household object shaped like a cylinder (such as a food can), 1 household object shaped like a cube (such as a toy block or cube-shaped tissue box), 1 household object shaped like a sphere (such as a ball), paper and pencil

Place the objects shaped like a cylinder, cube, and sphere on the floor for your child (so that you don't have to worry about objects rolling off the table). Ask him or her questions about the shapes, such as the following:

- *Which shapes roll?* (cylinder and sphere)

- *Which shapes stack?* (cylinder and cube)

- *Which shape has corners?* (cube)

- *Which shape has faces that are squares?* (cube)

- *Which shape has faces that are circles?* (cylinder)

Have your child hold the cylinder and then the cube on a piece of paper while you trace around one face of each object. Ask your child to name the flat shapes you drew (circle and square) and tell you how they are alike and different. Encourage your child to use the circle and square to make a drawing or design.

Compare Shapes

Name _____

Direct your child's attention to the shapes poster below the clock. Have your child color all the shapes with 3 sides. Then direct your child's attention to the top shelf. Tell your child to color the shapes that have corners one color and shapes that have no corners another color. Have your child color the rest of the picture.

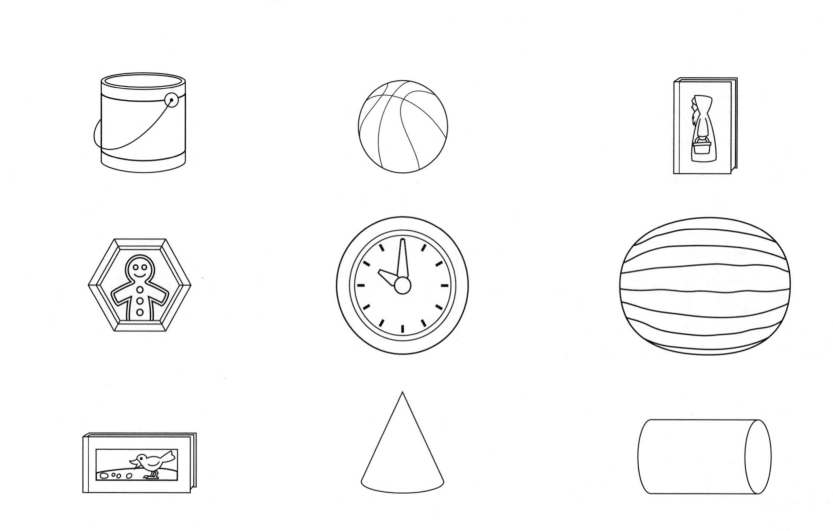

Guide your child to look for shapes that are alike in some way. Have your child color all the shapes that have corners red. Then have your child color all solids that have faces that are circles blue.

Compare Shapes

Name _____

Example

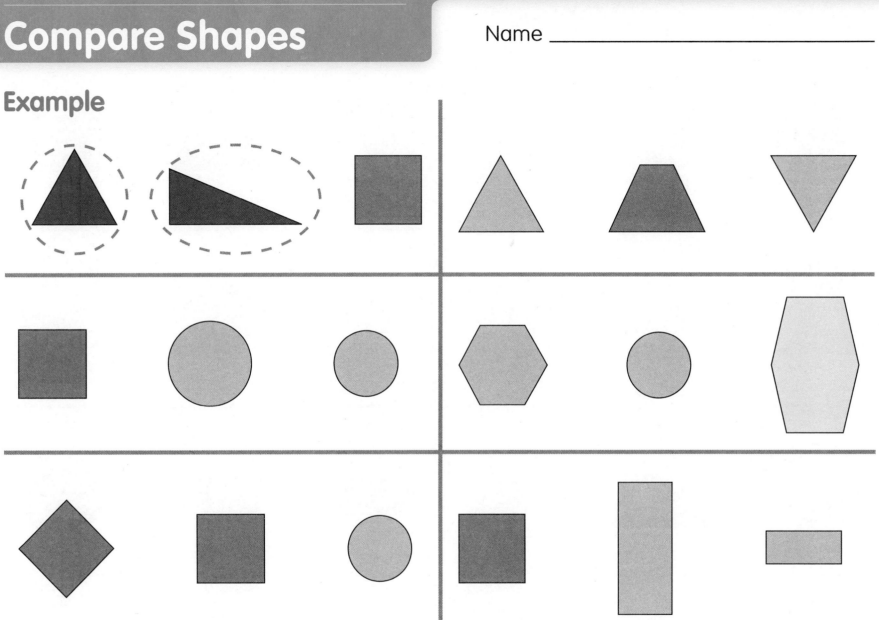

Guide your child to ring (circle) the two shapes that are most alike. Have your child focus his or her attention on the number of sides, the types of corners, or sides that are the same length. Guide your child to describe both what is alike and what is different.

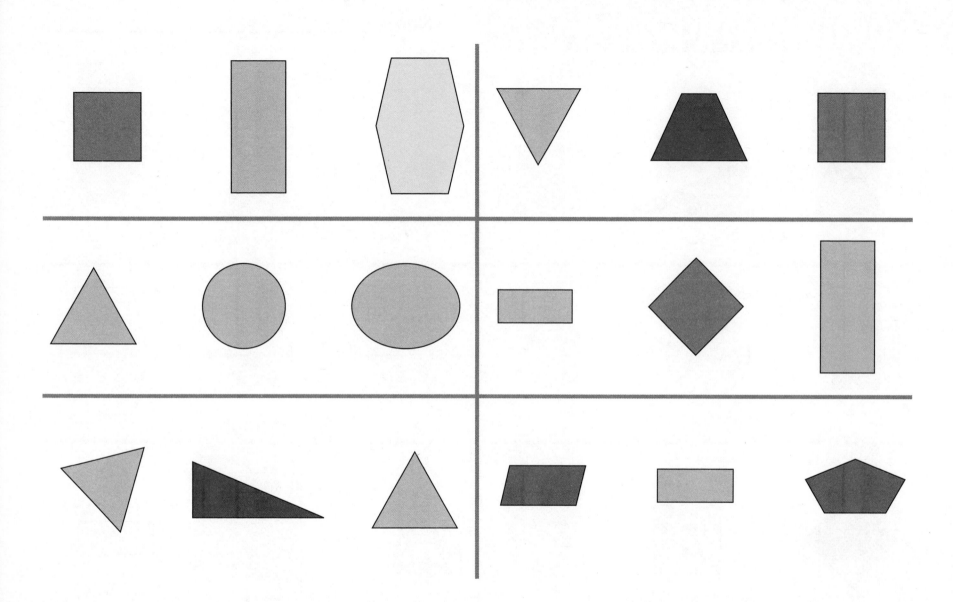

Guide your child to ring (circle) the two shapes that are most alike. Have your child focus his or her attention on the number of sides, the types of corners, or sides that are the same length. Guide your child to describe both what is alike and what is different.

Compare Shapes

Name _____

Example

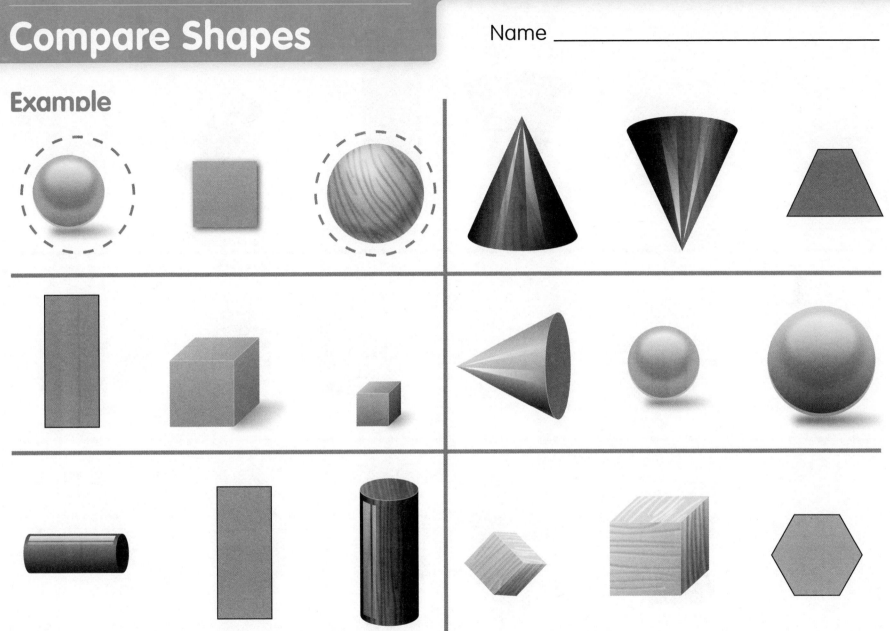

Guide your child to ring (circle) the two shapes that are most alike. Have your child focus his or her attention on whether the shapes are flat or solid and what kind of solid. Guide your child to describe both what is alike and what is different.

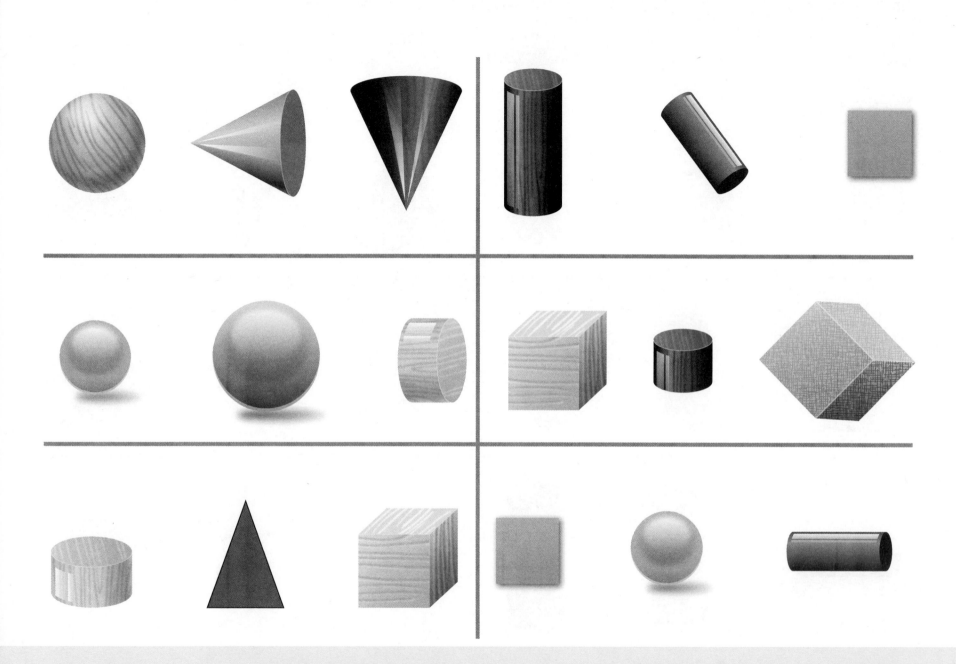

Guide your child to ring (circle) the two shapes that are most alike. Have your child focus his or her attention on whether the shapes are flat or solid and what kind of solid. Guide your child to describe both what is alike and what is different.

Dear Family,

This week your child is learning to build shapes.

Shapes can be put together to form larger shapes. For example, 2 squares can be put together to form a rectangle.

Also, 2 triangles can be put together to from a square and 4 triangles can be put together to form a rectangle.

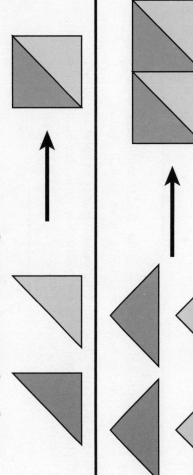

Learning to place shapes side by side to form larger shapes will help your child build a foundation for work in later grades with equal parts, fractions, and area.

Invite your child to share what he or she knows about building shapes by doing the following activity together.

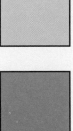

NEXT

Materials: 12 or more toothpicks (or other straight objects such as small craft sticks or straws cut into same-size pieces)

Ask your child to use some of the toothpicks to build a square. Then, providing assistance as needed, have your child add toothpicks to show how a rectangle can be built from two squares.

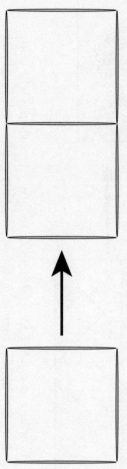

For an additional challenge, ask your child to build a rectangle from 3 squares and to build a large square from 4 small squares.

Then have your child put toothpicks together to build any shape, picture, or design. If you wish, help your child glue his or her toothpick arrangement to a sheet of paper.

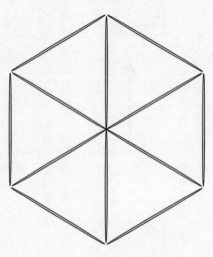

Build Shapes

Name _____

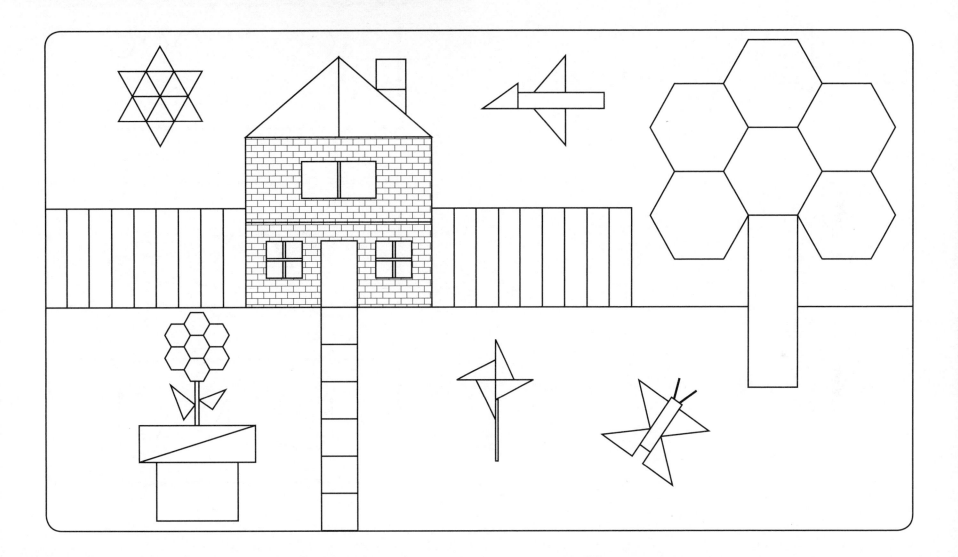

Have your child use one color to color a rectangle that is made from triangles. Then ask your child to use a second color to color a square that is made from smaller squares and a third color to color a triangle that is made from smaller triangles. Have your child color the rest of the picture.

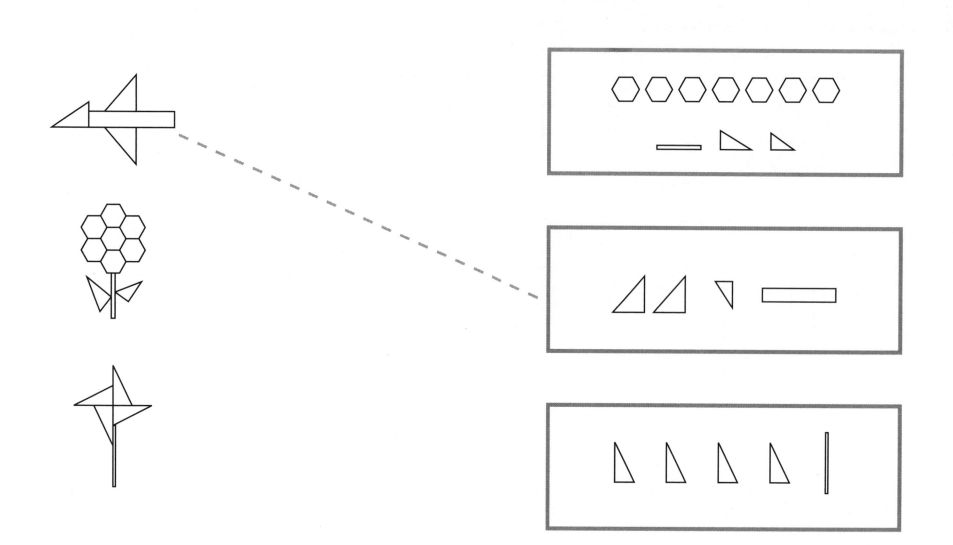

Guide your child to identify small shapes within a larger shape. Have your child look at the different shapes used to make each object. Then have your child draw lines to match each object to the group of smaller shapes used to make that object.

Build Shapes

Name _____

Example

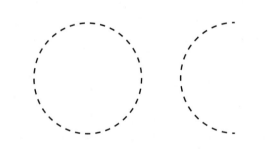

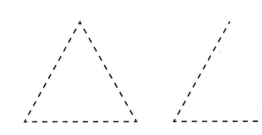

Guide your child to trace a shape, complete a partial shape, and then draw another of the same shape. After tracing the first of each shape, discuss its features, such as the number of sides and corners, and guide your child to include those features in his or her work.

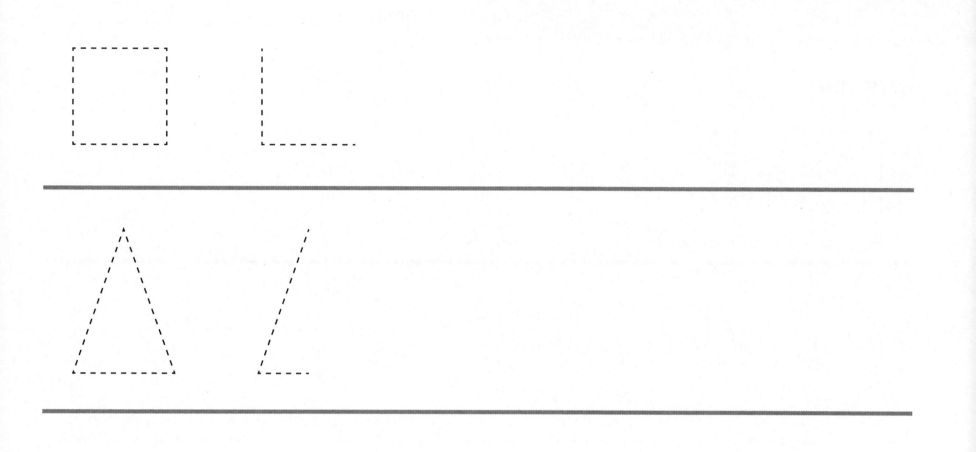

In the first two rows, guide your child to trace a shape, complete a partial shape, and then draw another of the same shape. After tracing the first of each shape, discuss its features, such as the number of sides and corners, and guide your child to include those features in his or her work. In the third row, ask your child to draw a rectangle.

Build Shapes

Name _____

Example

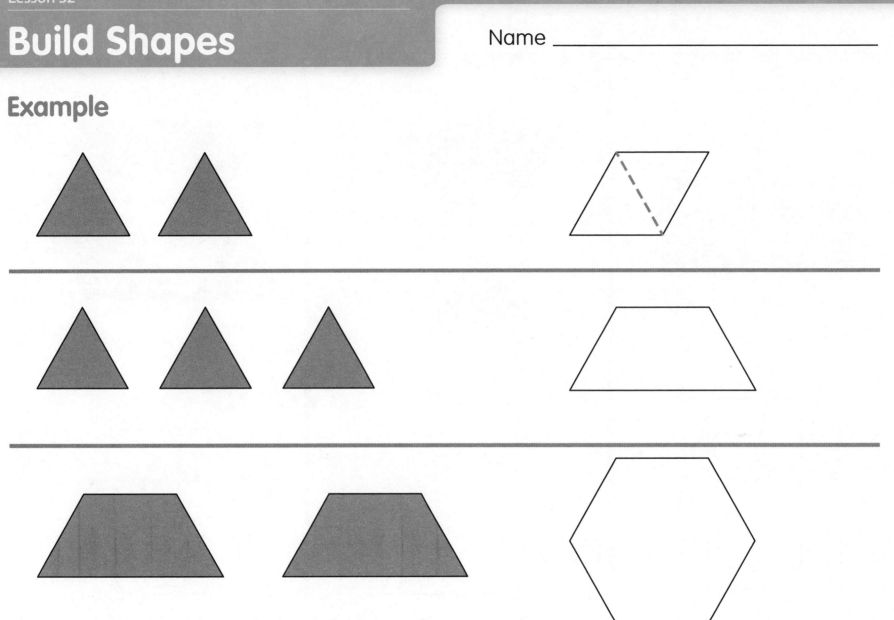

Guide your child to use shapes like the gray shapes shown to make each outlined shape at the right. Have your child use pattern blocks or shapes cut out from the Pattern Blocks sheet to try different arrangements for making the outlined shape at the right. Have your child draw lines to show how the smaller shapes fit into the outlined shape. **Materials: Teacher Resource 19: Pattern Blocks, scissors**

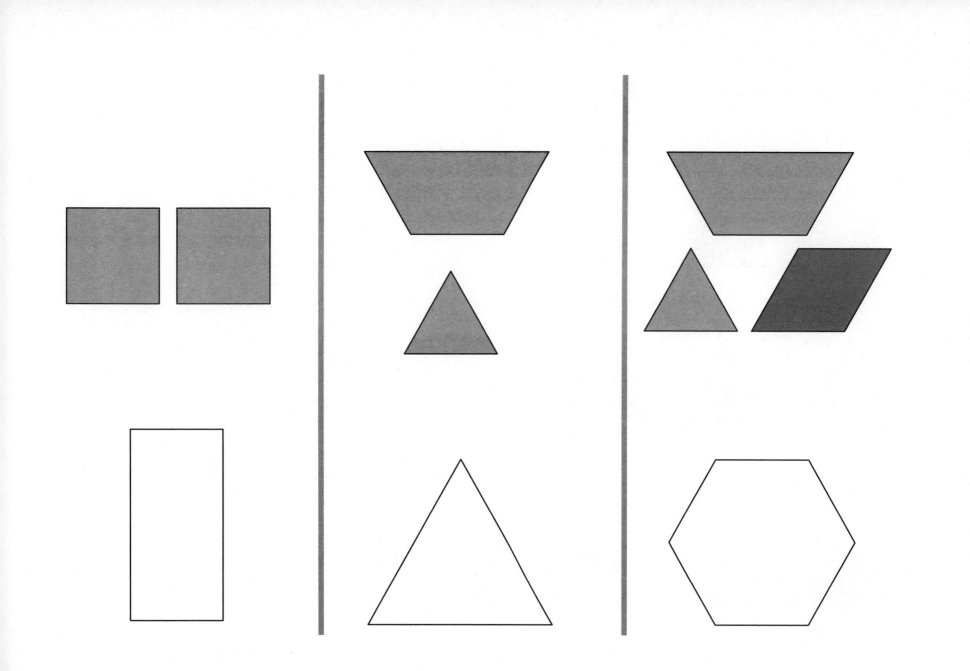

Guide your child to use shapes like the gray shapes shown to make each outlined shape below. Have your child use pattern blocks or shapes cut out from the Pattern Blocks sheet to try different arrangements for making the outlined shape below. Have your child draw lines to show how the smaller shapes fit into the outlined shape. **Materials: Teacher Resource 19: Pattern Blocks, scissors**

Shapes

Name _____

3 sides   ◯ face

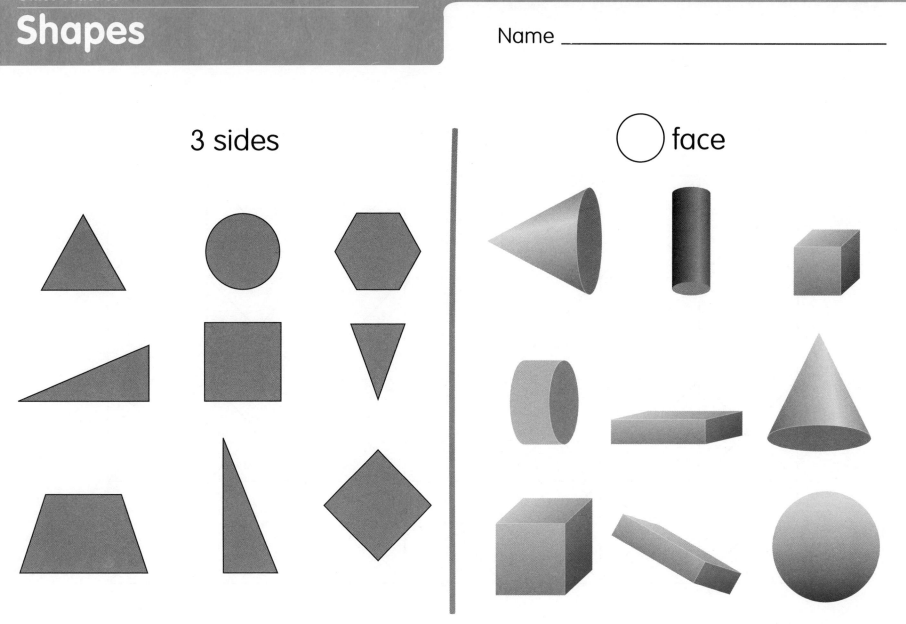

Have children analyze the flat shapes and solids and look for those with the given characteristic. On the left, children ring (circle) figures with three sides. On the right, children ring solids with a circular face.

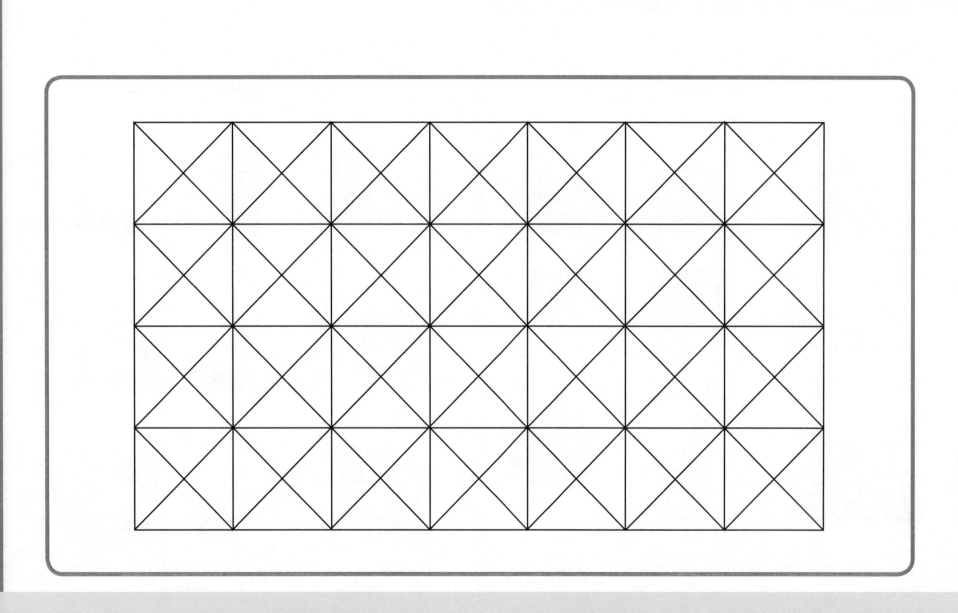

Have children combine shapes to make a picture. Have children use the guidelines to color triangles and squares and make a picture or pattern of their own.

Shape Cover-Up

Name _____

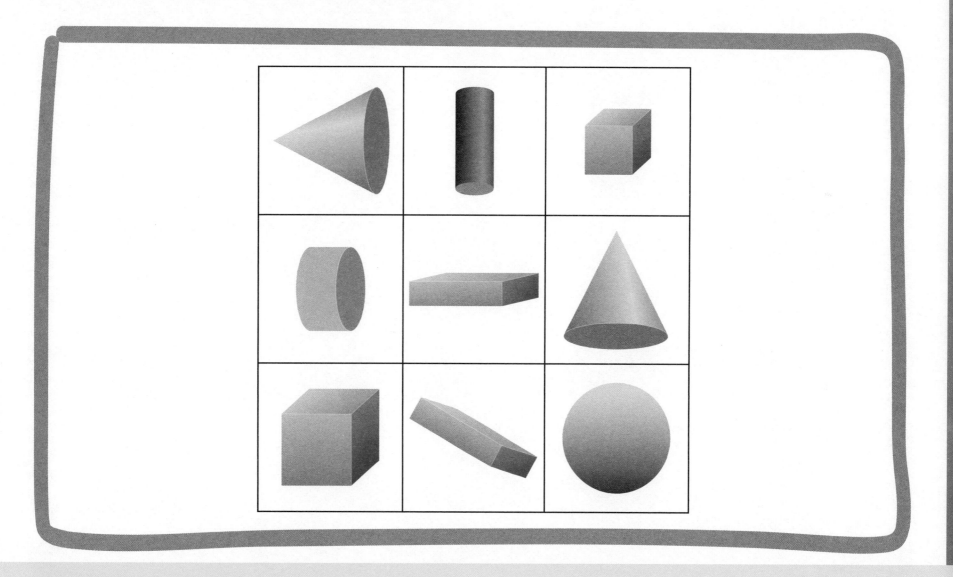

Materials For each child: 1 set of Shape Cards, Shape Cover-Up Game Board

How to Play Take a shape card from the stack. Look for that exact shape on your game board. If the shape is on your board, cover it with the card. If the shape is not on your board, put the card on the bottom of the stack and end your turn. The first person to cover every shape wins.

Table of Contents
Fluency Practice

Name _____

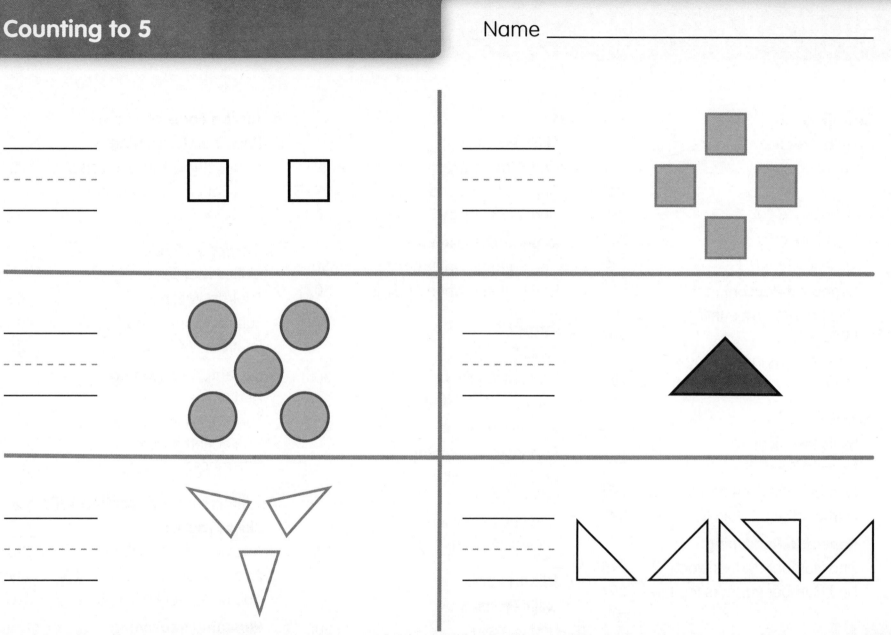

Have children count the number of objects in each group and write the number.

Counting to 10

_____

_ _ _ _ _ _ _ _ _ _ _ _ _ _ _ _

_____

_ _ _ _ _ _ _ _ _ _ _ _ _ _ _ _

_____

_ _ _ _ _ _ _ _ _ _ _ _ _ _ _ _

_____

_ _ _ _ _ _ _ _ _ _ _ _ _ _ _ _

_____

_ _ _ _ _ _ _ _ _ _ _ _ _ _ _ _

_____

_ _ _ _ _ _ _ _ _ _ _ _ _ _ _ _

Have children count the number of objects in each group and write the number.

Counting to 20

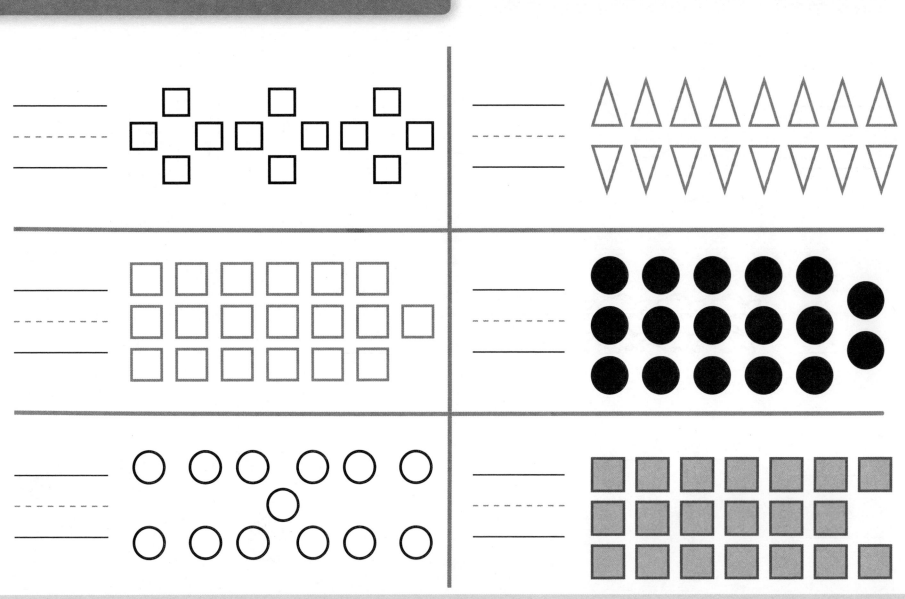

Have children count the number of shapes in each group and write the number.

Name _____

24   25   _____
            - - - - - - -
            _____

_____   41   42
- - - - - - -
_____

43   _____   45
      - - - - - - -
      _____

33   34   _____
            - - - - - - -
            _____

_____   38   39
- - - - - - -
_____

_____   29   _____   31
           - - - - - - -
           _____

27   _____   29
      - - - - - - -
      _____

48   49   _____
            - - - - - - -
            _____

Guide children to count and find the missing number. Have children write the missing number in each list.

Name _____

52   53   _____

79   _____   81

76   _____   78

_____   64   65

_____   70   71

98   99   _____

87   88   _____

58   _____   60

Guide children to count and find the missing number. Have children write the missing number in each list.

Find Patterns in Counting by Tens—Repeated Reasoning

Name _____

1	2	3	4	5	6	7	8	9	10
11	12	13	14	15	16	17	18	19	☐
21	22	23	24	25	26	27	28	29	30
31	32	33	34	35	36	37	38	39	40
41	42	43	44	45	46	47	48	49	☐
51	52	53	54	55	56	57	58	59	60
61	62	63	64	65	66	67	68	69	☐
71	72	73	74	75	76	77	78	79	80
81	82	83	84	85	86	87	88	89	90
91	92	93	94	95	96	97	98	99	☐

_____

- - - - - - - -

_____

_____

- - - - - - - -

_____

_____

- - - - - - - -

_____

_____

- - - - - - - -

_____

Guide children to point to the numbers in the far right column of the chart as they count by tens to 100. When they get to a blank box, have children write the missing number on the lines next to that box.

Talk About It Look at the numbers in the top row of the chart. Then look at the numbers in the far right column. How is counting by tens like counting by ones?

Find Patterns in Counting by Ones—Repeated Reasoning

Name _____

1	2	3	4	5	6	7	8	9	10
11	12	13	14	15	16		18	19	20
21	22	23	24	25	26	27	28	29	30
31	32	33		35	36	37	38	39	40
41	42	43	44	45	46	47	48	49	50
51	52	53	54	55	56	57	58		60
61	62	63	64	65	66	67	68	69	70
71	72	73	74	75	76	77	78	79	80
	82	83	84	85	86	87	88	89	90
91	92	93	94	95	96	97	98	99	100

_____

- - - - - - - - -

_____

_____

- - - - - - - - -

_____

_____

- - - - - - - - -

_____

_____

- - - - - - - - -

_____

Guide children to point to the numbers on the chart as they count by ones to 100. When they get to a blank box, have children write the missing number on the lines next to that row.

Talk About It   How are the numbers in each row alike? How are the numbers in each column alike? What patterns do you see in the numbers as you count to 100?

Name _____

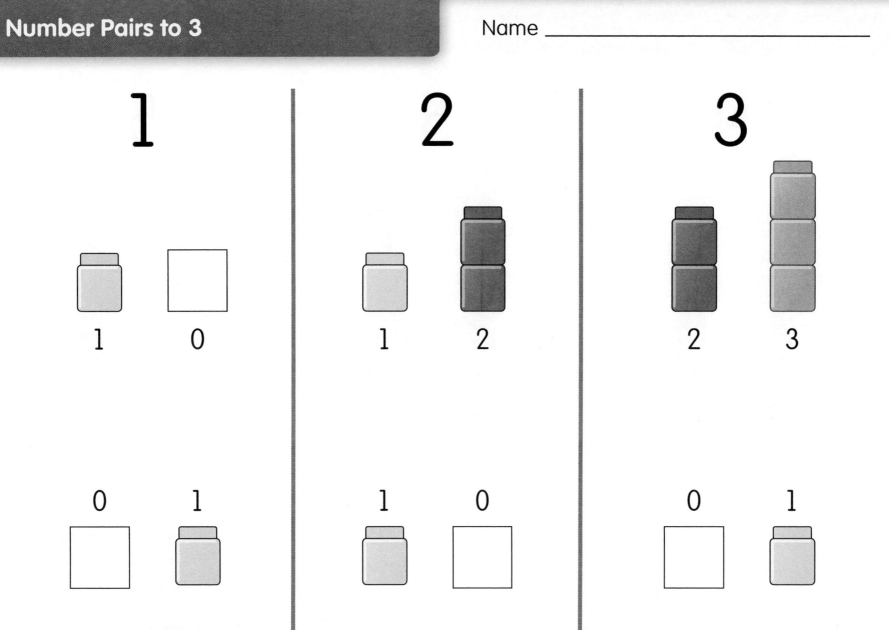

1

1	0

0	1

2

1	2

1	0

3

2	3

0	1

Guide children to draw lines that connect pieces at the top to pieces at the bottom to make trains of 1, 2, and 3.

Name _____

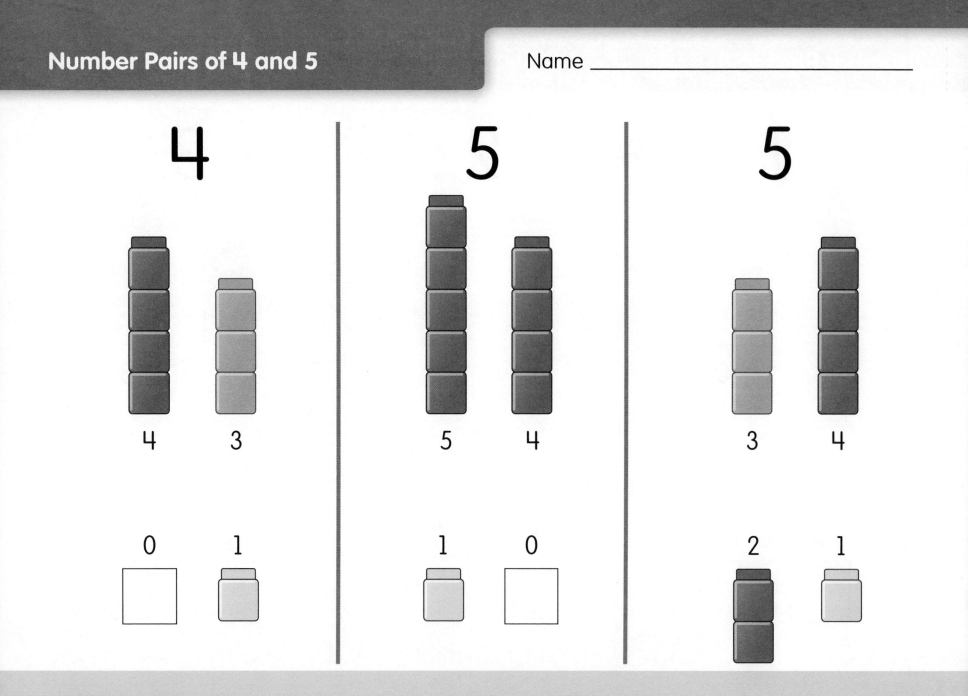

Guide children to draw lines that connect pieces at the top to pieces at the bottom to make trains of 4 and 5.

Number Pairs Within 5

Name _____

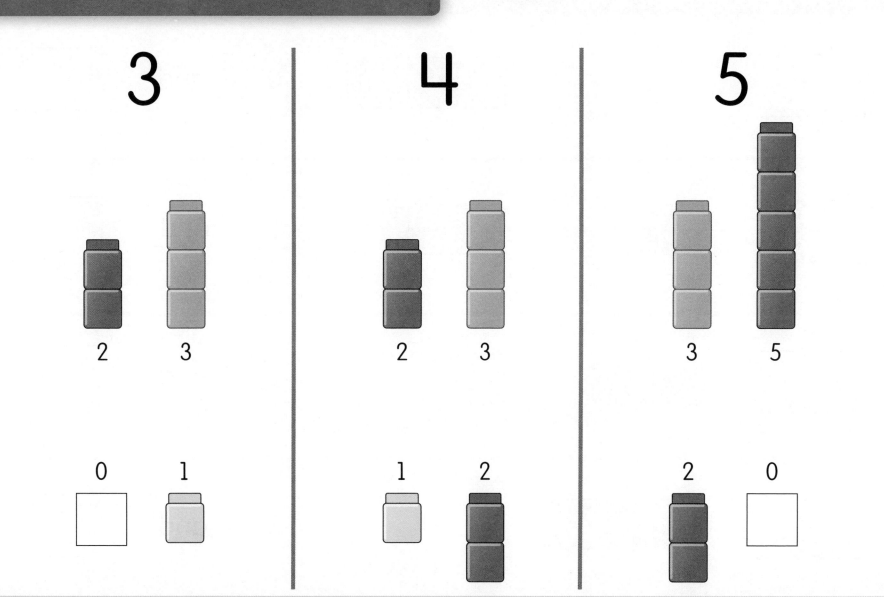

3　　　　**4**　　　　**5**

2　　3　　　2　　3　　　3　　5

0　　1　　　1　　2　　　2　　0

Guide children to draw lines that connect pieces at the top to pieces at the bottom to make trains of 3, 4, and 5.

Find Number Partners
for 3—Repeated Reasoning

Name _____

3   0   and   _____

3   ▪   3   1   and   _____

3   ▪   2   and   _____

3   ▪   3   and   _____

Guide children to write pairs of numbers that make 3. Have children trace the 3. Then ask them to write the missing number that is used to make 3 in each picture.

Talk About It   How does the first number in the number pair change from row to row? How does the second number change from row to row?

Find Number Partners
for 4—Repeated Reasoning

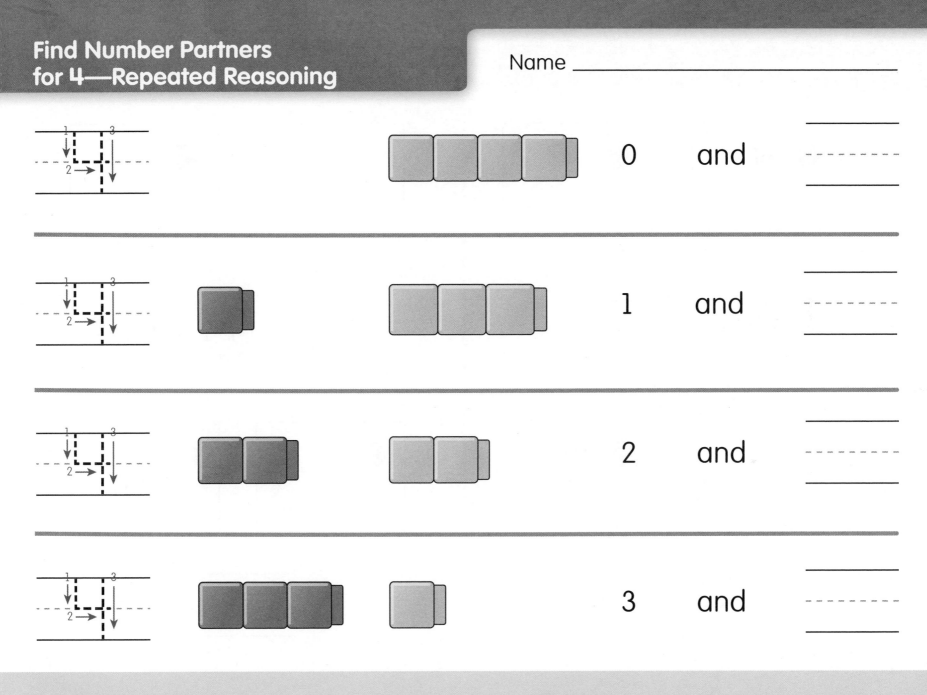

0   and   _____

1   and   _____

2   and   _____

3   and   _____

Guide children to write pairs of numbers that make 4. Have children trace the 4. Then ask them to write the missing number that is used to make 4 in each picture.

Talk About It   How does the first number in the number pair change from row to row? How does the second number change from row to row?

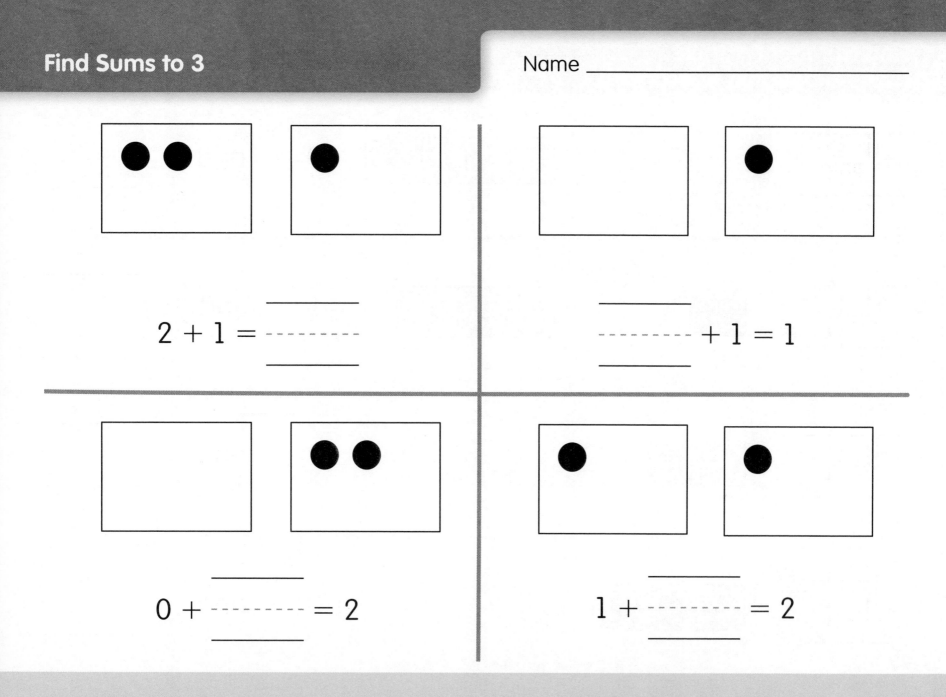

$$2 + 1 = \text{------}$$

$$\text{------} + 1 = 1$$

$$0 + \text{------} = 2$$

$$1 + \text{------} = 2$$

Guide children to write number sentences to match the dot cards. Have children write the missing number in each number sentence.

Name _____

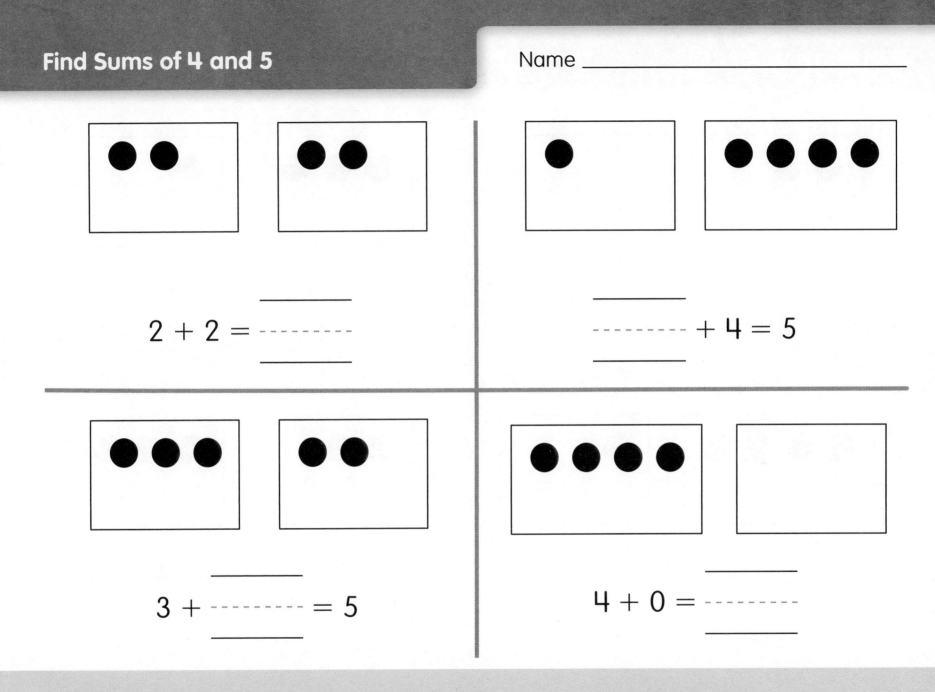

$2 + 2 =$ _____

_____ $+ 4 = 5$

$3 +$ _____ $= 5$

$4 + 0 =$ _____

Guide children to write number sentences to match the dot cards. Have children write the missing number in each number sentence.

Name _____

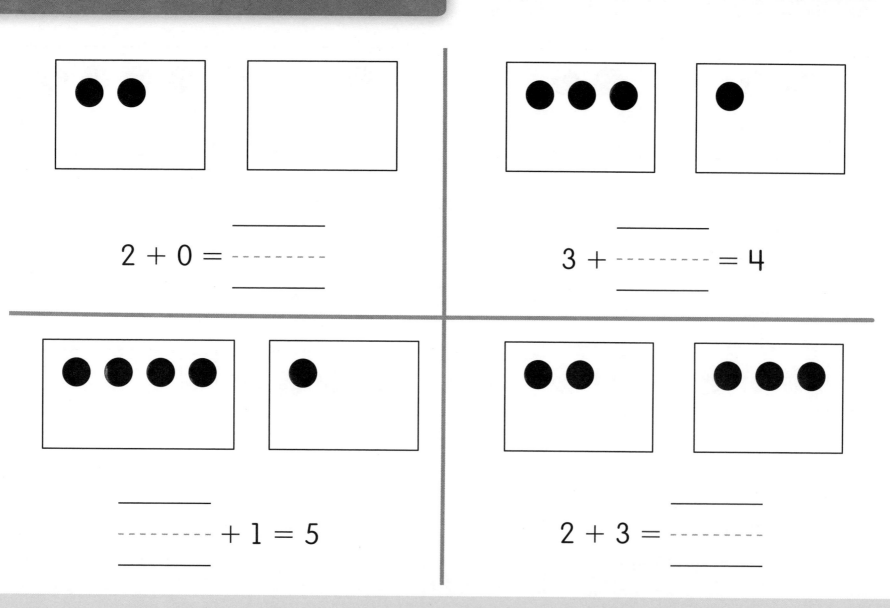

$2 + 0 =$ _____

$3 +$ _____ $= 4$

_____ $+ 1 = 5$

$2 + 3 =$ _____

Guide children to write number sentences to match the dot cards. Have children write the missing number in each number sentence.

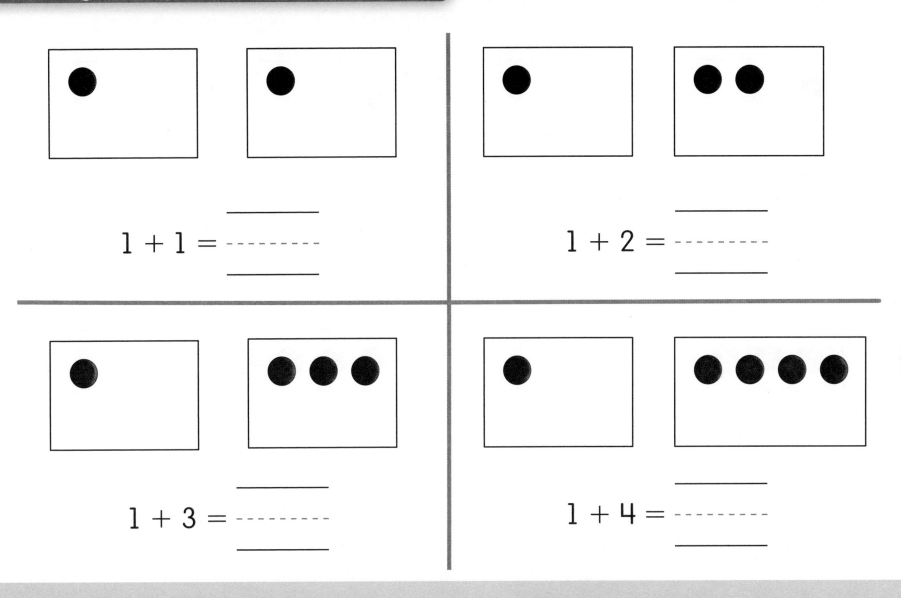

$1 + 1 =$ ------------

$1 + 2 =$ ------------

$1 + 3 =$ ------------

$1 + 4 =$ ------------

Guide children to write number sentences to match the dot cards. Have children write the total in each number sentence.

<u>**Talk About It**</u>   What number is added in every problem? How do the other numbers being added change from problem to problem? How do the totals change from problem to problem?

Name _____

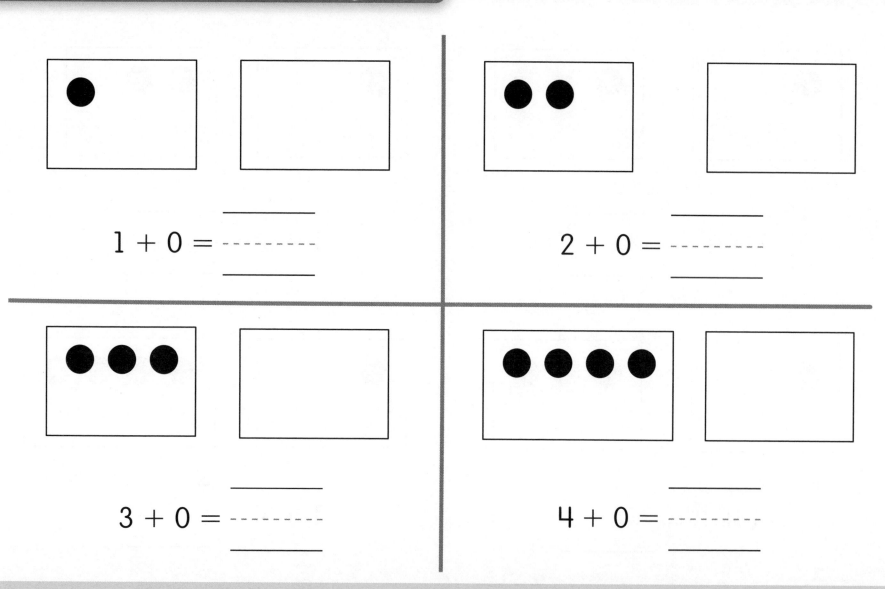

$1 + 0 =$ _____

$2 + 0 =$ _____

$3 + 0 =$ _____

$4 + 0 =$ _____

Guide children to write number sentences to match the dot cards. Have children write the total in each number sentence.

<u>**Talk About It**</u>   What number is added in every problem? How do the other numbers being added change from problem to problem? What is the total when you add 0 to a number?

Name _____

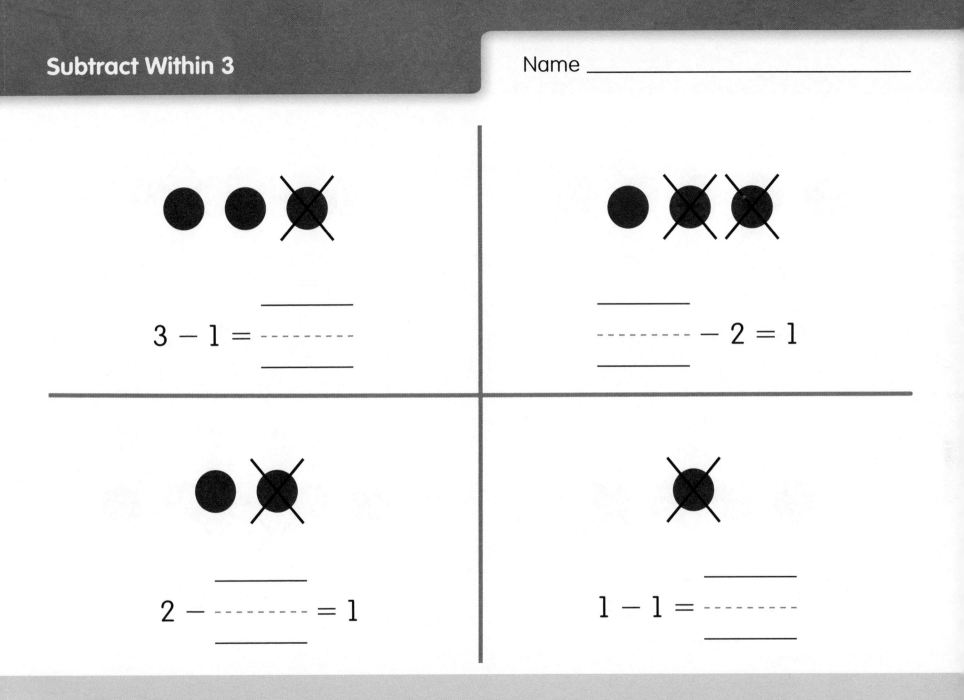

$3 - 1 =$ ------------

_____ $- 2 = 1$

$2 -$ ------------ $= 1$

$1 - 1 =$ ------------

Guide children to write number sentences to match the pictures. Have children write the missing number in each subtraction sentence.

Name _____

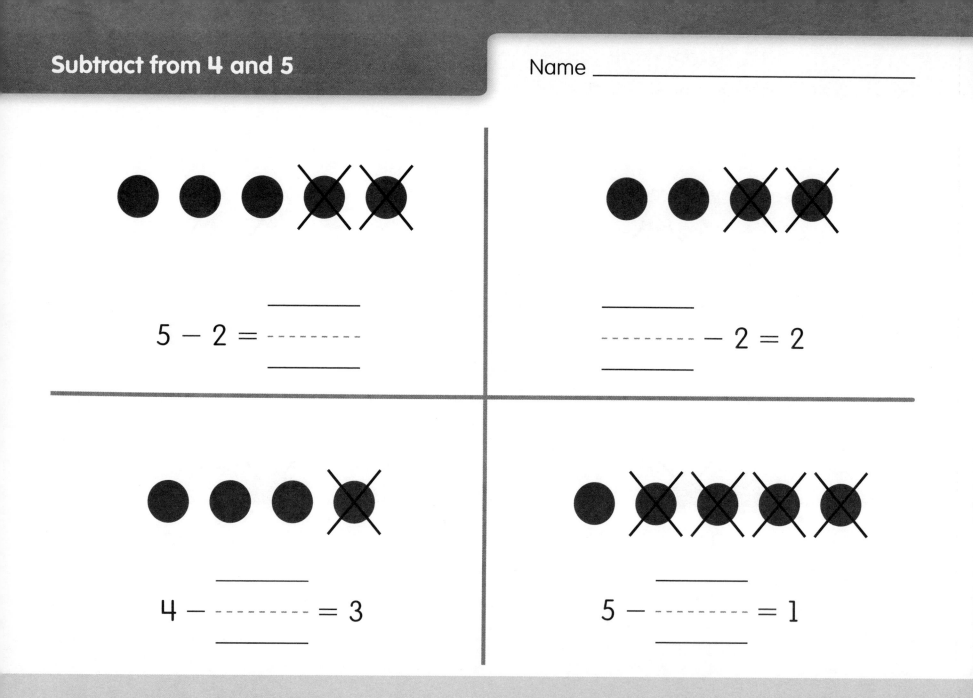

$5 - 2 =$ _____

_____ $- 2 = 2$

$4 -$ _____ $= 3$

$5 -$ _____ $= 1$

Guide children to write number sentences to match the pictures. Have children write the missing number in each subtraction sentence.

Name _____

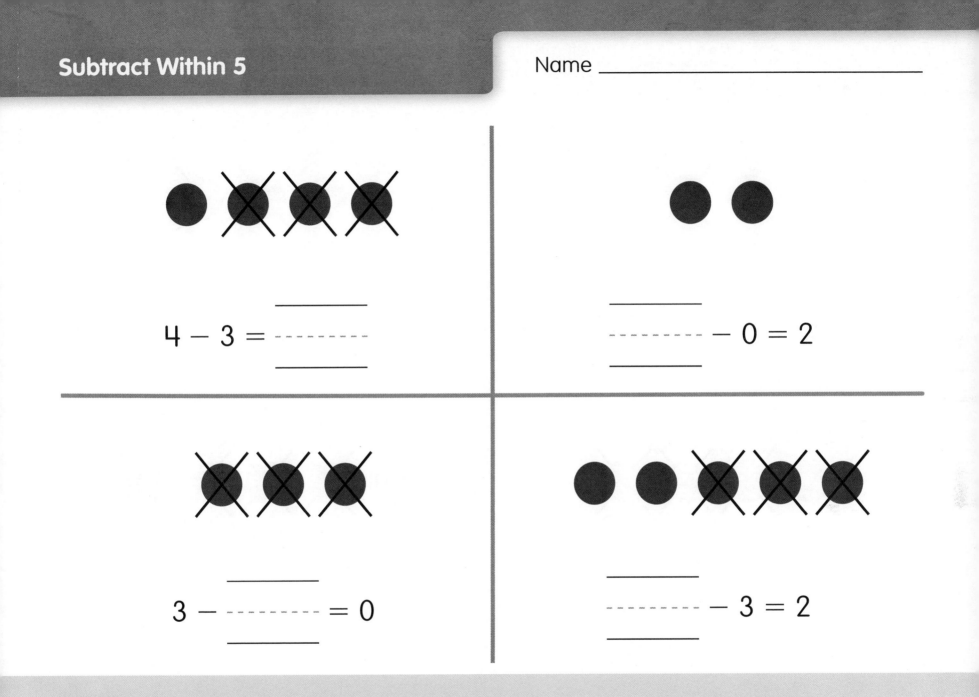

$4 - 3 =$ _____ (_____)

_____ $- 0 = 2$

$3 -$ _____ $= 0$

_____ $- 3 = 2$

Guide children to write number sentences to match the pictures. Have children write the missing number in each subtraction sentence.

Find Patterns with Differences of 1—Repeated Reasoning

Name _____

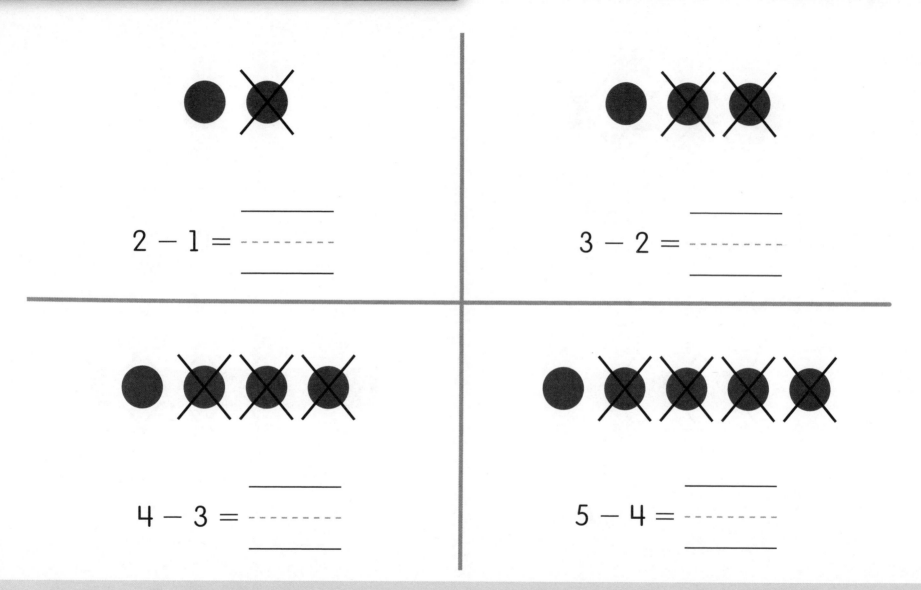

$2 - 1 =$ _____

$3 - 2 =$ _____

$4 - 3 =$ _____

$5 - 4 =$ _____

Guide children to write number sentences to match the pictures. Have children write the number they get for each subtraction sentence.

Talk About It   How are the problems alike? How does the number you start with change from problem to problem? How does the amount taken away change from problem to problem?

Find Patterns When Subtracting from 4—Repeated Reasoning

Name _____

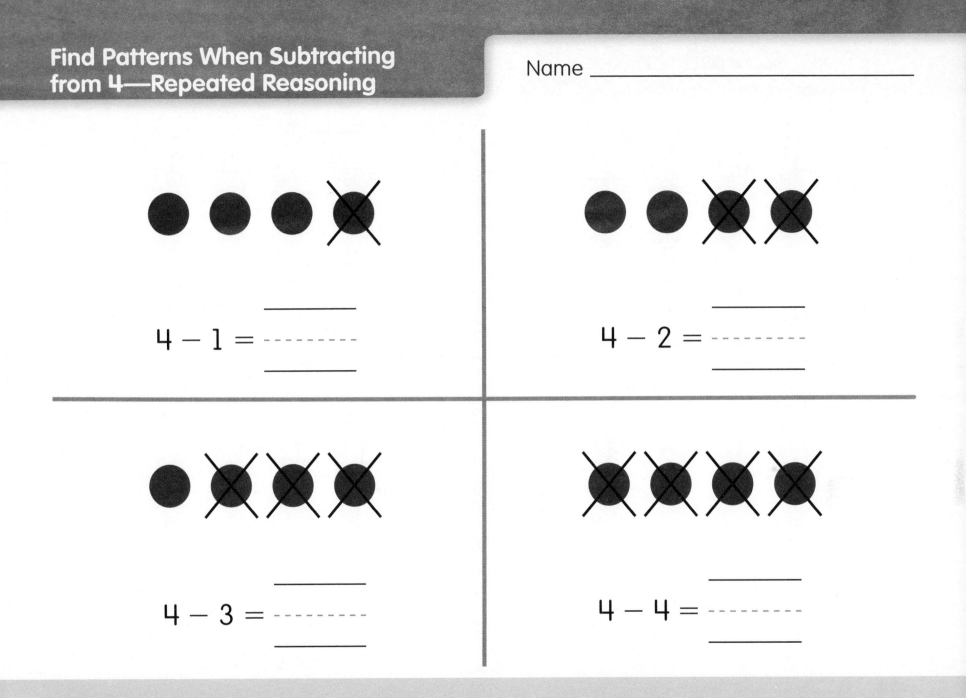

$4 - 1 =$ _____

$4 - 2 =$ _____

$4 - 3 =$ _____

$4 - 4 =$ _____

Guide children to write number sentences to match the pictures. Have children write the number they get for each subtraction sentence.

Talk About It   How are the problems alike? Look at the amounts taken away and the numbers you get. What patterns do you see?

Name _____

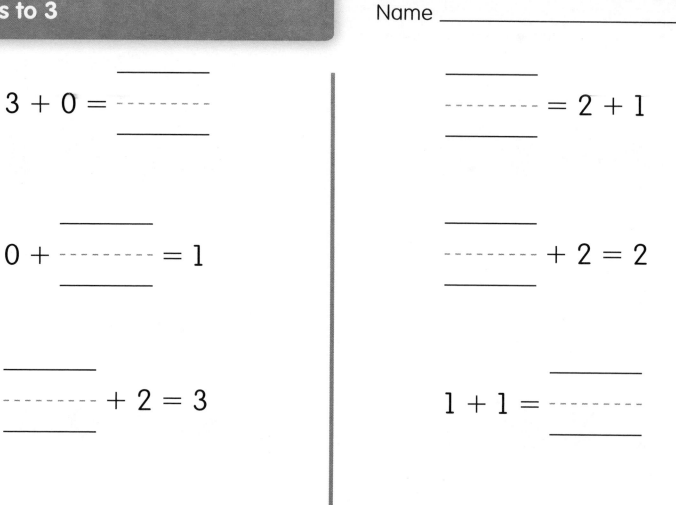

$$3 + 0 = \underline{}$$

$$\underline{} = 2 + 1$$

$$0 + \underline{} = 1$$

$$\underline{} + 2 = 2$$

$$\underline{} + 2 = 3$$

$$1 + 1 = \underline{}$$

$$\underline{} = 0 + 0$$

$$1 + \underline{} = 1$$

Have children write the missing number in each addition sentence.

$0 + 4 = \underline{}$

$\underline{} = 3 + 2$

$5 + \underline{} = 5$

$\underline{} + 3 = 4$

$\underline{} = 3 + 1$

$2 + \underline{} = 4$

$\underline{} + 3 = 5$

$1 + 4 = \underline{}$

Have children write the missing number in each addition sentence.

$$2 + 0 = \underline{}$$

$$2 + \underline{} = 3$$

$$\underline{} = 2 + 2$$

$$\underline{} + 5 = 5$$

$$\underline{} = 4 + 1$$

$$\underline{} + 1 = 2$$

$$0 + \underline{} = 3$$

$$1 + 3 = \underline{}$$

Have children write the missing number in each addition sentence.

Name _____

$$2 + 0 = \text{-----}$$

$$2 + 1 = \text{-----}$$

$$2 + 2 = \text{-----}$$

$$2 + 3 = \text{-----}$$

$$3 + 0 = \text{-----}$$

$$3 + 1 = \text{-----}$$

$$3 + 2 = \text{-----}$$

Have children write the total for each addition sentence. Encourage children to look for patterns in the numbers being added and the totals.

Talk About It How do the numbers being added change in each column? How are the numbers being added in each row different? What patterns do you see in the totals in each column? in the rows?

Find Patterns in Number Partners—Repeated Reasoning

Name _____

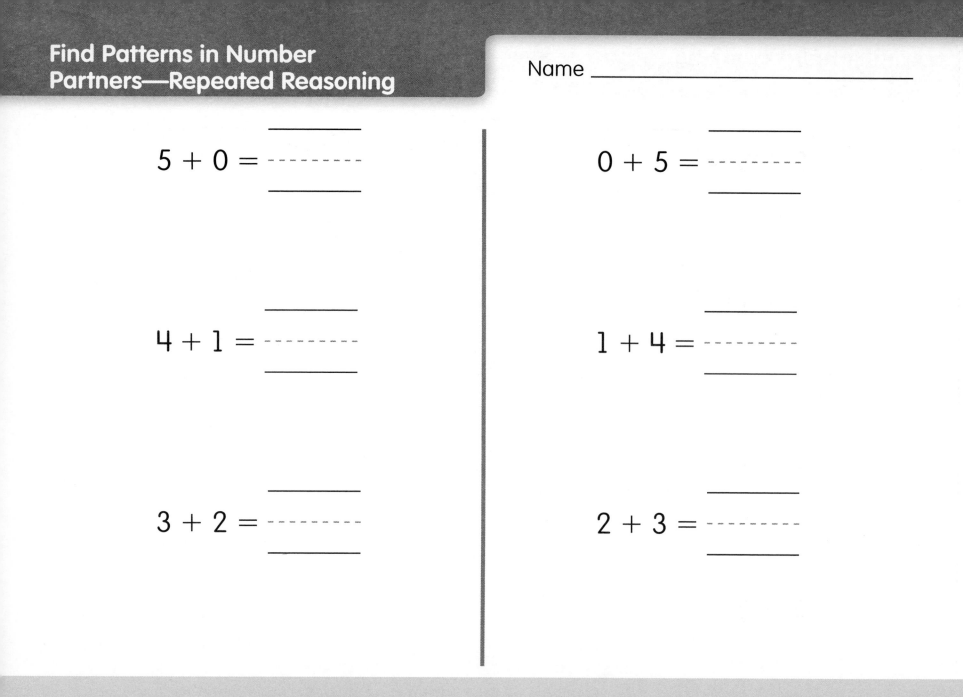

$$5 + 0 = \rule{2cm}{0.4pt}$$

$$0 + 5 = \rule{2cm}{0.4pt}$$

$$4 + 1 = \rule{2cm}{0.4pt}$$

$$1 + 4 = \rule{2cm}{0.4pt}$$

$$3 + 2 = \rule{2cm}{0.4pt}$$

$$2 + 3 = \rule{2cm}{0.4pt}$$

Have children write the total for each addition sentence. Encourage children to look for patterns in the numbers being added.

Talk About It How do the numbers being added change going down each column? How are the numbers being added in each row alike? How are they different?

Name _____

$$3 - 3 = \underline{}$$

$$\underline{} = 3 - 1$$

$$2 - \underline{} = 0$$

$$0 - \underline{} = 0$$

$$\underline{} - 1 = 0$$

$$2 - 1 = \underline{}$$

$$\underline{} = 3 - 0$$

$$\underline{} - 2 = 1$$

Have children write the missing number in each subtraction sentence.

Name _____

4 − 3 = ____

____ = 5 − 1

5 − ____ = 0

4 − ____ = 2

____ − 0 = 4

4 − 1 = ____

____ = 5 − 3

____ − 2 = 3

Have children write the missing number in each subtraction sentence.

Name _____

4 − 4 = ----------

_____ = 4 − 1

5 − ---------- = 1

2 − ---------- = 2

---------- − 2 = 1

5 − 0 = ----------

---------- = 1 − 0

---------- − 1 = 1

Have children write the missing number in each subtraction sentence.

Name _____

$$5 - 5 = \text{\underline{\hspace{2cm}}}$$

$$5 - 2 = \text{\underline{\hspace{2cm}}}$$

$$5 - 4 = \text{\underline{\hspace{2cm}}}$$

$$5 - 1 = \text{\underline{\hspace{2cm}}}$$

$$5 - 3 = \text{\underline{\hspace{2cm}}}$$

$$5 - 0 = \text{\underline{\hspace{2cm}}}$$

Have children write the number they get for each subtraction sentence.

Talk About It How are the problems alike? How does the amount taken away change from problem to problem? How does the number you get change from problem to problem?

Find Patterns with Differences of 2 and 3—Repeated Reasoning

Name _____

$$5 - 3 = \text{------}$$

$$4 - 2 = \text{------}$$

$$3 - 1 = \text{------}$$

$$5 - 2 = \text{------}$$

$$4 - 1 = \text{------}$$

$$3 - 0 = \text{------}$$

Have children write the number they get for each subtraction sentence.

Talk About It How are the problems in each column alike? What patterns do you see in the numbers you start with and the numbers being subtracted in each column?

Name _____

$$0 + 2 = \text{\_\_\_\_}$$

$$\text{\_\_\_\_} = 2 - 1$$

$$1 - \text{\_\_\_\_} = 0$$

$$\text{\_\_\_\_} - 0 = 0$$

$$\text{\_\_\_\_} - 2 = 1$$

$$3 - 1 = \text{\_\_\_\_}$$

$$\text{\_\_\_\_} = 1 + 0$$

$$2 + \text{\_\_\_\_} = 3$$

Have children write the missing number in each number sentence.

Add or Subtract from 4 and 5

Name ____________________

$2 + 3 =$ ____

____ $= 4 - 3$

____ $= 4 + 0$

$5 - 3 =$ ____

$4 -$ ____ $= 4$

____ $+ 2 = 5$

____ $- 1 = 4$

$3 +$ ____ $= 4$

Have children write the missing number in each number sentence.

$$2 + 0 = \underline{}$$

$$\underline{} - 3 = 0$$

$$\underline{} = 4 + 1$$

$$4 - \underline{} = 3$$

$$\underline{} = 5 - 2$$

$$2 + \underline{} = 4$$

$$\underline{} + 2 = 3$$

$$2 - 2 = \underline{}$$

Have children write the missing number in each number sentence.

Name _____

$2 + 3 =$ _____

$3 + 2 =$ _____

$3 + 1 =$ _____

$1 + 3 =$ _____

$1 + 2 =$ _____

$2 + 1 =$ _____

$0 + 2 =$ _____

$2 + 0 =$ _____

Have children write the totals for the addition sentences in each row.

Talk About It How are the problems in each row alike? What do you notice about the numbers being added in each row?

Name _____

$5 - 5 =$ _____

$4 - 4 =$ _____

$3 - 3 =$ _____

$2 - 2 =$ _____

$5 - 0 =$ _____

$4 - 0 =$ _____

$3 - 0 =$ _____

$2 - 0 =$ _____

Have children write the number they get for each subtraction sentence.

Talk About It How are the problems in the left column alike? How are the problems in the right column alike? What patterns do you see?